# QUEER ALLIANCES

# QUEER
# ALLIANCES

How Power Shapes Political Movement Formation

*Erin Mayo-Adam*

STANFORD UNIVERSITY PRESS —— STANFORD, CALIFORNIA

Stanford University Press
Stanford, California

Printed in the United States of America on acid-free, archival-quality paper

Library of Congress Cataloging-in-Publication Data

Names: Mayo-Adam, Erin, author.
Title: Queer alliances : how power shapes political movement formation /
    Erin Mayo-Adam.
Description: Stanford, California : Stanford University Press, 2020. |
    Includes bibliographical references and index.
Identifiers: LCCN 2020008429 (print) | LCCN 2020008430 (ebook) | ISBN
    9781503610354 (cloth) | ISBN 9781503612792 (paperback) | ISBN
    9781503612808 (ebook)
Subjects: LCSH: Sexual minorities—Political activity—Washington (State) |
    Sexual minorities—Political activity—Arizona. | Immigrants—Political
    activity—Washington (State) | Immigrants—Political activity—Arizona.
    | Labor movement—Washington (State) | Labor movement—Arizona. |
    Coalitions—Washington (State) | Coalitions—Arizona.
Classification: LCC HQ73.73.U6 M39 2020 (print) | LCC HQ73.73.U6
    (ebook) | DDC 306.7609791—dc23
LC record available at https://lccn.loc.gov/2020008429
LC ebook record available at https://lccn.loc.gov/2020008430

Base cover image: pixabay | raw pixel
Cover design: Rob Ehle

*For Addy*

# CONTENTS

# ACKNOWLEDGMENTS

A book is at once a personal and collective accomplishment. This project would not have been possible without the network of scholars who read drafts of the manuscript and provided critical feedback, as well as the family, friends, and community workers who have served as a constant source of support and encouragement.

The intellectual curiosity that inspired this project began really when I was an undergraduate student at California State University, Long Beach (CSULB). At CSULB, I had the opportunity to work with outstanding faculty. I will never forget the law and social change class I took as an undergraduate student with Renee Cramer, the teacher and mentor who first introduced me to the study of law, not from the perspective of attorneys and law school professors, but from the perspective of political activists and ordinary people whose lives and struggles both shape and are shaped by the law.

This project would not have been possible without my amazing faculty mentors at the University of Washington, especially Michael McCann, George Lovell, Rachel Cichowski, and Chandan Reddy, who believed in a project that centered the voices of local activists and community workers over national organization leaders. I feel so grateful to have had the opportunity to work with George Lovell, who has enriched my intellectual curiosity in labor and political movement research. Working with Michael McCann has been far more wonderful than I ever could have imagined. Michael is an absolutely phenomenal mentor, who has the unique ability to constructively criticize while developing and building up the important contributions of new academic research. Michael and George also always encouraged me to be actively engaged in the communities at the center of this project, a remarkable and, unfortunately, rare form of mentorship that I have learned is crucial for the formation of innovative qualitative research.

I have also been fortunate to have found support for this project in the broader law and society and political science academic communities. Susan Burgess, Dara Strolovitch, Naomi Murakawa, Anna Maria Marshall, Anna Sampaio, Scott Barclay, Ellen Ann Andersen, Zein Murib, Andrew Flores, Michael Bosia, and Jennifer Gaboury all helped me directly with the research and writing of this book by providing me with valuable feedback at academic conferences and beyond. I owe a debt of gratitude to the Law and Society Association's Law and Social Movements Collaborative Research Network, the American Political Science Association's Sexuality and Politics Section, and the Western Political Science Association. All three associations have enabled me to workshop sections of this book for years and have provided me with the crucial feedback necessary to complete this project.

This book grew out of my article "Intersectional Coalitions: The Paradoxes of Rights-Based Movement Building in LGBTQ and Immigrant Communities," published in 2017 in the *Law & Society Review*. I am grateful to the journal's editors, Jeannine Bell, Susan Sterett, and Margot Young, and to the anonymous reviewers whose critical comments and suggestions helped move the ideas in my journal article into a book manuscript.

I am further immensely grateful for the supportive faculty network I have found at Hunter College, City University of New York (CUNY). In particular, I am indebted to Lina Newton, Sanford Schram, Carolyn Somerville, Charles Tien, and Roger Karapin, who provided me with advice and feedback throughout the publication process. I am especially grateful for Lina Newton, who introduced me to CUNY's Faculty Fellowship Publication Program, where I had the opportunity to workshop portions of the manuscript. In this program, Nivedita Majumdar, Stanley Thangaraj, Jill Rosenthal, Steven Swarbrick, Brais Outes-Leon, William Ryan, and Angela Ridinger-Dotterman all provided comments and suggestions that helped shape the manuscript for an interdisciplinary audience.

Furthermore, this book would not have been possible without the community support of my academic activist friends and colleagues, who have encouraged me to think about my research in ways that challenge conventional understandings of political movement dynamics. I am especially grateful for the various people who awakened my interest in political movement building and helped me develop some of the theoretical concepts embedded in these pages through grassroots community organizing, including Riddhi Mehta-Neugebauer, David Lopez, Paige Sechrest, Seth Trenchard, Jonathan Beck, Betsy Cooper, Heather Pool, Kirstine Taylor, Allison Rank, Kiku Huckle, Hannah Walker, Sergio Garcia-Rios, Kassra Oskooii, Heather Evans, Tanya Kawarki, and Caterina Rost.

This book was funded in part by Hunter College, CUNY, a grant provided by the CUNY faculty union (Professional Staff Congress-CUNY), and the CUNY Book Completion Award. My fieldwork and an early draft of the manuscript were funded by the University of Washington Political Science Department's David Olson research grant, the Harry Bridges Labor Center's Graduate Student Research Grant, and an American Dissertation Fellowship award from the American Association of University Women. I am also grateful for the resources provided by Hunter College Libraries, the Roosevelt House Public Policy Institute at Hunter College, Arizona State University's School of Politics and Global Studies, Arizona State University Libraries, the Comparative Law and Society Studies Center at the University of Washington, and the Washington Institute for the Study of Inequality and Race.

I also thank Michelle Lipinski, who believed in this book and helped it become a reality. The editorial team at Stanford University Press provided valuable assistance throughout the publication process and were a welcome source of advice and encouragement.

In addition to the intellectual and academic support, this project would not have been possible without the personal and emotional support of my family and friends. In particular, I thank my parents (Joan Adam and John Adam), my sister (Christine Adam), and friends who encouraged my research, including Chris Price, April Catherine Amante, and Ray Lader. I also thank my wife, Meghan Mayo-Adam, for her unconditional support, reassurance, and encouragement.

Finally, and most important, I thank the organization leaders, advocates, activists, and community workers who participated in this study and whose work serves as the motivation behind this book and as its backbone. Their extraordinary movement building in the face of insurmountable odds—both from within and outside their own communities—is awe-inspiring. Their phenomenal work in the struggle against oppression far surpasses the confines of academic research. It is my hope that this book will provide a window into the tireless advocacy and community organizing of these grassroots workers who continue to persevere in the face of racism, xenophobia, homophobia, and transphobia in their everyday lives.

Introduction

# QUEER ALLIANCES

Political movements are dynamic and volatile entities that are never formed, but always forming. When we talk about political movements, we tend to construct them as monolithic, linear entities with clear goals and trajectories. This characterization is misleading. Most movements grow and contract through a series of rapid bursts of energy that captivate our attention for a moment and then dissipate, leaving those who lived through them feeling galvanized, empowered, disoriented, dejected. This is perhaps most apparent if we see movements through the eyes of the advocates and community members who are closest to the center of their fury.

In order to better understand the phenomenon of political movement formation, let's turn to some examples of grassroots organizing. In April 2010, Arizona's governor signed Senate Bill (SB) 1070. SB 1070 was an omnibus anti-immigration bill that enabled local law enforcement officers to stop and question people who they have reason to believe are undocumented immigrants. When signing the new legislation, then governor Jan Brewer proudly claimed that the legislation ensured that the "constitutional rights of all in Arizona remain[ed] solid, stable, and steadfast."[1] In many ways, SB 1070 has had a profound impact on politics in Arizona and has ignited struggles to protect against threats to constitutional rights—but probably not quite in the manner imagined by Governor Brewer and other conservative politicians and activists who passed SB 1070 with the goal of curtailing the flow of migrants into the state. The signing of SB 1070 awakened the re-formation of political movement building in Arizona; initiated a fervor of coalition advocacy that spanned the immigrant, labor, and Latinx communities; and fueled a growing grassroots queer migrant justice movement.

This re-formed movement was, by some accounts, wildly successful. Six years after SB 1070 was signed into law, much of the law had been dismantled through lawsuits, and the state senator who authored it was forced out of office through an embarrassing recall election. Sheriff Joe Arpaio, who infamously and aggressively enforced SB 1070 and federal immigration law in Maricopa County, lost a series of humiliating civil rights lawsuits. In 2016, due in large part to the political movement organizing that grew in response to SB 1070, Arpaio lost his reelection campaign to a Democrat after serving twenty-four years as the Maricopa County sheriff. That same year, a successful ballot initiative campaign increased the minimum wage across the state and required employers to provide paid sick leave.[2] An institutionalized grassroots advocacy coalition had expanded in Arizona.

Juan, a community organizer with the queer migrant movement in Arizona whom I interviewed for this book, was one of the individuals who became more involved in movement building as a result of SB 1070. Juan and his peers first created a queer migrant organization in the state to call attention to the experiences of those who identified as members of the queer and/or trans, and migrant communities. According to Juan, the queer and trans migrant organizing born out SB 1070 ultimately "rippled" into an array of organizing spaces in the state. The queer migrant community conducted several political actions and educational forums in the 2010s. During the afternoon I spent with him, Juan recalled in awestruck terms how he and other queer migrant activists pushed for new imaginings of movement, community, and being in the wake of the devastating anti-immigration law. In one action orchestrated by queer migrant activists, the pop star Lady Gaga publicly condemned SB 1070 when her 2010 Monster Ball Tour came to Phoenix. In another, activists forced space for a queer and trans migrant contingent in the Phoenix Pride parade, capturing the attention of local media and the crowd in what they argued had become a mainstream LGBTQ movement space, dominated by large corporate funders and mostly white gay men and lesbians. For

Juan and many other queer migrant community workers I met during my fieldwork, the 2010s were a powerful moment for re-imagining and challenging the limits of political movement organizing that they argued centered heteronormative experiences and discrete rights-based goals that rarely served queer migrant interests.

This book examines how political movement coalitions, like those that emerged in Arizona in the aftermath of SB 1070, unite and fracture around campaigns to achieve legal rights wins and thwart rights losses. What factors contribute to movement formation, and what factors limit movement expansion? How do intense legal rights advocacy moments impact movement formation? I argue that political movement formation has paradoxical effects that simultaneously involve the creation of new possibilities and the re-entrenchment of hierarchical power. I illuminate these paradoxical effects through a multimethod study conducted in 2014 and 2015 that includes an interpretive analysis of the language that movement actors use to describe their experiences of movement formation at the grassroots in two state contexts: Arizona and Washington State.

On the surface, the expansion of cross-community movement coalitions around episodic rights campaigns can appear to be mostly a successful illustration of how divergent minority communities come together and advance human rights. But discrete rights advances and movement expansion can also come at a cost. This was especially apparent in the Referendum 74 campaign for marriage equality in Washington State. Emilio was an advocate with the LGBTQ, Latinx, and undocumented immigrant communities in Washington. Emilio, like many other organizers and advocates affiliated with these communities in Washington, felt even further marginalized and exploited by the state's same-sex marriage campaign. During our conversation, Emilio directly criticized mainstream LGBTQ movement advocates for claiming that marriage equality was an important issue for the queer migrant and undocumented immigrant movements that grew in Washington State, Arizona, and nationally throughout the late 2000s and 2010s:

Emilio: For a long time, many LGBTQ folks who are white or many gay folks who were fighting for marriage equality saw equality just in that, just in marriage, which is sort of a very singular issue to think about equality and equity. And I think that's different for undocumented folks because why does it matter if we are married if we are both undocumented?[3]

For many people like Emilio, marriage equality served as an issue that centered the experiences of white gay men and lesbians who had citizenship status and who saw equality "just in marriage," and who, thus, no longer felt the need to continue mobilizing for LGBTQ justice once same-sex marriage was legalized nationwide. As a result, a lot of funding for LGBTQ rights issues evaporated after marriage equality, leaving organizations that purported to serve all LGBTQ people, including queer and trans undocumented migrants, trans people, and LGBTQ people of color, in a severely under-resourced position in the immediate aftermath of the win. According to Emilio, in a statement echoed by other advocates, the de-mobilization that occurred in the aftermath of the successful Referendum 74 campaign for marriage equality exemplified "white LGBTQ folks not really understanding the whole idea of white privilege."

Movement expansion around the Referendum 74 campaign in Washington and, to a lesser degree, against SB 1070 in Arizona involved the contraction of agendas in ways that benefited the most mainstream members of minority communities, those perceived as the most politically and socially acceptable, "deserving" minorities, at the expense of people like Juan and Emilio. Hierarchical power dynamics responsible for the centering of wealth, whiteness, and masculinity in the US are not confined to political institutions; they pollute political movement organizing as well. Both cases demonstrate how episodic rights campaigns can paradoxically expand and contract political movements. In the following pages, I argue that alliances that form across divergent movements often unite and fracture in frenzied bursts around legal rights struggles rather than along a linear trajectory forward toward progress, and that even the most egalitarian aims often coincide with the consolidation of hierarchical power.

In making this argument, this book draws from political movement and law and society scholarship. I define *movements* as *political* phenomena represented by "continuous process[es] from generation to decline," in line with scholars who adopt a political process model of movements, and, thus, study movement formation by looking at how movement actors take advantage of political opportunity structures and respond to structural constraints.[4] I enhance this understanding of movements by further envisioning political movements as entities composed of a series of shifting inter- and intra-movement coalitions.

Recently, sociology scholars have called attention to the failure of most empirical studies of political movements to recognize that movements themselves are composed of formal *and* informal coalitional networks of organizations.[5] Most political movement scholarship assumes a structural homogeneity to movements, and, for this reason, many political movement studies focus on one or a small core of organizations that claim to represent a given minority movement. This is especially true of scholarship on what Eskridge calls contemporary "identity-based movements": the collection of movements that arose out of the mass protests of the 1950s and 1960s, including the civil rights movement, the women's rights movement, the gay rights movement, and the disability rights movement.[6] Scholarship on identity-based political movements tends to focus on one or a few legal or national political organizations because of the limits of available organizational data.[7] The focus on a small set of national organizations reinforces constructions of political movements in the classroom and in popular media that center the narratives of a small core of the most well-resourced leaders. This inevitably results in the marginalization of the role that grassroots advocacy networks play in movements for social change.

Today, there is a wide array of historical accounts of the role that national political and legal organizations like Human Rights Campaign, Lambda Legal, and Freedom to Marry played in advancing same-sex marriage across the US.[8] However, there are very few accounts that focus on the complex roles that local actors played in the struggle for marriage equality or how LGBTQ rights campaigns and coalitions contributed to and limited movement building, with a few notable exceptions.[9] The dearth of empirical studies on local advocacy networks is understandable. Grassroots networks, like those networks that developed in response to SB 1070 in Arizona and the Referendum 74 marriage equality campaign in Washington State, are not easily mapped. These networks are composed of collectives of constantly shifting formal and informal organizations and alliances. At the local level, it is common for organizations to emerge for several years and then disappear, only to be replaced by new formations that may or may not include some of the same movement actors. The various struggles that local actors are involved in are not always archived or well documented.

Statewide ballot measure campaigns that collect enough signatures to appear on the ballot in a general election may generate a lot of paperwork and media coverage, but campaigns that fail to make it onto the ballot, legislative campaigns that are centered in state capitals, and local court case campaigns that do not make it to an appellate court often do not. This is especially true in the 2000s, when mass layoffs at local news media outlets resulted in severe under-reporting on local politics, and campaign websites and organizations were likely to appear for a few months during intense advocacy moments and dissolve once a campaign ended.

This book seeks to fill this research gap through an in-depth examination of grassroots coalition building within the LGBTQ and immigrant movement communities in Washington State and Arizona. By analyzing the formation of political movement alliances, this study destabilizes contemporary understandings of identity-based movements which assume that movement formation can primarily be found within a small collective of national organizations that represent one subject position. Instead, I advance a conceptual, methodological shift by analyzing political movements through alliances across a multiplicity of organizations and groups that hold an array of intersecting subject positions across intersecting structural hierarchies. This book employs a queer methodology that destabilizes homogenous and monolithic constructions of political movements that focus on mostly mainstream movement actors. In the same vein as the work of queer studies scholars, this book seeks to draw attention to other forms of political movement, other constructions of community, and other understandings of subjectivity.[10] When examining political movements, it does not make sense to confine our understandings to national organizations dedicated to specific minority populations alone. National organizations tend to get involved in movement activity very late in the formation process and often claim credit for rights wins without engaging in any on-the-ground advocacy. Rather than form at the national level, movements expand at the local level through the advocacy work of people like Juan and Emilio—people who build grassroots organizations and alliances that are capable of responding to and halting threats to minority communities as they arise.

Constructing movements as expansionist entities that defy specific organizational ties and transcend individual subject-position boundaries is consistent with the critiques of scholars who decry monolithic understandings of activism and political movement studies that center organizational formation.[11] In the same vein as Majic, who, through her study of sex-worker rights advocacy in California,[12] argues that activists often simultaneously work in nonprofit organizations and conduct non-organizational movement activism, this study recognizes that advocacy networks are both within and outside formal organizations. The coalitions in this study encompass formal nonprofit organizations and advocacy organizations, and informal organizations that are composed of volunteers who unite under a common name and mission but have not applied for formal nonprofit status with the Internal Revenue Service (IRS). I argue that movement actors are not confined to the limits of formal organizations in their advocacy. Further, I contend that scholars should not only evaluate movements based on outcomes but also study political movements through the expansion and contraction of inter- and intra-movement coalitions. Movements should be measured not only by their ability to attain discrete rights goals but also by their potential to expand into new struggles against legal and political power.

## Case Selection

This book examines LGBTQ and immigrant rights movement formation through case studies of two states: Washington and Arizona. My goal is to illustrate the complexity of political movement formation, to demonstrate the need for more attention to coalitions in studies of rights-based movements, and to explain how political movement advocacy is often connected to hierarchical power dynamics. I have identified Washington and Arizona as my core cases for several reasons. Washington and Arizona provide a good pairing because some similarities make it possible to study movement formation in each state, while other sharp differences between the two states mean that they can together reveal considerable complexity in movement mobilization at the local level and in the various roles that grassroots advocacy networks play in coalition formation. The two state variables described here are chosen not because they are perfectly independent and thus suitable for a linear causal analysis. This study is not an analysis of what causes rights wins or rights losses. Instead, my project is designed to reveal *how* political movement coalitions unite and fracture and *why* hierarchical power dynamics often persist in political movement formation.

As a threshold matter, inter- and intra-movement coalitions that span the LGBTQ and immigrant communities have formed in each state at the grassroots level. These coalitions formed around the same time that these communities experienced political setbacks. In Washington, there were few signs of effective cross-community coalition work in the early 2000s. In 2005, only one immigrant rights organization (Hate Free Zone, now OneAmerica) signed onto an amicus brief filed by civic and community leaders in support of gay and lesbian couples fighting for marriage equality in the case *Andersen v. King County*. By contrast, during the 2012 Referendum 74 campaign for marriage equality, a wide array of organizations that represent immigrant communities endorsed the referendum. Similarly, in Arizona, when the state passed a same-sex marriage ban in 2008, the statewide campaign to thwart the initiative included no visible partnerships with immigrant rights organizations or organizations representing communities of color. Since then, coalitions between LGBTQ and immigrant movement organizations have formed at the local level in Arizona.[13] These new coalitions feature organizations and communities that have historically been marginalized in political movement spaces. In both states, queer migrant community spaces were formed by people like Juan and Emilio, the community workers discussed at the beginning of this introduction. These new organizing spaces became increasingly important in pushing the boundaries of traditional political movement organizing during this time.

Although the timing of coalition formation is similar across the two cases, there is important variation in Washington and Arizona on other dimensions. This includes variation across the two states (1) in the different ways that movement advances develop through political and legal venues, (2) in the dissimilar sequence of political and legal wins and losses, and (3) in the overall political culture. The Washington and Arizona cases show that rights losses and wins can provide an impetus for coalition building regardless of whether losses and wins come in the courts or through political processes. In Washington State, movement advances usually occur through political processes such as ballot initiative and legislative campaigns. In Arizona, by contrast, these political processes are almost entirely closed off for movements because the state legislative and executive branches are controlled by many legislators committed to anti-immigration, religious freedom, and right-to-work policies.

Consequently, when movement wins do occur in Arizona, they often materialize through court campaigns that challenge the limits of state laws that movement actors argue violate the constitutional rights of minorities or through counter-campaigns designed to halt the advancement of anti-progressive issues.

In addition to the different ways that movement advances manifest in the two states, the sequence of advances also varies across Washington and Arizona, particularly for the LGBTQ and immigrant rights movements. Throughout the mid-2000s and 2010s, following significant policy losses in the 1990s, the LGBTQ and immigrant rights movements advanced a series of discrete rights wins in Washington. During this time, Washington experienced the institutionalization of in-state tuition for undocumented college students, the passage of an LGBTQ-inclusive nondiscrimination act, the legalization of marriage equality, and the passage of a law providing state financial aid for undocumented students. By contrast, throughout the same period of time in Arizona, legislators and voters instituted a series of debilitating rights losses for LGBTQ, Latinx, and immigrant rights organizations. Between 2000 and 2010 alone, Arizona enacted a stringent voter ID law that also limited access to state public benefits for undocumented persons, banned in-state tuition for undocumented students, passed a constitutional ban on same-sex marriage, and passed SB 1070.

Despite contradictory trajectories of rights wins and losses, inter- and intra-movement coalitions have emerged in the LGBTQ and immigrant communities in each state, due in large part to the political organizing of marginalized communities. By looking at both Arizona and Washington, contrasting cases of coalition development, this book provides a broader account of inter- and intra-movement coalition formation than studies that look only at national organizations, examine states with similar demographics and similar political contexts, or focus on a small subset of legal or political organizations rather than the coalitions of organizations that compose movements.

## Methodology: Studying Political Movement Formation in a Contested Terrain

I rely primarily on the sociolegal and historical context framework used by political movement and law and society scholars to identify the context within which groups form inter- and intra-movement coalitions and the impact that the politics of rights has on movement formation.[14] The analysis presented here details how political movement coalitions expand and contract movement mobilization at the local level, the role that intersectionally marginalized people play in movement expansion and contraction, and the relationship between episodic rights campaigns and social change as illuminated through fifty-one semi-structured, in-depth interviews with LGBTQ, labor, and immigrant community leaders and advocates; more than thirty participant observations; and organization and newspaper archives. I conducted interviews and participant observations between December 2014 and July 2015 in Washington State and August 2015 and October 2015 in Arizona. I conducted twenty-five interviews in Washington and twenty-six in Arizona. Interview protocols are included in appendix 3. The use of in-depth interviews is particularly well suited for investigations of identity politics, legal mobilization, and intersectional alliances, as it "is useful for uncovering aspects of a phenomenon that may remain hidden, [and] because . . . [the] trust that can be established between the researcher and subject in an in-person interview is invaluable when encouraging subjects to define issues for themselves."[15] The goal of this study is to develop a bottom-up, grassroots lens to delineate how inter- and intra-movement coalition formation contributes to mobilization.

The purpose of my chosen methodology is to explore how advocacy in different institutional and non-institutional forums contributed to and limited the formation of inter- and intra-movement coalitions. The results presented are meant to convey the experiences expressed during the course of my research in a manner that considers and reflects on my own positionality as a researcher and subject. For a broader discussion of the methodology employed in this book, including how I conducted the study in a manner that considered my own positionality, please see appendix 2.

The chapters that follow focus on those individuals who have been involved in large, statewide campaigns and more localized, municipal efforts that focus on issues important to LGBTQ, immigrant, and labor communities. All interviewee names used in this book have been replaced with pseudonyms; and identifiable details, such as the names of organizations that interviewees worked for, have been eliminated or altered in order to protect interviewee confidentiality. Confidentiality was necessary in order to give interviewees the space needed to reflect openly on their experiences with political movement formation without damaging their relationships with other movement actors. The life experiences recounted by interviewees are personal advocacy stories, which, in many cases, played out against a background of racism, classism, homophobia, transphobia, and sexism. The chapters in this book include excerpts from some, though not all, of these advocacy stories that delineate some of the factors that drive coalition unity and movement expansion as well as those that fracture and divide political movement coalitions.

## Understanding Movement Mobilization through Rights Episodes

In order to describe intense rights advocacy moments in a language that best reflects interviewee experiences, I develop the concept of *rights episodes*. Rights episodes are intense rights-based advocacy moments, or "vortexes" and "fires," according to interviewees who experienced them, that paradoxically both expand and contract political movements. Terms like *vortex* and *fire* underscore how movement actors often see rights episodes as agenda-setting and priority-shifting moments that are in many ways beyond their control. These intense advocacy moments form around political and legal rights campaigns. They can also expand over time through smaller episodic rights moments that culminate in a massive rights episode. This is what happened in Washington State, where smaller rights episodes around court cases, legislation, and ballot initiatives built the momentum necessary to set the stage for the massive marriage equality rights episode in 2012.

Rights episodes expand political movement mobilization by contributing to the formation of coalitions within and across different types of movement organizations. These moments contribute to coalition formation because they emphasize how different organizations have similar political movement or civil rights pasts, and they highlight a common core of opponents. At the same time, rights episodes have paradoxical implications for movements. They tend to exacerbate the factors that contribute to movement contraction because they focus movement mobilization around discrete campaigns and reinforce historic inequities within and across movements.

Rights episodes are a variant of the concept of *political opportunity structures and constraints*.[16] Research on political movements uses this concept to capture "the importance of the broader political system in structuring opportunities" that expand collective action and political constraints that limit collective action.[17] Scholars use the concept of political opportunity structures to explain how political movements generate or form and are also constrained through changes in networked political structures of formal power relations within a given political context. Building off this scholarship, I construct rights episodes as a type of, or subset of, political opportunity structures. When local political networks shift due to external actions, these actions can open a political opportunity through the formation of an intense rights-based advocacy moment or rights episode, and this episode, in turn, can simultaneously place constraints on movement formation.

Rights episodes occur when a networked political advocacy environment suddenly opens, as described in figure I.1, "Rights Episode Formation." As this figure illustrates, a political network shifts and a new rights episode is created when a new political action, such as a change in public support or a change in political control, suddenly creates the possibility for a movement to achieve a long-standing rights win or enables a counter-movement to initiate a rights threat. This, in turn, creates an episodic vortex around achieving a rights win or thwarting a rights loss that spurs the formation and expansion of movement coalitions. Although the newly formed rights episode contributes to movement mobilization and expansion, the episodic struggle also constrains movement formation around this discrete rights-based advocacy moment, which complicates future political movement advocacy after the episode dissipates.

### Inter- and Intra-Movement Coalitions

In examining the complexities of movement formation to advance legal rights wins and thwart rights losses, I focus on two levels of coalition formation in the LGBTQ and immigrant communities in Washington State and Arizona: (1) across- or inter-movement coalitions and (2) within- or intra-movement coalitions. These coalitions form both within and across mainstream and marginalized movement organizations, as delineated in figure I.2, "Mainstream and Marginalized Organization Alignment."

The organizations that compose political movement coalitions often encompass both political (i.e., policy- and/or litigation-focused) organizations and health and human service organizations that represent the

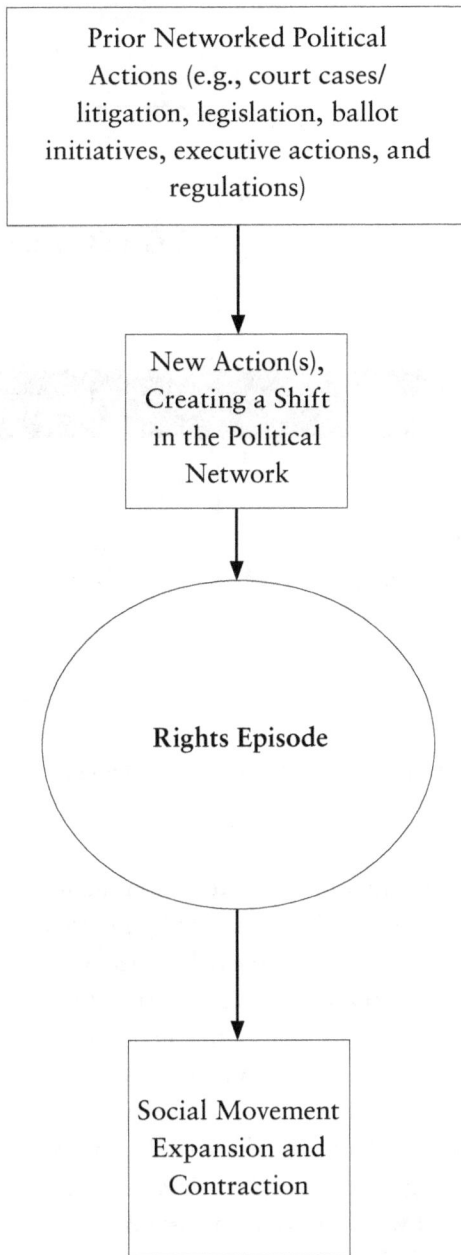

FIGURE I.1. Rights Episode Formation

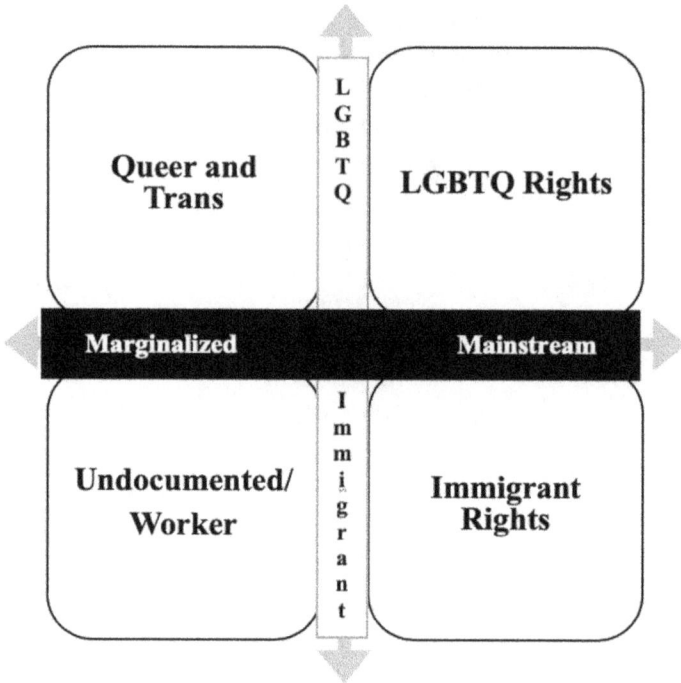

FIGURE I.2. Mainstream and Marginalized Organization Alignment

different minority communities depicted in this figure. This book enhances past scholarship on political movements by problematizing what counts as a movement. Rather than relatively homogenous entities composed of either policy-focused organizations *or* organizations that focus on litigation, the movements in this study are composed of coalitions of policy, litigation, protest, and health and human services organizations that represent minority communities.

In theory, coalition building may seem like an obvious way for movements to achieve rights wins and to thwart losses. However, coalition building across and within movements is a difficult and delicate process in practice, especially in contexts where the multiplicity of organizations that represent minority communities are rivals with one another when it comes to fundraising and grant applications. This has a great deal to do with how power dynamics influence the way that movement organizations align. For example, as illustrated in figure I.2, the separate organizations that exist within the LGBTQ and immigrant movements coalesce around four divisions driven by differences based on policy and subject position. Along the marginalized end of the movement advocacy spectrum, queer and trans organizations united around what mainstream groups perceived as more radical issues during the course of this study, such as prison abolition and trans inclusive health care. Marginalized groups that represent undocumented people and undocumented workers united behind such issues as forming a union to help fight exploitative labor practices, de-militarizing the border, and ending immigration detention. Along the mainstream end of the movement advocacy spectrum depicted in the figure, LGBTQ rights organizations united behind rights-based issues such as marriage equality and adding sexual orientation and gender identity and expression to anti-discrimination policy; immigrant rights organizations united behind Comprehensive Immigration Reform.

Recognizing the complex inter- and intra-movement dynamics that compose coalitions builds on the work of scholars such as Jane Ward, whose study of three queer organizations in Los Angeles reveals that mainstream organizations often employ marginalized subject positions when doing so is considered profitable, and suppress these subject positions when they are considered "unpredictable, unprofessional, messy, or defiant."[18] As in prior research, the policy positions and subject positions represented within the organizations in this study are frequently constrained by intersecting structural hierarchies that limit funding to one subject position but not others and, thus, constrain the set of possibilities available for all movement actors. For example, immigration advocacy is often limited by funding policies (in both public and private agencies) that encourage organizations to serve some immigrant populations over other, more disadvantaged communities. Disadvantaged communities are part of intersectionally marginalized subgroups within movement communities.[19] These intersectionally marginalized subgroups are composed of people whose subject positions encompass multiple marginalized sociopolitical groups, such as those who identify as part of both queer and migrant groups.

Many contemporary sociological and anthropological scholars in law and society argue that legal and political discourses or discursive practices shape how individuals understand their relationships with the world through the formation of collective subjectivities or subject positions.[20]

For example, a person's enacted and intersubjective understanding of their gender, race, and ethnicity is informed by discourses or discursive practices performed through social, legal, and political systems.[21] People can adopt multiple subject positions throughout their lives.[22] In this study, many interviewees adopt intersectionally marginalized subject positions. Someone has an intersectionally marginalized subject position if their understanding of self encompasses an LGBTQ and an immigrant or migrant subject position or another combination of subject positions associated with minority groups. For a more detailed description of the language I use in this book to describe different subject positions and identities, please see appendix 1.

Recognizing the existence of complex inter- and intra-movement coalitions composed of organizations of people who hold different subject positions destabilizes the tendency in social movement and sociolegal scholarship to understand political movements as unitary and static entities. By contrast, the boundaries of political movements are often somewhat arbitrary, always contestable, and openly contested. I argue that political movements are best understood as a dynamic series of shifting coalitions rather than as monolithic bodies that have clear, singular goals or directions. The groups that compose the shifting coalitions that constitute movements are unequally situated. Hierarchical power dynamics determine to a large extent which interests are centered within coalitions, or are considered the agenda of the mainstream movement, and which interests are considered marginal. As a result, the interests of groups that represent the most privileged or advantaged members of minority communities are frequently constructed as a movement's core, while comparatively less privileged, disadvantaged intersectionally marginalized groups (e.g., LGBTQ people of color, trans and queer people, and undocumented immigrants), and the interests that matter to them, are placed at the margins. In other words, movements are coalitions that are constantly changing, and every movement that comes together will tend to reinforce fractures based on differential power.

## Legal Mobilization, Rights, and Political Movement Formation

This is not to say that legal rights do not matter in political movement formation. Rights matter tremendously, but more for the extent to which they facilitate the expansion of inter- and intra-movement coalitions than as discrete policy ends or goals.[23] Hence, this book draws from law and society scholarship on legal mobilization in adopting a holistic understanding of rights and in analyzing how advocates mobilize legal rights at the grass roots in struggles for social change.[24] Instead of confining rights to litigation alone, legal mobilization scholars argue that rights are constituted through norms, symbols, and discourses in social and political life. Rights encompass not only court cases and judicial decisions but also grassroots aspirations—or how activists adopt new formations of rights from the bottom up.[25]

Many law and social change scholars examine which institutions are appropriate strategic choices for movement actors involved in struggles to obtain rights wins.[26] Their studies often focus on judicial decisions made by the US Supreme Court and on conversations with legal elites, without engaging with the experiences of grassroots movement actors. This book challenges this scholarship through an examination of in-depth interviews conducted with local movement actors who understand rights mostly as means or tools rather than ends. During my fieldwork, many interviewees were puzzled when I asked them what role they thought the law played in movements for social change. What did I mean by the law? Was I asking about a court case or legislation? Was I asking about legislation designed to benefit political movements, such as the DREAM Act, or harmful laws that increased criminalization? For movement actors, the law exists in every movement-based action.

Understanding rights as episodes that travel through a variety of different political and legal venues builds on the work of many legal mobilization scholars who adopt a broader conceptualization of what the law is, in ways that reflect the lived experiences of movement actors. Legal mobilization scholars have pointed out that the "law" encompasses institutionalized legal strategies, legal norms and symbols, and legal rights discourse.[27] Leading legal mobilization researchers argue that one appropriate way to measure legal reform efforts is not only by "initial goals, local scale conflict or immediate outcomes" but also by "lasting impacts on subsequent struggles—i.e., whether they are successfully contained or potentially expansionist in nature."[28]

Although legal mobilization research strives to create a dynamic, multidimensional account of political movement formation, some legal mobilization scholarship, like some political movement scholarship, assumes a focus on unidimensional, national, and single-axis political movements, especially scholarship on LGBTQ movement formation. These studies tend to examine political movements by focusing on just a few leading organizations that have seemingly clear goals and trajectories. As a result, these studies can miss the full complexity of political movements, which often develop out of inter- and intra-movement coalitions or a larger number of organizations of varying size, sophistication, and visibility. For example, legal mobilization research that studies LGBTQ movement formation tends to look to national litigation organizations or to focus on the extent to which a limited number of movement organizations advance issues that predominately concern white gay men and lesbians through either legislation or litigation.[29] These studies, though pioneering in their contributions to research on the potential and limits of the law, do not engage with how intense rights advocacy moments impact coalition dynamics across an array of minority communities. This book enhances contemporary legal mobilization scholarship—particularly scholarship that has focused on LGBTQ movement formation—by focusing on local organizations and grassroots inter- and intra-movement alliances rather than on national litigation- or policy-focused organizations alone.

## Outline of the Book

Coalitions form in paradoxical ways, simultaneously expanding and constraining political movement formation. The coalitions that emerged around statewide campaigns in this study expanded movements by mobilizing and activating new groups, creating a sense of inter- and intra-movement unity, and bringing more community awareness to smaller organizations that represent intersectional and more marginalized movement constituencies. However, as the coalitions in this project expanded movements, they also constrained them, limiting the issues and opportunities available for marginalized group members, driving resources toward larger organizations that serve comparatively more privileged members of minority communities, and reinforcing historic power inequities within political movements. I present this argument across four chapters.

Chapter 1 theorizes how rights episodes impact social movement formation, examined through the lens of the Referendum 74 campaign for marriage equality in Washington State. Many scholars see movements through the lens of single organizations that can easily pick and choose between using litigation or using political venues to accomplish social change.[30] Conceiving of rights as "episodes," however, emphasizes that much of group-driven social movement politics is not grand strategizing or tactical decisions about whether to fight in court or at the legislature. Rather, groups involved in political movement struggles are responding to different circumstances and threats, and no one has perfect agency or a purely strategic way of thinking. Chapter 1 makes this apparent by explaining the dynamics of Washington State's marriage equality rights episode—the largest rights episode that occurred during the course of my research in Washington State. The chapter includes a historical analysis of the formation of the marriage equality rights episode and an examination of its effects on cross-community alliances in the state.

Chapter 2 is a historical analysis of coalition alignment around immigrant rights in Arizona, focusing on the rights episode that emerged out of SB 1070 in 2010, the infamous "show me your papers" law. Following the passage of SB 1070, marginalized immigrant and queer and trans movement organizations in Arizona constructed a civic engagement coalition that conducted voter registration drives and get-out-the-vote efforts to increase their political capacity in the state. Through this expansive coalition, marginalized organizations largely built the political power necessary to engage in future movement struggles, including the recent successful campaign to remove Sheriff Joe Arpaio from office. At the same time, SB 1070 also had some containing effects on movement mobilization by funneling movement advocacy into cyclical campaigns and centering the experiences of the most privileged constituencies within minority populations. Through an analysis of Arizona's SB 1070, a defensive rights episode that activated an entire generation, this chapter further articulates my understanding of how rights struggles can operate as episodes that paradoxically at once expand and ossify political movements.

Chapter 3 addresses how the inter- and intra-movement coalitions described in the preceding chapters formed and why these coalitions were often unable to successfully pursue issues designed to uproot power. This chapter delineates, based on an analysis of patterns across in-depth interviews with organization leaders, advocates, and community workers, which factors contributed to the simultaneous expansion and contraction of inter- and intra-movement coalitions in Washington and Arizona. This chapter further develops how coalitions unite and fracture through the construction of a shared past narrative and a common core of opponents.[31] I argue that the creation of a narrative of a common political movement past based on shared opponents facilitated the formation of coalitions in both states and, in doing so, expanded movement mobilization. Movement constituents formed inter- and intra-movement coalitions in Washington and Arizona by constructing narratives and building relationships around the idea that individuals and groups involved in these coalitions were part of one community that shared a common political movement past, or "civil rights" past, and the same opponents. This enabled the new relationships built between and across seemingly disparate movements to last beyond episodic rights campaigns, in some circumstances contributing to movement expansion and mobilization over time. However, the formation of this collective past simultaneously constrained political movements by reinforcing historic exclusions based on power. Chapter 3 ends with a discussion of how the formation of inter- and intra-movement alliances within both states tended to fracture and contain movements.

Chapter 4 examines how intersectionally marginalized people within movements have in some contexts strategically pushed back against the movement contraction discussed in the previous chapters. Members of intersectionally marginalized subgroups helped both mainstream and marginalized organizations thwart the constraining effects of movement formation in some circumstances. I argue that these *intersectional translators* are tactically important because (1) they combat the constraints of a discrete rights focus by demonstrating how this is strategically short-sighted and how adopting a long-term commitment to undoing systemic oppression is in the interests of coalition partners, and (2) they call attention to the fact that inadequate commitment to the most marginal is a failure to advance justice. Using original data constructed from in-depth interviews and participant observations conducted with movement actors in Washington State and Arizona, chapter 4 demonstrates how intersectional translators create opportunities for political movement formation through participating in and intentionally utilizing rights campaigns as resources for more expansionist ends; through the construction of new groups and subgroups; and through educational outreach and in-depth conversations across and within mainstream and marginalized movement organizations.

The concluding chapter offers suggestions, based on the analysis related in each chapter, for avoiding marginalization and movement containment in some contexts. I delineate four ways that political movement actors can minimize coalition fragmentation: (1) by constructing a shared movement past and highlighting common opponents both during and after rights campaigns; (2) by devoting more resources to marginalized groups and individuals and providing opportunities for them to lead coalition organizing; (3) by adopting an expansionist commitment to movement formation through a politics of solidarity and through strategically using rights campaigns to further this commitment; and (4) by forming non-partisan institutionalized grassroots advocacy networks that exist in separate spaces than Democratic or Republican party politics. These suggestions are difficult to implement in all settings and contexts. Nevertheless, they serve as aspirational guidelines for pushing back against the hierarchical power dynamics that exist in our society and frequently manifest in political movement organizing. This chapter ends with an examination of specific inter- and intra-movement coalitions that have successfully adopted some of these suggestions. I focus especially on the coalitions formed to thwart attacks on the trans community in Washington (the Washington SAFE Alliance and Washington Won't Discriminate), the coalition to remove Sheriff Joe Arpaio in Arizona (the Bazta Arpaio campaign), and select campaigns outside the two states at the center of this book, such as the student movement against gun violence and the #RedForEd teacher's movement.

This book constructs a new theoretical framework for explaining how rights operate in movements for social change; this framework centers the standpoint of activists through an analysis of in-depth interviews conducted with grassroots activists engaged in political movement coalition building. In doing so, it examines the extent to which rights struggles expand movements within heavily constrained political contexts as well as limit the opportunities for movement building available for oppressed communities. We should understand rights struggles as episodes: intense advocacy moments created when external events alter a local political network, creating for the first time the possibility for a major legal rights advance or loss. These intense legal rights advocacy moments can result in the formation of inter- and intra-movement coalitions and thus expand political movement mobilization. At the same time, these moments also involve the further exclusion of intersectionally disadvantaged organizations and people within movements—people like Juan and Emilio, the queer migrant community workers whose stories opened this introduction. In describing the marriage equality movement, Emilio pointed out how the movement was "unrealistic" for his community because most undocumented immigrants cannot obtain immigration status through marriage. Similarly, Juan saw the struggle for marriage as part of an exclusive "gay agenda" that was unconcerned with issues that most impacted the queer migrant community. Same-sex marriage was a rights win for the LGBTQ community, but it was also a limiting, exclusive win that sidelined the interests of Juan's and Emilio's communities and reinforced the interests of more advantaged lesbian and gay people over others. The following pages delve into contradictions in legal rights advocacy that aims to achieve an egalitarian goal while simultaneously furthering the marginalization of others. In doing so, this book examines the extent to which inter- and intra-movement coalitions formed to win rights or thwart rights losses represent and serve intersectionally marginalized communities—groups in political movements that are often absent in contemporary accounts of political movement formation.

Chapter 1

# A "NEUTRON STAR"

Marriage Equality and Created Rights Episodes

Bianca: I was dismayed, but not actually surprised, to notice that [mainstream LGBTQ organization] had effectively collapsed, *and the analogy was the neutron star*. That you had this hot, bright, burning ball of energy that was providing life and so much movement and progression that had collapsed to almost nothing and it was still hot, but it was super dense, and it had almost a gravitational pull of its own. It wasn't quite a black hole, but it wasn't providing the impetus anymore. It wasn't a viable source of light and energy anymore. [emphasis added]

The organization leaders and advocates I interviewed for this book used similar terminology to describe intense rights-based advocacy moments. They would call these moments "fires," "explosions," "machines," "hurricanes," "vortexes," and "neutron stars." Each analogy captures how heated rights struggles can sometimes manifest into mobilizing moments, or *rights episodes*, that activate new organizations and facilitate partnerships at the same time that they contain political movements by focusing advocacy around discrete issues that usually do not serve the interests of marginalized people. How do struggles to obtain rights wins and thwart rights losses impact political movements? How do they contribute to and/ or inhibit the formation of inter- and intra-movement coalitions?

Scholars are increasingly sophisticated about how they study the implications of rights struggles and litigation on political movements. Many law and society scholars examine the role that law plays in movements for social change by focusing on litigation alone, arguing that litigation largely contains political movements by provoking electoral and policy setbacks that usually thwart any rights victory achieved in court.[1] For this reason, these scholars imply that the law, understood as litigation, is not an appropriate strategic choice for movement actors in struggles for social change. Other legal scholars who focus on litigation highlight the expansionist potential within legal rights wins, arguing that rights can serve as a useful strategic choice for political movements.[2]

Law and social change studies that focus on litigation can assume that movement actors are in a position to select one type of political tactic or forum (e.g., either legislation or litigation) in social change struggles. One manifestation of this assumption is research that sets up dichotomies between different political venues without considering how access to these forums differs depending on context. These studies often construct litigation and other political tactics, such as legislation and ballot initiative campaigns, within separate spheres rather than as networked political forums that influence one another. For these scholars, the courts are a "hollow hope" for advancing social change, and, thus, their findings suggest that some political venues such as legislatures and executive agencies are better suited for the advancement of political movement goals and for winning rights.[3]

Studies that construct social change models based on assumptions that political and legal venues are the same in each context present several problems for movement advocates. First, the opportunities available for movement actors are deeply constrained and dependent on the political environment. For example, progressive advocates in states with Republican legislatures with political ideologies that differ from their own have very little opportunity to advance anything perceived as partisan, progressive legislation. Indeed, most of the legislative struggles that progressive advocates organize in these state contexts focus on stopping legislation that harms the communities they serve. In this context, courts sometimes do protect minority communities whose lives are threatened by toxic legislation that infringes on their constitutional rights. Court wins that prevent the advancement of harmful legislation, such as legislation that takes away anti-discrimination protections for LGBTQ people or creates new criminal penalties for migrants, can become vehicles for empowering minority communities to mobilize in hostile environments.[4] It is important to note, however, that litigation strategies can also backfire and constrain the ability to advance movement goals. For example, courts provide little opportunity to advance rights in political contexts where the courts are controlled by conservative judges who are unwilling to interpret constitutional rights in ways that broadly benefit minority communities. This is what happened with LGBTQ movement advocacy in Washington State. In Washington, a court case loss constrained movement actors' ability to strategically use state courts as venues for achieving marriage equality, but also enabled the formation of a rights episode around marriage equality in the state's legislature and at the ballot box.

Second, political movement advocates' ability to make strategic choices between political venues is tempered by the actions of opponent groups. Political movements do not exist in vacuums; they develop in concert with opponents and counter-movements that dictate what choices are available for progressive advocates as opponent groups attempt to maintain the status quo. During my fieldwork, I witnessed movement organizations scrap entire agendas and strategies when opponent organizations and legislators introduced legislation or filed a lawsuit that required immediate action. Movement actors, particularly those who are concerned with rights-based ideological struggles that do not offer material outcomes for most members of a minority community, are largely dependent on opposition strategies and agendas, which frequently dictate how rights battles are waged.[5] Even when movement actors pursue a specific strategy, they do not have complete control over how this strategy will manifest in the real world, where opponent groups mobilize to thwart a rights win and even the best planned messaging and organizing strategies can fail to persuade the public. In this context, strategic choices among political venues are intensely constrained.

Finally, scholarship that constructs political venues within separate spaces does not delve into the various ways in which different political and legal venues are deeply networked. Court decisions can constrain or expand the extent to which legislatures can be strategically used as venues for change, while new legislation can constrain or expand political opportunities that enable the possibility for change through litigation. In movement struggles, different political and legal forums are so intertwined that it is often impossible to distill them into separate variables. Struggles over rights often involve intense advocacy fights that develop between movement organizations and opponent groups and play out over a variety of different types of institutions. These episodic advocacy moments encourage groups to use all the strategies and tactics they have in their arsenals, including referencing court decisions during legislative hearings to argue why a piece of legislation should or should not get enacted, and citing legislation during court hearings to persuade the judiciary. The courts constrain the types of laws that legislatures can enact and the type of language that appears in ballot initiatives. Contemporary Supreme Court precedent that is used to determine the contours of fundamental rights requires courts to consider legislative intent and political histories, including the laws that state legislatures have and have not passed, when deciding cases.

For these reasons, constructing political and legal strategies as distinct rather than overlapping and intertwined is not useful for movement advocates whose experience with movement advocacy emphasizes the myriad ways political and legal venues are interconnected. Strategy for movement advocates is more about being prepared for the next rights episode when it arises rather than about focusing on different types of political and legal venues. This is not to say that scholars who argue that litigation can have negative effects on movements are incorrect. Certainly, litigation that can constrain opportunities for change is often a harmful strategy for political movements. However, scholarship that focuses only on litigation without also considering the ways in which litigation is networked with other political forums can overdetermine the extent to which litigation is constraining.

I argue that campaigns to obtain rights wins and thwart losses are used as strategic tools (or as means rather than only as ends) by political movements across a multiplicity of interconnected legal and political forums. It is unrealistic for scholars to assume that it is always beneficial for movement actors to focus on pursuing change in courts *or* in other political venues. Movement actors are rarely wedded to one venue or another, because opportunities for change can open at a moment's notice or close swiftly in the face of new opponent threats, disrupting and realigning movement agendas and priorities. This infamously occurred in the LGBTQ rights movement in the 1980s, when the AIDS epidemic, combined with the ascent of right-wing politicians, forced movement actors to mobilize behind HIV/AIDS, derailing organization agendas

practically overnight. Because the conditions in which political movements operate are constantly changing, efforts at centering one type of
forum or tactic or issue in the pursuit of social change are not likely to
pay off. Instead, the strategy for grassroots movement actors is often to
be prepared in the long term for when the next intense rights episode will
activate and mobilize a mass movement. Political movement struggles are
unstable, hydra-like creatures that coalesce and divide as they attempt
to be responsive to myriad short-term threats that constrain choices,
delimit opportunities, and complicate long-term goals. These rippling
effects impact future political movement struggles, making it easier and
more difficult to organize around new issues depending on how much the
advocacy moment contributes to the unification and division of movement
alliances. These paradoxical effects of rights episodes are easily seen in
the development and decline of the marriage equality rights episode in
Washington State.

## Washington's Political Ethos: Liberalism in a Politically Divided State

Washington is a politically divided state. Western Washington, which
consists of a progressive urban stronghold in Seattle and the greater
Puget Sound region, has long housed Democratic and pro-labor voters
alongside a few Republican-leaning billionaires. Eastern Washington, by
contrast, houses the state's rural agricultural region and consists of voters who align with the political ideologies of conservative and religious
right politicians.[6] Despite the political division in the state between the
eastern and western regions, Washington is often characterized as a liberal or "blue" state because Democratic-leaning Western Washington is
also the most populous area of the state and nearly always carries the
state to the left in national elections. Because most people in Washington
live in Seattle and the Puget Sound region, the politics of Seattle permeate throughout the state, much to the consternation and resentment of
many Eastern Washingtonians. Although Washington's state capitol is
in Olympia, most of the statewide political movement organizations and
labor unions are in Seattle. For this reason, it is common for advocates
to live in Seattle, base much of their organizing in the city, and travel to
Olympia each January for the start of the legislative session in a "Seattle-
to-Olympia public policy pipeline." Because of the large influence that

Seattle, the state's progressive center, has on Washington politics, and because most statewide movement organizations are based in the city, Seattle provides a window into the dynamics that shape liberalism in Washington State.

## A Radical Past in a City with a "Dual Personality"

According to Washington State historian James Gregory, Seattle is a city with a "dual personality" and "strong echoes of a radical past."[7] The city's dual personality stems from the presence of both progressive labor activists and business billionaires within city limits. Today, Seattle and the greater Puget Sound region are home to some of the wealthiest men in the nation, including Amazon's Jeff Bezos and Microsoft's Bill Gates. These billionaires own and influence large swaths of the city, which underwent a tech and business boom during this study, driven by such companies as Amazon, Microsoft, and Alaska Airlines, whose headquarters are in the Puget Sound area. Although the tech boom is recent, the Puget Sound region has long encompassed wealthy international corporations—from the companies that profited off the Puget Sound area's major seaport in the 1800s to the Boeing aerospace company, which was founded in the area in the early 1900s and is one of the state's largest employers today. These corporations have tense and complicated relationships with progressive political movement advocates in Western Washington. Although Western Washington's corporations often support political movement campaigns, such as the campaign to include LGBTQ status within the state's anti-discrimination laws in 2006 and the marriage equality campaign in 2012, they also support fiscally conservative policies aimed at weakening the labor movement in Washington. They have also donated to anti-union Democratic and Republican legislators in the past.[8] In 2012, executives at Microsoft helped Republicans capture the Washington State Senate with the assistance of a few fiscally conservative Democrats who decided to work with Republican state senators in the Majority Coalition Caucus. Republicans controlled the state senate during the course of this study, with Democrats ultimately gaining control of the chamber in the 2016 general election.

The liberal conservatism of large businesses and their CEOs in the Puget Sound region has contributed to the fracturing of progressive movement organizations in the state in ways that align with the critiques of scholars such as Ward,[9] who shows that mainstream organizations take up and reject marginalized community goals based on the whims of profitability. Many mainstream movement organizations apply for and accept funding from these companies when engaging in rights campaigns; others, especially marginalized organizations and those on the receiving end of anti-union efforts, are critical of the role these businesses play in local movement politics. This is just one facet of the long history of in-fighting in progressive circles in Washington, which prevented many organizations from forming sustained campaign alliances in the past. Movement organizations have overcome some of these divisions through the formation of expansive cross-community coalitions. However, although today's inter- and intra-movement coalitions often appear intersectional (because they include organizations from an array of different communities), they have difficulty maintaining unity and mobilization in the long term as campaign dynamics inevitably bring out these historic divisions.

## DIVERGENT SUBJECT POSITIONS ACROSS
## MOVEMENT COMMUNITIES IN SEATTLE

In addition to historic divisions over the role that large businesses should play in political movement campaigns, movement organizations also have a long history of political division because they represent communities that hold different subject positions within Washington's radical past. One subject position lies within Washington's historic labor activism. The state's labor movement past goes back to the late 1800s when the Puget Sound region experienced an economic boom in industrial sectors that attracted members of Eugene Debs's Social Democracy of America, an influx that ultimately spurred the creation of one of the largest branches of the Socialist Party in the nation in Washington State.[10] By 1936, the large impact that the Communist Party had in the state led then postmaster general James Farley to jokingly refer to the state as "the Soviet of Washington."[11] As late as 1964, about 45 percent of people in Washington held union memberships.[12] Although Washington's union membership has declined dramatically since 1964 along with that of the rest of the country, Washington still has one of the largest union memberships in the nation and was the fifth most unionized state in the US in 2017.[13]

A second subject position is based in Seattle's racial and ethnic minority and immigrant communities. These activist communities formed through grassroots organizing both for economic justice and against segregation, discrimination, and racial violence in Washington. Seattle, in particular, has a long history of racial segregation, from housing to access to restaurants, hotels, hospitals, and employment.[14] Although visible segregation in Seattle has diminished over time and Seattle's suburbs are some of the most diverse in the country, Seattle is still, in many ways, a de facto segregated city. This has a lot to do with how initial housing patterns were created through racially restrictive housing covenants that prevented homeowners in certain areas of the city from selling to minorities.[15] Furthermore, many unions in the state initially blocked racial minorities from union membership, spurring campaigns to end discriminatory hiring practices, such as the desegregation campaign at Boeing in the late 1930s and early 1940s, which sought to end the company's failure to hire black workers.[16] During World War II, Washington State's large Japanese American population was forced into internment camps. When they returned after the war, many were unable to regain access to their homes and businesses.[17] Steven, one of the interviewees who participated in this study, recalled the destructive impact that internment had on his family. Steven's grandparents lost their family farm after they were removed to an internment camp, and his grandfather, who "couldn't take the thought of starting over again," died a few weeks before the war ended.

Currently, Seattle is considered one of the whitest cities in the US, with a white population of 67 percent, according to demographic information from the last US Census. However, whiteness varies by neighborhood, with the most diversity in a few city neighborhoods and just outside the city's limits—an illustration of how Seattle's segregated past continues to shape the present.[18] Seattle's segregated past explains how organizations that represent immigrant communities and communities of color formed apart from political movement organizations in the area that serve the state's white liberal-leaning population. When movement organizations formed to address long-standing segregation, discrimination, and racial violence, they operated in tension with white progressive movement spaces. Yet, despite the history of racial discrimination and violence, Washington has historically been in some ways more egalitarian than other states when it comes to race. For example, Washington was one of the only states that did not pass racial anti-miscegenation laws in the nineteenth and twentieth centuries. Over time and through grassroots campaigns, racial tensions across movement organizations have somewhat diminished; however, these divisions still permeate local political movement campaigns, presenting significant barriers to the formation of inter- and intra-movement coalitions.

A third subject position is based in Seattle's LGBTQ community, which, through grassroots activism, has moved from a position of invisibility and exile to a highly visible component of the state's political fabric. In the late 1800s, non-heterosexuality was treated as a criminal activity, and low-wage workers who engaged in same-sex sexual conduct were convicted under the state's anti-sodomy law.[19] Organizations and bars serving gay men and lesbians existed in Washington before the late 1960s; it was during this time period that Seattle gay and lesbian activists became more visible in local progressive circles and challenged the notion that non-heterosexuality is a social perversion that should be criminalized. After the 1969 New York City Stonewall uprising, the gay liberation movement spread to Washington State.[20] Through the grassroots advocacy of gay liberationists in Seattle, the city passed an employment anti-discrimination ordinance that prohibited discrimination based on sexual orientation in 1973, and a housing anti-discrimination ordinance that prohibited discrimination based on sexual orientation in housing in 1975.[21] As the gay liberation movement grew into the LGBTQ movement of today, divisions arose in the movement over tactics and the inclusion of queer and trans communities, racial and ethnic minorities, immigrants, and labor activism. Because of the historical divisions across the various political movement communities that compose Washington's progressive center, political movement coalitions, when they formed, were often weak. After individual campaigns, many early coalitions quickly fragmented due to political in-fighting. This began to change in the 2000s, in the various political campaigns leading up to the Referendum 74 campaign for marriage equality, which marked a historic alignment across the politically divided communities that make up progressive politics in Washington. How did new coalitions form across and within these political movement communities? Were they able to expand into new political movement struggles, or did they reinforce historic inequities, fragmenting movements in the immediate aftermath of a rights win?

An Offensive Rights Episode: The Formation of the
Washington State Referendum 74 Campaign for Marriage Equality

Political campaigns and court cases that advance human rights rarely
occur in isolation. Rather, they are often part of an intertwined sequence
of intense advocacy moments, or smaller campaigns, that build over time
and seemingly ignite overnight. This is certainly true of the Referendum
74 campaign for marriage equality. The Referendum 74 campaign was
built on four decades of episodic rights moments. Each moment built off
the last, expanding the array of opportunities available for advocates
and, eventually, expanding the array of communities and organizations
that worked together in coalition to advance same-sex marriage. When
lesbian and gay activists first began to fight for marriage equality in
Washington State, they did so largely alone, without the support of political officials or other progressive political movements. Through a series
of prior networked rights episodes, movement actors constructed cross-
community coalitions that ultimately formed the backbone of the massive Washington United for Marriage coalition in 2012, which included
over five hundred organizations at its peak.

Advocacy around statewide rights campaigns has appeared intersectional
in Washington State for several decades. Today, Washington campaigns are
led by a multiplicity of organizations that represent an array of minority communities and special interests. In order to have any statewide mobilization
capacity, these groups have to operate in a somewhat intersectional manner,
building alliances and coalitions wherever needed in order to obtain statewide
rights advances. However, the alliances of the past were much more limited
than they are today. These prior statewide campaigns around rights func-
tioned as a series of smaller rights episodes that created the network of opportunities available for movement actors in Washington State. In the 2010s,
this network began to shift in favor of LGBTQ movement advocates who
wanted to win same-sex marriage for Washington. When the public became
more supportive of same-sex marriage, and major political officials, most notably President Barack Obama, endorsed marriage equality, an opening was
created in the fabric of Washington's political network, which facilitated the
development of a massive rights episode. Suddenly, the legislative and ballot
initiative process presented a viable opportunity for winning same-sex marriage for the first time. Figure 1.1 depicts the formation of the Referendum
74 rights episode in Washington State.

```
┌─────────────────────────────────┐
│  Prior Networked Political Actions │
│     (e.g., *Singer v. Hara*, state │
│   DOMA, Anderson-Murray Anti-     │
│   Discrimination Act, *Andersen v.* │
│   *King County*, Referendum 71)    │
└─────────────────────────────────┘
                  │
                  ▼
        ┌─────────────────────┐
        │  New Action(s), Creating │
        │   a Shift in the Political │
        │   Network (public and    │
        │  presidential support for │
        │   marriage equality)     │
        └─────────────────────┘
                  │
                  ▼
              ╭─────────╮
             (  Referendum 74 Offensive  )
             (   Rights Episode          )
              ╰─────────╯
                  │
                  ▼
          ┌───────────────┐
          │ Social Movement │
          │ Expansion and  │
          │  Contraction   │
          └───────────────┘
```

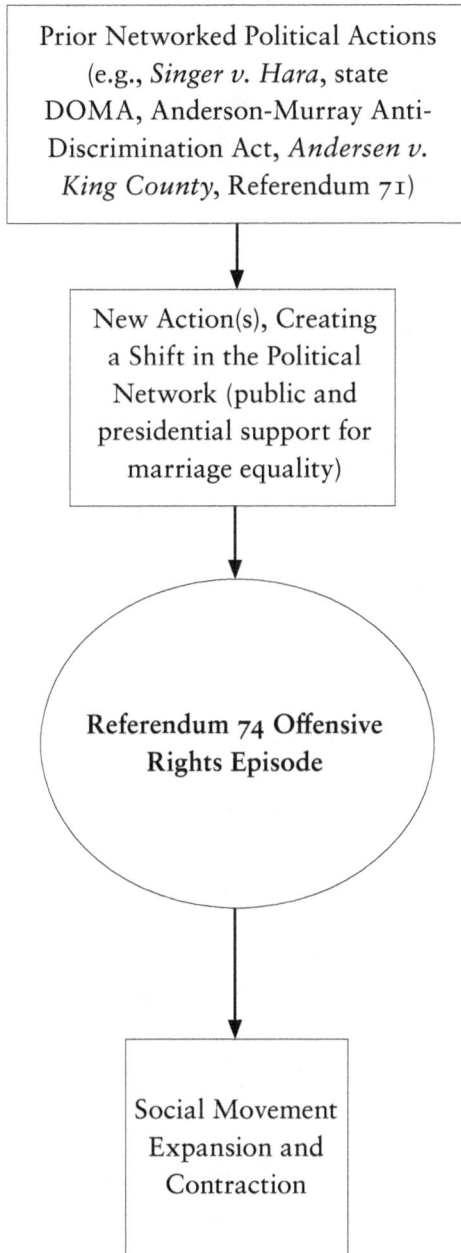

FIGURE 1.1. Formation of the Referendum 74 Offensive Rights Episode

Figure 1.1 illustrates how the Referendum 74 rights episode (i.e., the campaign for marriage equality) emerged out of networked political and legal arenas wherein prior events overlapped with and influenced the formation of new episodic rights moments. In Washington, the state's network consisted of a series of episodic moments prior to the formation of the marriage equality rights episode in 2012. These included a state appellate court case that determined in 1974 that there was no state constitutional right to same-sex marriage (*Singer v. Hara*); a state Defense of Marriage Act (DOMA) in 1998, which limited marriage to heterosexual couples; a law that expanded anti-discrimination protections in the state to include sexual orientation and gender identity (the Anderson-Murray Anti-Discrimination Act); a state supreme court case that determined in 2006 that there was no state constitutional right to marriage (*Andersen v. King County*); and a referendum in 2009 that expanded the rights and benefits available to domestic partners in the state (Referendum 71). These episodic moments occurred across a variety of political and legal forums and are indicative of an ongoing struggle between movement and counter-movement forces on LGBTQ rights issues in Washington. The next sections explore each of these episodic moments in greater detail and delineate how the marriage equality rights episode emerged out of a shift in the state's political and legal network.

"LAUGHED OUT OF COURT": POLITICAL FAILURE
IN THE EARLY STAGES OF THE CONTEMPORARY
LGBTQ RIGHTS MOVEMENT

It is possible to trace the origins of the struggle for marriage equality in Washington State back to September 20, 1971, when Paul Barwick and Faygele Ben Miriam (then named John Singer) went to the King County auditor's office to request a marriage license.[22] Barwick and Ben Miriam were part of the Seattle chapter of the Gay Liberation Front and considered themselves radical activists in the "business of gay liberation."[23] Lloyd Hara, then King County auditor, swiftly rejected their application for a marriage license and the couple sued, testing the boundaries of Washington State's newly adopted Equal Rights Amendment (ERA), which used gender-neutral language, prohibiting discrimination on the basis of "sex."[24] The ERA, which altered the Washington State Constitution, stated that "equality of rights and responsibility under the law shall not be denied or abridged on account of sex."[25]

At the time, Barwick and Ben Miriam believed that the state ERA could provide a new opportunity for the recognition of same-sex marriage through a court case. In the appellate court case *Singer v. Hara*, Barwick and Ben Miriam argued, based on the text of the new ERA, that it was unconstitutional for Washington State to deny same-sex couples the right to marry because of their sex. The appellate court roundly rejected Barwick and Ben Miriam's argument, holding that the couple was not denied a marriage license because of their sex, or "status as males," but, rather, because the state recognizes "that our society as a whole views marriage as the appropriate and desirable forum for procreation and the rearing of children."[26] Barwick and Ben Miriam still had an equal right to marry, but they could only do so for procreative purposes with a person of the opposite sex, according to the court.

When referencing *Singer v. Hara* years later, lesbian and gay community advocates would say that Barwick and Ben Miriam were "laughed out of court," that their case was treated as a ridiculous legal exercise with no real possibility of success.[27] However, the events that preceded the case are representative of how the fight for marriage equality would progress in Washington over several decades: as an intertwined political struggle that encompassed multiple forums and tactics. In *Singer*, activists decided to sue because they felt that a state constitutional amendment (the ERA), recently passed in two political forums (the legislature and the ballot box), provided a new opportunity for change in the courts. Much of the court decision was dedicated to interpreting whether the amendment intended to create a new right to same-sex marriage. The case constituted the first in a series of smaller rights episodes culminating in the successful marriage equality rights episode in 2012.

A State Defense of Marriage Act (DOMA)

The interconnectedness of political and legal forums is also apparent in other struggles over same-sex marriage that developed over time in Washington. Twenty-four years after *Singer v. Hara*, prior court cases were used during legislative debates as the Washington State legislature considered passing a state Defense of Marriage Act (DOMA). Washington's DOMA further clarified that the state limited marriage to two-person heterosexual couples and would not recognize same-sex marriages conducted legally in other states. The Washington State DOMA passed in 1998 after nearly a decade of statewide advocacy that centered on pro- and anti-LGBTQ ballot initiative campaigns. The advocacy around the ballot initiatives in the 1990s marked the beginning of inter- and intra-movement coalition building in the LGBTQ, labor, and immigrant movements in Washington.

During the 1990s, a number of ballot measures helped form a backbone of common experiences of discrimination and a common core of opponents across the LGBTQ and racial justice movements in Washington, which aided in the formation of movement coalitions. These coalitions began to form in the early 1990s through various initiative campaigns and then grew through the 2000s, reaching their greatest capacity in 2012 during the Referendum 74 campaign for marriage equality. The ballot initiatives that contributed to the formation of inter- and intra-movement coalitions in Washington by emphasizing common opponents included (1) a pair of failed anti-LGBTQ initiatives in 1994 (Initiative 608 and Initiative 610); (2) a failed pro-LGBTQ movement initiative in 1997 that sought to pass anti-discrimination protections for lesbian and gay people (Initiative 677); and (3) a successful anti–affirmative action initiative in 1998 (Initiative 200).

The dual anti-LGBTQ initiatives in 1994 sought to ban all localities from passing civil rights laws that protected LGBTQ people from discrimination, prohibit schools from teaching non-heterosexuality as an appropriate lifestyle, and bar lesbians and gay men from being adoptive or foster parents.[28] These initiatives were fueled by an uptick in countermovement advocacy in Washington State and Oregon that likely occurred as a result of the 1993 lawsuit in Hawaii, *Baehr v. Lewin*, which provided a legal rationale for recognizing same-sex marriage as a constitutional right.[29] When LGBTQ movement opponents initiated both ballot campaigns, LGBTQ rights advocates formed the statewide advocacy organization Hands Off Washington for the purpose of fighting the initiatives and building partnerships with other minority community organizations, labor unions, and political organizations in Washington.

In interviews about the formation of Hands Off Washington in the documentary *We're Here to Stay*, LGBTQ advocates argued that tensions ran high around issues of representation and identity during this time.

Advocates struggled to form lasting and genuine partnerships with other organizations and individuals. The first executive director of Hands Off Washington, Karen Cooper, illuminated how, despite building what was then one of the most racially, economically, and politically diverse coalitions in support of LGBTQ rights in the state's history, the partnerships that formed were intensely volatile and unstable:

> Karen Cooper: We had many, many people working for a common goal that had never worked together before, didn't know each other, sometimes knew each other and didn't like each other. [We] came from all kinds of different backgrounds, classes, political experience, lack of political experiences, Republicans, Democrats, conservatives, liberals. And these folks were all struggling to work together on a common goal on an issue that was so intensely personal. An example I've always used about why the campaign was difficult was that, let's say we're ordering some tablets and whether we're going to get yellow tablets or white tablets and nobody cares. However, at Hands Off Washington that could become a huge issue. The minorest of decisions, the smallest of decisions could become major battlegrounds because people's lives were being threatened, people's lives were at stake, so everything became highly charged with emotion.[30]

Despite the fragile nature of the coalitions that formed in the early 1990s, LGBTQ movement advocates were able to gain the support of some organizations that represented communities of color in the state by emphasizing common opponents. Specifically, LGBTQ activists discovered during opposition research that the Citizen's Alliance, one of the LGBTQ opponent coalitions at the time, had ties to the white supremacist populist party and the Ku Klux Klan. LGBTQ activists argued that they were able to use this information to convince some community of color organizations to join LGBTQ community-led coalitions in the 1990s.[31]

Other individuals associated with the LGBTQ rights movement at that time emphasized tensions around coalition formation. Patrick Hogan was an advocate with Bigot Busters, a Seattle-based grassroots group that formed in response to the anti-LGBTQ initiatives of the early 1990s. Bigot Busters engaged in what many other LGBTQ advocates saw as unacceptable and radical tactics, such as following opponents at shopping malls as the opponents attempted to gather signatures to place the anti-LGBTQ initiatives on the ballot, and intervening to explain why shoppers should refuse to sign.[32] In the following quotation, Hogan argues that, in addition to friction around representation and identity, movement actors divided over these tactical approaches:

> Patrick Hogan: There was an element of the community that always felt that the street activists, the radicals if you will, or you know the Queer Nation/ACT UP types were just giving everyone a bad name. And I think a lot of the friction came from that as well. You know, that this wasn't something that was acceptable somehow.[33]

From friction over political and racial identity to the types of tactics the political movement should pursue, divisions characterized the campaign to stop the anti-LGBTQ initiatives in the early 1990s. These fissures, along with the failed pro-LGBTQ movement ballot initiative campaign in 1997, eventually contributed to the dissolution of Hands Off Washington in the early 2000s.

Washington passed its state Defense of Marriage Act (DOMA) after the LGBTQ movement in the state was hobbled by the failure of Initiative 677, the 1997 ballot initiative that proposed expanding Washington State anti-discrimination law to cover sexual orientation.[34] The initiative failed by nearly 20 percentage points despite support from then governor Gary Locke, possibly because the initiative appeared on the ballot along with a pro-gun measure supported by the National Rifle Association, driving up conservative voter turnout.[35] Washington State has a history of opponent groups, led by conservative activist Tim Eyman, placing counter-movement issues on the ballot in order to drive up conservative voter turnout during general elections. This tactic was famously used across the nation in 2004 when conservative activists placed constitutional amendments limiting marriage to two-person heterosexual couples on eleven state ballots in order to increase conservative voter turnout for then president George W. Bush in state electoral races.[36] However, opponent messaging (which was based in a moral panic about homosexuality harming children) during the 1997 ballot initiative campaign likely played a role in the initiative's defeat as well.[37]

Activated by the loss of Initiative 677, opponents swiftly worked to pass a statewide DOMA in the 1998 legislative session, with bipartisan, veto-proof support for a bill. During one floor debate of the proposed DOMA, legislators argued that the DOMA was necessary to clarify that *Singer v. Hara*'s prohibition on same-sex marriage applied throughout Washington State and not only in the appellate court district in which it was decided.[38] In arguing for the DOMA, State Representative Larry Sheahan contended that legislative action was necessary "to guide the courts," which have said that "if an issue is brought before the legislature, even if it fails, . . . that can be brought into play when [looking] into legislative intent."[39] In arguing against the state DOMA, then state representatives Dow Constantine and Ed Murray maintained that legislative action was unnecessary because *Singer v. Hara* prohibited same-sex couples from marrying already and the US Congress had enacted a federal DOMA, which granted states the ability to refuse to recognize same-sex marriages granted in other states.[40] During the floor debate on Washington's DOMA, discussions of what *Singer v. Hara* did and did not do were used by legislators to persuade their colleagues. Ultimately, both Republicans and Democrats in the Washington State legislature passed the DOMA, overriding a veto from then governor Gary Locke.[41]

Due to the networked way that the struggle over same-sex marriage developed in Washington State, Melo argues that the various battles over marriage equality in Washington illustrate that political campaigns can build off one another over time, creating new political opportunities for change.[42] Although it is certainly true that the sequence of political campaigns built off one another in Washington State, this construction does not occur along a linear trajectory from legislation to court case or vice versa. Instead, legislation and litigation, as political tactics, are interwoven with each other. The continual use of references to different tactics in varying political forums demonstrates that each forum does not exist in a separate sphere but, rather, is intimately interconnected with others—and is not necessarily on a forward path that leads to progress.

No Longer a Laughing Matter:
Possibilities in a Tough Courtroom Battle

The struggle over marriage equality in Washington clearly grew over time in a series of smaller rights episodes that involved court cases, legislation, and ballot initiatives. Following the enactment of a state DOMA in 1998, the next rights episode around same-sex marriage emerged through the court cases *Andersen v. King County* and *Castle v. State*, two lower court cases that were ultimately consolidated under the name *Andersen v. King County* and heard by the Washington State Supreme Court in 2006. Advocates within Washington State's lesbian and gay community believed that an opportunity for marriage equality was opening nationwide after the Massachusetts Supreme Court legalized same-sex marriage in the state in 2003 through *Goodridge v. Department of Public Health* and as public support for marriage equality grew.[43] These advocates felt that *Goodridge* provided a legal framework for arguing in the Washington State courts for the right to marry. Much had changed in Washington since *Singer v. Hara.* The state's LGBTQ community had fought for and against numerous local ordinances, state bills, and ballot initiatives by the early 2000s. This, along with the increased political representation of LGBTQ people in the state and shifts in national politics around the LGBTQ rights movement, created a climate in Washington that lesbian and gay advocates believed would enable the state's supreme court to legalize same-sex marriage in *Andersen v. King County.*

Despite changes in the national and local political networks, however, LGBTQ advocates were wary of initiating a court case in Washington State. Washington Supreme Court justices are elected, unlike in other states, including Massachusetts. Hence, LGBTQ advocates feared that marriage equality was still unpopular enough nationwide in the early 2000s to influence how the Washington justices would decide *Andersen v. King County.* Many LGBTQ advocates wondered whether it would be better to wait a few years to pursue a lawsuit once public opinion shifted even more and after more states legalized same-sex marriage. Ultimately, some advocates believed that they were forced to risk a case when, in 2004, Dan Savage, the openly gay editor of the alt-weekly newspaper *The Stranger* applied for a marriage license in Washington State with a lesbian friend in an attempt to demonstrate the absurdity of a state DOMA that forced gay men to marry women if they wanted access to marriage.[44] These local LGBTQ advocates decided to file same-sex marriage lawsuits with couples who they believed better represented normative marriage ideals in order to prevent Dan Savage from initiating a lawsuit as a less than ideal plaintiff without the backing of the LGBTQ legal advocacy network. In other words, the dynamics underlying the decision to pursue a marriage equality lawsuit in Washington are an example of how an unplanned new political action can derail movement strategy, forcing advocates to respond to the new threat at a moment's notice.[45]

Despite increasing support for same-sex marriage, LGBTQ political movement mobilization was still constrained. In an amicus curiae brief filed by leaders of communities of color in support of the lesbian and gay plaintiffs in *Andersen v. King County*, interested amici included the state's Asian American Bar Association, the state's Latino/a Bar Association, and the state's African American Bar Association rather than membership-driven civil rights movement organizations. The only civil rights organization that signed the brief was Hate Free Zone of Washington (now OneAmerica). The amicus brief also included a list of leaders of civil rights organizations that represent communities of color, but *without their organizational affiliations*. Hate Free Zone's decision to intervene was not made lightly or without opposition. Years later, when reflecting on the organization's decision to support same-sex couples in *Andersen*, Pramila Jayapal (the founder of Hate Free Zone, who later became a congressional representative) recalled a heated debate among the organization's membership that centered on issues of faith that fostered deep conversations among the organization's members.[46]

Ultimately, *Andersen v. King County* failed to legalize same-sex marriage in Washington State, despite the expectations of LGBTQ rights advocates who believed that they would win marriage equality at the state supreme court. Once again, the court referenced state legislation in reaching this decision. For example, when considering whether lesbian and gay people are a suspect class, the court discussed the 2006 Anderson-Murray Anti-Discrimination Act, which prohibited discrimination based on sexual orientation and gender identity and expression in public accommodations. Unfortunately for the plaintiffs and lesbian and gay community advocates, the court referenced this legislation to support the argument that lesbian and gay people are politically powerful, as they were able to use the legislative process to pass LGBTQ-friendly legislation. This argument supported the court's conclusion that lesbian and gay people are not a suspect class, so a law that discriminates on the basis of sexual orientation, here the state DOMA, was not subject to a heightened-scrutiny constitutional test that likely would have resulted in the state DOMA's demise.[47]

Lesbian and gay advocates also credited the 2004 election for the court loss. As noted earlier, in Washington State, supreme court justices are elected into office. During the 2004 election, one characterized by increased conservative voter turnout due in part to ballot initiative campaigns against same-sex marriage in states across the US, Faith Ireland, the liberal and pro–marriage equality state supreme court candidate, lost the election to the more conservative Jim Johnson. This shifted the balance on the state supreme court against same-sex marriage.[48] Even though the lesbian and gay community lost the *Andersen v. King County* case, language in the court's opinion criticized the legislature for passing the DOMA.[49] At the end of the *Andersen* case, recognizing the harms caused by the failure to extend marriage to same-sex couples, the court admonished the legislature, asserting that, "given the clear hardship faced by same-sex couples evidenced in this lawsuit, the legislature may want to reexamine the impact of marriage laws on all citizens of this state." The court's explicit language calling on the legislature to pass protective legislation for same-sex couples contributed to the formation of a new political opening to advance marriage benefits for same-sex couples.[50]

## "Everything but Marriage": The Referendum 71 Campaign

*Andersen v. King County* altered the political context in Washington and created the possibility for advocates to advance a law that for the first time expanded domestic partnerships to encompass all the rights and benefits of marriage, in what at the time was the largest episodic rights moment in the struggle for marriage equality. In 2009, the LG-BTQ rights movement in Washington mobilized behind a campaign for domestic partnerships, newly bolstered by a court opinion that explicitly stated that there was no reason why "the legislature or the people acting through initiative process would be foreclosed from extending the right to marry to gay and lesbian couples in Washington."[51] After the *Andersen* case, legislators moved to expand domestic partner benefits in Washington State. This effort peaked with the passage of SB 5688 in 2009, the "everything but marriage" law, which expanded previous domestic partnership laws in the state by adding domestic partnerships to all remaining areas of state law that addressed married couples.[52]

Once again, floor debates in the legislature addressed case law. Legislators on both sides of the aisle discussed legal precedent to persuade their colleagues. State Senator Val Stevens discussed both *Singer v. Hara* and *Andersen v. King County* to support the argument that courts in the state have historically opposed same-sex marriage. Pointing to these cases, Senator Stevens argued during floor debate that legislators should vote against SB 5688 because "domestic partnership equals marriage," contravening legal precedent.[53] By contrast, State Senator Ed Murray argued that, although Senator Stevens was "correct when she described the process that the courts went through when they ruled DOMA constitutional, the courts also said the legislature offered gay and lesbian citizens of this state a remedy and that's what we're doing with this bill"—a clear reference to language the court used in *Andersen* asserting that the legislature had the authority to determine how the state should recognize same-sex relationships.[54] SB 5688 ultimately passed and was signed into law by then governor Christine Gregoire.[55] However, Washington State has a referendum process that allows citizens to refer acts of the legislature to the people through a petition process.[56] Opponent groups, led by Larry Stickney, the president of the Washington Values Alliance, filed Referendum 71 and collected enough signatures to place the referendum on the November 2009 general election ballot.[57]

Ballot initiative campaigns, like the Referendum 71 "everything but marriage" campaign, provide a unique opportunity for movement expansion. According to Rachel, an advocate who worked with an organization that builds cross-community coalition campaigns in Washington, rights campaigns are important political opportunities because they enable deep conversations across and within minority communities:

> Rachel: The opportunity with a campaign of course is that, as you're door knocking, as you're canvassing, as you're doing training with people, as you're developing commercials and radio sound bites, you are having as well a cultural conversation that is revealing people's kind of unspoken homophobia and transphobia. And then you help them shift.

The "cultural conversation" that emerges in a ballot initiative campaign is also in place in rights campaigns around court cases and legislation as well, though to a lesser degree. Recall that Representative Jayapal and other Hate Free Zone (now OneAmerica) leaders also had deep conversations with their organization's members when the group decided to support same-sex couples in *Andersen v. King County*. However, ballot initiatives require even more focused conversations between members of disparate communities and a larger degree of statewide mobilization to get out the vote necessary to secure a win. Referendum 71 ultimately expanded the coalition of organizations that supported the rights of same-sex couples as a result of the "cultural conversations" that occurred during the campaign. The new coalition included a collective of organizations that represented immigrants and communities of color, a clear expansion from *Andersen v. King County*, when only Hate Free Zone and minority bar associations intervened to support same-sex couples. Thirty-one organizations that represented immigrants and communities of color ultimately endorsed Referendum 71.[58]

## A "NEUTRON STAR": MARRIAGE EQUALITY AND THE REFERENDUM 74 RIGHTS EPISODE

Voters approved Referendum 71, ending the episodic moment that emerged around legislation expanding domestic partnerships in 2009.[59] Each of the smaller episodic rights moments described thus far is indicative of an expanding LGBTQ movement in Washington State, which mobilized over time by aligning with other movement organizations affiliated with the labor, immigrant, and racial justice movements in the state. This was especially true of the labor movement. A large number of labor organizations filed an amicus brief in support of same-sex couples in *Andersen v. King County*, and the labor movement both endorsed and provided significant resources to help pass Referendum 71.[60] The Referendum 74 campaign for marriage equality, which emerged in 2012, would expand the movement even further, pulling virtually every progressive organization in the state into a vortex around the rights episode.

In November 2011, a coalition of labor, civil liberties, immigrant, community of color, and religious organizations, calling themselves Washington United for Marriage, announced their intention to launch a campaign to legalize same-sex marriage in Washington State in 2012.[61] This coalition started to act in Washington State in response to the shifting political network, prompted by an increase of public and political support for same-sex marriage. The state's political network shifted further when President Obama publicly endorsed same-sex marriage in 2012.[62] As with Referendum 71, advocates began the marriage equality rights episode at the legislature with the understanding that a referendum was certain. Movement leaders who decided to introduce marriage equality legislation likely selected 2012 because it was a presidential election year, which would increase Democratic turnout in Washington State, and because new polling data suggested that public opinion in Washington was shifting in support of same-sex marriage.[63] In early 2012, Democrats, with the support of some Republicans, introduced SB 6239 in the Washington State legislature to legalize same-sex marriage.

Once again, legislators referred to litigation during floor debate as they attempted to persuade their colleagues to support or oppose SB 6239. For instance, State Senator Dan Swecker argued that doctors and "ordinary workers" who oppose same-sex marriage "would be subject to discrimination lawsuits if they chose not to offer their services due to their religious or moral beliefs." By contrast, State Senator Debbie Regala drew an analogy between the legalization of same-sex marriage and *Loving v. Virginia* (338 U.S. 1 [1967]), the 1967 US Supreme Court case that declared state bans on interracial marriage unconstitutional, a court case that legitimated her own interracial marriage.[64] In the Washington House of Representatives, Representative Jamie Pedersen opened floor debate by reading from the Ninth Circuit Court opinion in *Hollingsworth v. Perry* to demonstrate why marriage matters for same-sex couples, and Representative Jay Rodne read from *Andersen v. King County* to illustrate that marriage should be limited to heterosexual marriages for procreative purposes.[65] The Washington State legislature ultimately passed SB 6239, legalizing same-sex marriage in Washington State, and the bill was signed into law by then governor Christine Gregoire.[66] Opponents quickly mobilized, forming their own coalition, Preserve Marriage Washington, and filed Referendum 74.[67] A court struggle over the language of the referendum ensued. A Thurston County court ultimately removed biased language from the referendum at the urging of marriage equality advocates. Following this short court battle, Preserve Marriage Washington collected enough signatures to place Referendum 74 on the November 2012 general election ballot.[68]

LGBTQ, labor, immigrant, and community of color advocates felt much better positioned during Referendum 74 than during Referendum 71. According to Emma—an advocate who helped construct the coalition of community of color and immigrant organizations that endorsed Referendum 74—the advocates, community workers, and organizers behind the campaign had professionalized and become more sophisticated through the prior, smaller rights advocacy moments:

> Emma: I think by the time—so R-71 was 2009, and then R-74 was 2012—I mean just in those three years it seems like the various POC [people of color] organizations that were involved in advocacy became a lot more sophisticated. So overall everyone—maybe because I personally had grown a lot professionally as well—so it just kind of seems like we all grew up together.

During interviews, organization leaders and advocates described how opponent attacks and shared experiences in previous episodic rights campaigns emphasized that labor, immigrant, community of color, and LGBTQ organizations were aligned in the same struggle, strengthening coalitional unity in support of marriage equality.

Here, Richard, a leader in an immigrant organization, describes why emphasizing shared experiences of discrimination and traditional understandings of family helped expand cross-movement mobilization during the rights episode:

> Richard: Our focus was family, number one family, so I think if you look at especially the radio ads that we would do, that we did, they were a father who was talking about his son who had come out to him and how he had banished him from the family essentially, and how he [the son] had passed away while he had been kept away from the family and how much guilt and how much regret he [the father] had about that decision. . . . So it was kind of a dialogue with him sharing his regret about that. So there was a focus on family.
>
> I think another thing we focused on was just overall discrimination. I mean as an organization our tagline is "Justice for All" and so when we talk about justice for all we talk about justice for everyone and that includes the LGBT community. And so, we really talked about it in terms of discrimination and people being treated differently. Something our members are acutely aware of is discrimination since they are discriminated against in a lot of ways. They are sensitive to people being treated differently because of factors that are beyond their control or because of who they are and how they identify. So those were the messages that we led with.

Through focusing on family narratives and sharing past experiences of discrimination, which necessarily invoke similar opponents, Richard's organization helped expand the coalition, drawing in members of immigrant communities and communities of color as well as more organizations that represented these communities.

The emphasis on family is also clearly depicted through the campaign ads produced for communities of color and immigrant communities. In the following excerpt from a campaign ad directed at the Latinx community, the language of the ad focuses on how lesbian and gay people are part of one family and one community with Latinx people:

> **Familia Es Familia:** Many Latinos know someone who is gay or lesbian. They are family members, neighbors, people we work with, and members of our church. **In the Latino community, we don't turn our backs on family.** No member of anyone's family—gay or straight—should have to face discrimination where they live, at their jobs, or when they hope to marry the person they love. **Latino families are stronger when they are together.** By supporting marriage for committed gay and lesbian couples, we strengthen *all* families in our community.[69]

This advertisement, produced by organizations that represent communities of color, strives to increase support for marriage equality by underscoring how lesbian and gay people are part of Latinx families and by comparing job discrimination to the exclusion of same-sex couples from state marriage and family law. The advertisement includes a photo of a lesbian couple who have been in a committed relationship for twenty-two years. The next page of the advertisement has a quote from Latinx community leader and state representative Luis Moscoso alongside his photo, a list of other Latinx community leaders, and a selection of local mainstream and marginalized Latinx and immigrant rights organizations in Washington State that endorse marriage equality.

The emphasis on family as a cornerstone of the community and on shared experiences of discrimination appeared in a variety of advertisements directed at communities of color with large immigrant constituencies in the Pacific Northwest. For instance, the following ad targeting the Asian/Pacific Islander (API) community describes similarities among LGBTQ and API families, same-sex marriage, and past discriminatory laws prohibiting interracial marriage:

# Love. Commitment. Family.
## WHY MARRIAGE MATTERS

### LATINOS FOR THE FREEDOM TO MARRY

**FAMILIA ES FAMILIA**

Many Latinos know someone who is gay or lesbian. They are our family members, neighbors, people we work with, and members of our church.

**In the Latino community, we don't turn our backs on family.** No member of anyone's family—gay or straight—should have to face discrimination where they live, at their jobs, or when they hope to marry the person they love.

**Latino families are stronger when they are together.** By supporting marriage for committed gay and lesbian couples, we strengthen *all* families in our community.

**MARRIAGE PROTECTS FAMILIES**

**Marriage gives couples the tools and the security to build a life together and to protect their families.** Couples get married because they want to be there for each other in sickness and in health, when times are good and when things get tough.

State and federal marriage laws provide a **safety net of legal and economic protections for married couples and their children**—including the ability to visit your spouse in the hospital and to transfer property, which can mean being able to remain in the family home when your spouse has passed away.

Nearly 42% of Latina lesbian couples, and nearly one in four Latino gay male couples are raising children. **Marriage helps Latino same-sex parents protect their families.**

**MARRIAGE SAYS "WE ARE FAMILY"**

**Marriage says "We are a family" in a way that no other word does.** Gay and lesbian couples may seem different from straight couples, but share similar values—like the importance of family and helping out our neighbors; worries—like making ends meet or the possibility of losing a job; and hopes and dreams—like finding that special someone to grow old with, and standing in front of friends and family to make a lifetime commitment.

**Most people don't understand what a domestic partnership is, but marriage is understood.** Marriage says that these two people belong to one another, that they have chosen each other above all others, that they take responsibility for each other, and that in times of crisis, they will be there for each other. **Marriage matters, and no one should be denied something so important.**

*"We've been together for 22 years, through joy and hardships. Marriage would give us the ability to protect one another and take care of each other as we get older."*

*-Martha and Laura, Federal Way*

### WhyMarriageMattersWashington.org

**IMAGES 1.1 AND 1.2.** Latinx community advertisement used during the Referendum 74 Campaign. Source: Image Given to Author by Interviewee.

# WHY MARRIAGE MATTERS TO WASHINGTON LATINOS

## REFLECTING OUR COMMUNITY VALUES

**Latinos are supporting marriage for same-sex couples because it reflects our community values.** We believe in loving our neighbor and treating others the way we would want to be treated.

Once we learn more about it, we realize that marriage matters to gay people in similar ways that it matters to everyone. Gay and lesbian couples want to get married to make a lifetime commitment to the person they love and to protect their families.

"As a state legislator, I voted to extend marriage to same-sex couples. As the father of a gay son, I want him to be able to marry the person he loves. I want him to have the chance to stand in front of our friends and family and make a commitment to cherish, honor, and love his partner. That's what marriage is."

-WA State Rep. Luis Moscoso (D-1)

## CIVIL MARRIAGE WILL NOT AFFECT YOUR CHURCH

Civil marriage for gay couples does not affect religious marriages, religious institutions, or clergy in any way. No religion would be forced to marry same-sex couples, or recognize same-sex marriages within the context of their religious beliefs.

## LATINO LEADERS AND GROUPS SUPPORTING MARRIAGE FOR SAME-SEX COUPLES
(*organizations listed for information purposes)

**Washington Latino Organizations and Leaders**
- Consejo
- Catholics for Marriage Equality
- Casa Latina (Seattle)
- Community to Community (Bellingham)
- Entre Hermanos (Seattle)
- El Centro de la Raza (Seattle)
- Latino Community Fund of Washington
- Northwest Immigrant Rights Project
- Seamar Community Health Centers
- Rep. Luis Moscoso (D-1)
- Jorge Quiroga, Catholics for Equality
- Jorge Barón, Executive Director, Northwest Immigrant Rights Project
- Ricardo García, founder, Radio KDNA* (Yakima)
- María Cuevas, Chicanos Studies, Yakima Valley Community College*

- Jean Hernandez, President, Edmonds Comm. College*
- Nina Martínez (Everett)
- Rogelio Riojas, CEO, Seamar Community Health Centers
- Noel Solano, MEChA GSE, Yakima Valley Community College*

**National Latino Organizations**
- National Council of La Raza
- League of United Latino American Citizens
- Mexican American Legal Defense and Educational Fund
- An more than 20 other respected national Latino groups

**Why Marriage Matters Washington** is a project of Pride Foundation, Western States Center and Freedom to Marry.

WhyMarriageMattersWashington.org

# Love. Commitment. Family.
## WHY MARRIAGE MATTERS

### ASIAN/PACIFIC ISLANDERS FOR THE FREEDOM TO MARRY

SAME-SEX COUPLES ARE PART OF OUR FAMILIES AND COMMUNITIES

Many Asian/Pacific Islanders (API) know someone who is gay: neighbors, friends, and even our own family members. Within Asian/Pacific Islander families, unity is important. The lack of acceptance and recognition of gay and lesbian people breaks families apart. **By accepting our gay and lesbian family members, we strengthen *all* families in our community**.

Nearly 25% of same-sex couples where at least one person is Asian are raising children; more than 33% of same-sex couples where at least one person is Pacific Islander or Hawaiian are raising kids. Marriage helps API same-sex parents protect their families.

REFLECTING OUR COMMUNITY VALUES AND HISTORY

**API communities support marriage for same-sex couples because it reflects our community values.** We believe in loving our neighbor and treating others the way we would want to be treated. Marriage is about loyalty, stability, and security. Once we learn more about it, we realize that marriage matters to gay people in similar ways that it matters to everyone. Gay and lesbian couples want to get married to make a lifetime commitment to the person they love and to protect their families.

**Asian/Pacific Islanders understand what it's like to face marriage discrimination**. As recently as the mid-1900s, anti-miscegenation laws prohibited interracial marriages. The Washington Filipino, Japanese, and Chinese communities joined with other communities of color in the 1930s to defeat state anti-miscegenation laws.

MARRIAGE SAYS "WE ARE FAMILY"

**Marriage says, "We are a family" in a way that no other word does.** Gay and lesbian couples may seem different from straight couples, but share similar values—like the importance of family and helping out our neighbors; worries—like making ends meet or the possibility of losing a job; and hopes and dreams—like finding that special someone to grow old with, and standing in front of friends and family to make a lifetime commitment.

"There are so many Asian/Pacific Islanders who are also lesbian, gay, bisexual and transgender. I don't see these communities as separate; we're all part of the larger community. Because API's have a history of being discriminated against, we have the moral authority and responsibility to advocate for fairness for all."

*– Kip Tokuda,*
*former state legislator,*
*children's advocate, and*
*Japanese-American*

WhyMarriageMattersWashington.org

**IMAGES 1.3 AND 1.4.** Asians/Pacific Islanders community advertisement used during the Referendum 74 Campaign. Source: Image Given to Author by Interviewee.

# WHY MARRIAGE MATTERS TO APIs in WASHINGTON

## MARRIAGE STRENGTHENS FAMILIES

State and federal marriage laws provide a safety net of legal and economic protections for married couples and their children—including the ability to visit your spouse in the hospital and to transfer property, which can mean being able to remain in the family home when your spouse has passed away.

**Most people don't understand what a domestic partnership is, but marriage is clear.** Marriage says that two people belong to one another, that they have chosen each other above all others, that they take responsibility for each other, and that in times of crisis, they will be there for each other. **Marriage matters, and no one should be denied something so important.**

"We have been together for 7 years, and we provide a loving home full of laughter for our three daughters. We want to give them the protection and equal status provided by marriage."

-Laina and Ina, Seattle

## DOES THIS CHANGE MARRIAGE FOR MY CHURCH?

**No.** Civil marriage for gay couples does not affect religious marriages, religious institutions, or clergy in any way. No religion would be forced to marry same-sex couples, or recognize same-sex marriages within the context of their religious beliefs.

## API COMMUNITIES SUPPORT MARRIAGE FOR SAME-SEX COUPLES

**Asian/Pacific Islander Organizations:**
- Asian Pacific Islander Americans for Civic Empowerment (APACE)
- Asian Pacific Islander Coalition of Washington (APIC)
- Asian Pacific American Labor Alliance (APALA ) – Seattle Chapter
- API Chaya
- Japanese American Citizens League Seattle Chapter
- Filipino Lawyers of Washington (FLOW)
- One America
- Organization of Chinese Americans of Greater Seattle (OCA)
- Vietnamese Friendship Association

**Asian/Pacific Islander Community Leaders:**
- Rep. Sharon Tomiko Santos (D-37)
- Rep. Cindy Ryu (D-32)
- Rep. Bob Hasegawa (D-11)
- Venerable Thich Nguyen An
- Doug Chin (OCA)
- Cindy Domingo (Seattle)
- Vu Le (Vietnamese Friendship Association)
- Akemi Matsumoto (Seattle)
- Faaluaina Pritchard (Puyallup)
- Bill Tashima (JACL-Seattle former president)
- Linh Thai (VOVINAM)
- Kip Tokuda (former state legislator)

Why Marriage Matters Washington is a project of Pride Foundation, Western States Center, and Freedom to Marry.

Pride
Foundation
WhyMarria... WESTERN STATES CENTER ...hington.o... FREEDOM TO MARRY

Reflecting Our Community Values and History: API communities support marriage for same-sex couples because it reflects our community values. We believe in loving our neighbor and treating others the way we would want to be treated. Marriage is about loyalty, stability, and security. Once we learn more about it, we realize that marriage matters to gay people in similar ways that it matters to everyone. Gay and lesbian couples want to get married to make a lifetime commitment to the person they love and to protect their families.

**Asian/Pacific Islanders understand what it's like to face marriage discrimination.** As recently as the mid-1900s, anti-miscegenation laws prohibited interracial marriages. The Washington Filipino, Japanese, and Chinese communities joined with other communities of color in the 1930s to defeat state anti-miscegenation laws. **Marriage says "we are family" in a way no other word does.** Gay and lesbian couples may seem different from straight couples, but share similar values—like the importance of family and helping out our neighbors; worries—like making ends meet or the possibility of losing a job; and hopes and dreams—like finding that special someone to grow old with, and standing in front of friends and family to make a lifetime commitment.[70]

As with the advertisement directed at the Latinx community, this ad highlights how same-sex marriage matches API community understandings of traditional, nuclear families. The advertisement, by emphasizing the civil rights struggles of the API community over the legalization of interracial marriage, highlights a common civil rights past shared by LGBTQ and API people. The advertisement is an example of how civil rights narratives unify coalition partners. In drawing attention to the similarities between denying same-sex couples and interracial couples the right to marry, the advertisement also calls attention to a common core of opponents. Both struggles were driven by religious and conservative opponents who used similar messaging and tactics based in moral fears that "undesirables" (here same-sex couples and interracial couples) should not be allowed to stain state-sanctioned civil marriages.

By emphasizing how multiple movements share a common movement past and common opponents, the series of smaller rights episodes that culminated in the marriage equality rights episode expanded inter- and intra-movement mobilization, building new coalitions and increasing cross-community partnerships. Eventually, when the US Supreme Court decided *Obergefell v. Hodges* in 2015, the case that legalized same-sex marriage nationwide, the court directly referred to the many "referenda, legislative debates, and grassroots campaigns," such as those that occurred in Washington State, when making the argument that there has been sufficient deliberation about marriage equality to justify federal judicial intervention.[71]

## The Limits of the Right to Marry

Organizing through deep conversations within immigrant communities and communities of color expands inter- and intra-movement coalitions by emphasizing how disparate subject positions (e.g., LGBTQ people and Latinxs) are part of one community, share historical struggles against discrimination and oppression, and have a common core of opponents. However, there are also important ways that this messaging and other mechanisms also constrained political movements. The emphasis on "one community" and on traditional two-person families as a core social value depicted in the advertisements shown earlier relies on an understanding of family and community that centers lesbian and gay couples that most closely mirror mainstream heterosexual families. This is certainly an expansion of what constitutes a legitimate family. Yet it is also a limited expansion that does not engage with a discussion of queer kinship networks that exist outside of nuclear families. Rights episodes like Referendum 74 hyper-focus on discrete, rights-based issues that allow little space for conversations about minority identities that exist outside of the mainstream. As a result, once the episode ends, there is little space for movement expansion beyond a created rights episode.

Voters ultimately approved Referendum 74, legalizing same-sex marriage throughout Washington State, but this win came at a cost. My data shows that after the marriage equality rights episode ended, movement mobilization largely dissipated because (1) movement expansion centered on winning discrete rights rather than on long-term cross-community mobilization; (2) the cyclical nature of the rights episode drained the resources of many of the  organizations involved in the campaign; and (3) the rights episode centered the experiences of the most mainstream, "acceptable" minorities rather than the experiences of those who held identities or were part of queer relationships that are perceived as less socially desirable. Interviewees frequently emphasized the constraining impacts of the marriage equality rights episode, with some recounting experiences of marginalization during the campaign. For example, Valeria is a community organizer who works with grassroots organizations that represent queer, trans, and undocumented people. In her interview, Valeria described marriage equality as a constraining rights episode that limited the imaginations of politicians and political movement advocates:

> Valeria: I think a lot of the groups I work with; marriage equality just isn't their issue. Period. And I think some people are happy that it passed, some people actively feel that it's taken away from the attention that should be paid to the actual issues facing queer people. And that the funding, in the same ways as the Comprehensive Immigration Reform [CIR] funding, has limited both a radical imagination and the strategies. The incredible focus on marriage equality has taken the focus away from the murders of trans women or policing or lack of access to health care that doesn't rely on you getting married and having somebody who already has a job who has access to health care.
>
> So those demands, you know, the marriage equality demand or the CIR demand, are, again, demands that are very palatable despite the opposition. Ultimately, the Republicans could imagine a world in which you have marriage equality, the Republicans probably imagine a world in which you have CIR even though there is still well-based opposition. They can't imagine a world and probably Democrats can't either  where policing is omitted in ways LGBT women, or trans women are no longer at risk in the ways that they are.

Although the marriage equality rights episode tended to expand political movement formation in some contexts—for example, by expanding the array of subject positions represented within mainstream movement spaces—it did not meaningfully incorporate political issues that matter to many marginalized people and organizations, and limited each movement's ability to "imagine" beyond discrete rights outcomes.

After marriage, much of the mobilization that had expanded over decades through multiple episodic rights campaigns dissolved. This is apparent in the rapid decline of mainstream LGBTQ organizations once the campaign ended, both in Washington State and in other state contexts.

In Washington State, as in many other states, mainstream LGBTQ organizations focused intensely around winning marriage equality in the 2000s. This was driven at first by opponent groups who worked to expand state-level DOMAs, forcing local organizations that may not have focused on marriage equality in the past to respond. Eventually, it became the primary focus of many state-based LGBTQ organizations at the urging of grassroots advocates as well.[72] State-based organizations still supported issues that mattered to other minority communities in political forums, demonstrating their commitment to other minority movements and expanding inter- and intra-movement coalitions in the process. However, for mainstream LGBTQ organizations, the movement was more about winning a discrete right—winning marriage—than about mobilizing in the long term. During the interviews, many advocates with immigrant and community of color organizations who worked on the Referendum 74 campaign were disenchanted with LGBTQ organizations for this reason. They felt that these organizations predominately cared about marriage, and that as far as the organizations were concerned, all other issues, including those that matter to the marginalized communities that the organizations claimed to serve, were secondary.

For some interviewees, the concern that marriage alone was the center of mainstream LGBTQ organizing was validated after Referendum 74, as LGBTQ organizations were crippled by funding losses. All of the mainstream organization leaders and advocates I interviewed for this study wanted to continue mobilizing after the achievement of marriage equality, and believed that an array of LGBTQ people for whom marriage equality was not a concern were left behind by the win. But the crippling effects of a rights episode is felt not only at the margins but in mainstream organizations as well. During the interviews, organization leaders and advocates described how mainstream LGBTQ organizing in Washington State was dealt a significant blow by the marriage equality rights episode. Organizations lost much of their funding after the Washington State marriage equality win because they did not simultaneously plan for another rights episode or otherwise reserve funding collected during the Referendum 74 campaign to ensure institutional longevity once money devoted to marriage equality disappeared. This, in turn, solidified the perception among many marginalized organizations that mainstream organizations are not concerned with issues that matter to more disadvantaged communities. Many marginalized organizations then placed the blame on mainstream organizations for centering the right to marry at the expense of more marginalized people, further fragmenting the relationships that had formed during the marriage equality rights episode in Washington State.

Washington's marriage equality rights episode took decades to develop, expanding into new partnerships and increasing mobilization around a discrete rights win in the process. This mobilization was often constrained because it was limited to winning rights rather than constructing a long-term sustainable movement, it centered the interests of the most privileged constituencies within the LGBTQ community, and it drained community organizations of funding and resources. The analysis presented here demonstrates that political movement formation does not always occur along a linear trajectory toward progress. The development of the marriage equality rights episode often did not move seamlessly forward from one political venue to another. Instead, the political spaces through which the episode developed were often overlapped and networked with one another, together delimiting intersecting hierarchical constraints placed on each phase of the episode's development. This suggests that, when analyzing the relationship between law and social change, scholars should not focus only on political venues in isolation but instead should also look to the intensely interwoven nature of the different political venues, which can vary depending on context, because struggles for rights move in paradoxical ways through political and legal spaces.

Chapter 2

# "SHOW ME YOUR PAPERS!"

SB 1070 and Defensive Rights Episodes

Diana: I first got involved in 2010, and it was after SB 1070 and the real-ization that our community, especially my family and myself, were being attacked and the fear once it was passed. . . . So that fear drove me to say, OK they're attacking us anyway and we've been with our head down, you know. What happens when we raise ourselves and we're together? And so I got involved with electoral work, with different organizations.

Jorge Martinez: I drive about 100 to 120 miles a day, and I see a lot of people get detained. Everyone says SB 1070 is in court. It's not in court. We're living it.[1]

Jorge Martinez worked as an ice cream truck driver in Arizona. He was also a member of Puente Movement, a migrant advocacy organization based in Phoenix. In the documentary *The State of Arizona*, Martinez talks about how he became politically active when people in his community started getting deported in greater numbers in the late 2000s, particularly in the aftermath of the Support Our Law Enforcement and Safe Neighbor-hoods Act, also known as Senate Bill (SB) 1070. SB 1070 was entrenched in a history of anti-immigrant law and policy that had a profound impact on Martinez's community in Arizona. In the documentary, people sometimes described the rise in immigration enforcement and deportations in the state using the word *disappeared*, a term that captures both the transnational experiences of Arizona's migrant workers who personally suffered the effects of government-enforced disappearances in many Latin American countries, and the anguish that undocumented and mixed-immigration-status families go through when a family member is banished from their home through US government deportation proceedings. Although SB 1070 was most known for its "show me your papers" provision, which allowed law enforcement officers to question and detain those who they reasonably suspect are undocumented immigrants, SB 1070 was really an omnibus bill that aimed to make "attrition through enforcement the public policy of all state and local government agencies in Arizona."[2] The goal of SB 1070 was to dramatically decrease Arizona's undocumented population. Immediately after the bill passed in 2010, the federal government filed a lawsuit challenging much of the law's constitutionality. Yet Martinez, and many of the participants in this study, who felt the impacts of SB 1070 in their daily lives, from increased anti-immigrant rhetoric to the deportation of friends and family members, contend that SB 1070 was "not in court"— they were "living it." SB 1070 was a *defensive rights episode* that deeply impacted (and still impacts) the lives of Arizona's migrant and Latinx communities and revitalized the immigrant rights movement in Arizona.

Rights episodes can be *offensive* or *defensive*. *Offensive*, or created, rights episodes are constructed by movement actors in order to secure a rights win, such as marriage equality or legal representation for undocumented people in immigration proceedings. By contrast, *defensive* rights episodes are created by movement opponents to take away minority rights through passing laws like SB 1070, which limits privacy rights and infringes on the right to equal protection of the law. When a defensive rights episode emerges, movement actors are forced to quickly respond and mobilize to prevent the loss of rights. Table 2.1 summarizes the similarities and differences between offensive and defensive rights episodes.

As with the Referendum 74 campaign for marriage equality in Washington State, SB 1070 tended to both expand and contract movement mobilization. However, rights episodes have different effects depending on context. Like Referendum 74, SB 1070 activated and grew coalition partnerships that expanded into new rights events at the same time that it contained movement mobilization. Yet, unlike Referendum 74, local coalition partnerships that formed through SB 1070 were able to expand into more sustained inter- and intra-movement alliances after the defensive rights episode had dissipated. In other words, SB 1070 had more potential for expansion than the Referendum 74 marriage equality rights episode.

TABLE 2.1. Comparison of Offensive and Defensive Rights Episodes

| Similarities | Differences |
| --- | --- |
| Both types of episodes expand through emphasizing a common political movement/civil rights past and shared opponents. | Marginalization in *offensive* episodes is usually driven by mainstream organizations who determine the agenda or priority for a rights win. |
| Both types of episodes contain movements around discrete campaigns. | Marginalization in *defensive* episodes is largely driven by opponents who create the rights threat. |
| Both types of episodes shift movement priorities, which manifests in a feeling of losing control of the agenda. | *Defensive* episodes have a greater capacity to expand inter- and intra-movement coalitions beyond a campaign cycle. |
| Both types of episodes reinforce marginalization and tokenization based on race, class, and gender hierarchies. | *Offensive* episodes also unify inter- and intra-movement coalitions, but have less potential for expansion. |

SB 1070 had this greater potential because it was a defensive episode, and there was, thus, an increased desperation in the rights advocacy moment that encouraged the formation of lasting alliances that center marginalized people and organizations. Furthermore, because SB 1070 was an omnibus bill with multiple components, it has not contracted as much as the single-issue-focused Referendum 74 campaign for marriage equality. SB 1070 also made it a crime to harbor or transport an undocumented person while committing a criminal offense and had an anti–sanctuary cities clause that allowed individuals to sue if cities or state government agencies refuse to enforce immigration law. The anti–sanctuary cities component has fostered more immigrant movement mobilization recently due to increased federal immigration enforcement under President Trump's administration.

The SB 1070 defensive rights episode influenced inter- and intra-movement coalition expansion while also containing movement mobilization, often mirroring the effects of the marriage equality rights episode in Washington State. Yet my interviews also indicate that SB 1070 had important differences, (1) because its defensive nature helped shift most of the blame for marginalization onto movement opponents rather than mainstream organizations, and (2) because it had a greater potential to expand coalitions formed during the heated advocacy moment beyond a single campaign cycle. In the end, SB 1070 had a dramatic impact on political movement formation in Arizona. The defensive rights episode assisted in the institutionalization of a grassroots advocacy network that included marginalized organizations and that became central to the electoral campaigning of mainstream political movement advocates. Through SB 1070, marginalized immigrant, labor, and LGBTQ movement organizations in Arizona constructed a civic engagement coalition that conducted voter registration drives and get-out-the-vote efforts to increase their political capacity in the state. Marginalized organizations accomplished this by working with mainstream organizations to get the votes needed to elect progressive candidates and then holding these candidates accountable for passing community-led public policies after electoral campaigns.

### Understanding the Roots of SB 1070:
### Southern Traditionalism, Frontier Values, and Law and Order

During my fieldwork, it was common for Arizonans to describe the state's anti-immigrant, anti-LGBTQ, and anti-worker politics by turning to the state's history. One interviewee, an attorney who has worked on immigrant and migrant rights cases, referenced the "historical discrimination, historical white privilege, historical dominance by the Anglo community" to describe the flood of anti-immigrant bills and ballot initiatives that materialized in the early 2000s and made SB 1070 possible. When I asked another interviewee to describe the greatest problems facing the Latinx and immigrant communities in Arizona, she responded by explaining what she called the "cult of racism" that has developed in the state. For Arizonans involved in the political movement struggles, SB 1070 was a new manifestation of an entrenched state ethos that involves the disenfranchisement and exclusion of minority communities by those in power and began with the formation of the Arizona-Mexico border.

The establishment of the US territory that would one day become Arizona in the mid-1800s gave way to what social scientist Mona Lynch calls Arizona's "long and bitter battle to shed its territorial status"— a battle that would last nearly fifty years.[3] This battle over Arizona's statehood brought out the "discriminatory attitudes" of Anglo Arizonans and American politicians.[4] When members of Congress proposed a joint Arizona–New Mexico statehood, Arizona demurred out of a concern that New Mexico had a Mexican population that was too large.[5] At the federal level, the resistance to annexing Arizona stemmed from a majority view in Congress that Arizona's political leaders were "radicals" who distrusted the federal government.[6] Influenced heavily by the influx of settlers from southern US states, Arizona's political culture was characterized by both the traditionalist values of Southern Democrats of the late 1800s and the frontier values of American settler communities of the time who migrated to the region through the westward expansion justified by Manifest Destiny ideology. Composed of a distrust of federal and state government and a pioneer culture that valued self-reliance and individualism, the political ethos that developed out of Arizona's founding continues to characterize the political climate in the state today.[7]

After the annexation of Arizona in 1912, a series of "hot moments" jarred the inhabitants of the region.[8] Each of these events centered on a period of economic expansion followed by economic recession or depression that directly impacted the state's Latinx migrant worker population. A racialized hierarchy dominated Arizona's politics in the early 1900s, and the state's economy relied heavily on cheap laborers who worked in harsh conditions. During a time period characterized by the racialized pseudoscience of eugenics and Social Darwinism, Mexican migrants were socially constructed by Anglo elites as a desirable source of cheap labor because of their purported "domesticated" and "passive nature."[9]

Throughout the 1900s, Arizona relied on and spurned migrant labor depending on the whims of a boom-and-bust economic cycle that played on the vulnerabilities of a state with a historically unstable economy. Following the Great Depression of the 1930s, the federal government initiated a forced "repatriation" program that resulted in the deportation of nearly one million Mexicans and Mexican Americans, including US citizens.[10] When the country needed laborers during World War II, the government instituted the temporary guest worker *Bracero* program to provide migrant workers predominately from Mexico with a pathway into Arizona as well as other states. Following a recession in 1953, the US Border Patrol conducted a deportation program whose title included a racial slur, indicative of the entrenched racial hierarchy that dominated

US politics in the 1950s. The border patrol's "Operation Wetback" forced the mass deportation of workers who came into the US.[11] Although the border patrol was supposed to target undocumented workers and not those who came into the US through the *Bracero* program, border patrol officers were indiscriminate as they conducted immigration sweeps. Each of these "hot moments" further embedded a racialized nativism in Arizona's political ethos that would resurge with force from time to time as Arizona's economy and immigrant population shifted and grew in future decades.

In addition to the federal programs described here, the state government has historically enacted hostile measures designed to marginalize its Latinx population. For example, until 1975, Arizona refused to provide election materials in Spanish or any language other than English. For this reason, when the US adopted the Voting Rights Act (VRA) in 1965, Arizona was the only entire state in the Southwest, other than Texas, that had to have proposed changes to its election laws precleared by the federal government under Section 5 of the VRA. Furthermore, Arizona has always been a segregated state, first through official state, local, and federal laws and then through de facto segregation in the aftermath of civil rights laws that largely eliminated de jure segregation.[12] Arizona's historical segregation and its inclusion in the VRA's Section 5 pre-clearance provisions are examples of the Southern traditionalist and segregationist values brought into the state by Anglo settlers.[13]

In addition to a political ethos based in the traditionalist values of Southern Democrats and pioneer individualism, Arizona developed a uniquely American frontier-style culture of harsh punishment and law-and-order politics.[14] This culture embedded demands for "cheap" and "harsh" punishment in the mythos that defined the state's Anglo community. This would prove a useful tool for Anglos in Arizona to politically implement a penitentiary and criminal justice system to socially control and solidify the underclass status of the state's Latinx, indigenous, black, and other minority communities. The system also violated constitutional and international human rights under the guise of remaining "cost effective."[15] The myth that politicians and law enforcement officials must go "above the law" to protect the state against foreigners and other "invaders," depicted universally as people of color in popular media, continues to haunt the political culture of the state generations after its inception.

Against this background, it becomes clearer why, in the late 1980s and early 1990s, Arizona resisted adopting Martin Luther King Jr. Day (MLK Day) as a holiday and passed a controversial constitutional amendment that made English the official language of the state. The amendment was eventually declared unconstitutional by the Arizona State Supreme Court in 1998 in *Ruiz v. Hull*.[16] The invalidation of Arizona's attempt to make English the state's official language is one of many examples of the net-worked political context that exists in Arizona, a state where legislation and ballot initiatives are sometimes passed in violation of the federal and state constitutions. For this reason, the courts have occasionally served as important political venues that check anti-immigrant and racist state laws and as mobilization sources for movement organizations.

Along with acknowledging the struggle to invalidate the amendment mandating English as the official language of the state, interviewees in-voked the MLK Day holiday struggle as one of a series of "hot moments" in explaining the culture out of which SB 1070 emerged in Arizona. When President Reagan pushed for the national adoption of a holiday to honor civil rights leader Martin Luther King Jr., Arizona's governor initially supported the move, although Arizona's then representative John McCain voted against the proposed holiday in Congress.[17] When Governor Evan Mecham assumed office in 1987, he pushed for a ballot initiative asking Arizonans to vote on whether the state should adopt the holiday. Two initiatives appeared on the ballot in 1990; each would have created the state holiday, but both failed in the face of opposition campaigns that emphasized the economic cost of an additional paid holiday and aligned MLK with "radicalism" and "communism"—messaging that played on the state's Southern traditionalist and frontier ethos.[18] When Arizonans failed to implement the holiday, the National Football League withdrew the planned 1993 Super Bowl from the state. This, along with millions of dollars in lost revenue from cancelled conferences, produced widespread outcry among Arizona's business and tourism industry (the second-largest industry in the state), which prompted another ballot initiative campaign that ultimately passed and finally enacted the holiday.[19]

Scholars have also connected Arizona's tough-on-crime ideology to the criminalization of non-heterosexuality and regulation of sexuality.[20] This is evident in Arizona through the enactment of anti-LGBTQ laws such as SB 1396, passed by Arizona legislators in 1991, which banned public school teachers from teaching anything that may promote "a homosexual lifestyle" in the wake of the HIV/AIDS epidemic.[21] One of the few state laws in the US that banned discussions of LGBTQ people in the classroom, Arizona's law required state public school curricula to adopt heterosexuality as the norm and exclude all other non-heterosexual forms of relationships from public education.[22] Critics aligned Arizona's law with the "anti–gay propaganda law" passed in Russia in 2013, which criminalized the "promotion" of non-heterosexuality among minors and led to international calls for a boycott of the 2014 Winter Olympics in Sochi, Russia.[23] SB 1396 was eventually repealed in 2019, shortly after state and national LGBTQ organizations filed a lawsuit challenging the law's constitutionality.[24]

Arizona's unique Southern traditionalist, law-and-order political ethos perhaps explains why rights movement opponent groups and politicians are so powerful in the state. Arizona is home to the national conservative legal advocacy group Alliance Defending Freedom (ADF) and a state-based conservative advocacy group, the Center for Arizona Policy. Often the leading force behind national anti-LGBTQ lawsuits, ADF was cofounded by James Dobson, the founder of the national anti-LGBTQ evangelical Christian group Focus on the Family. Arizona has also been a testing ground for national anti-immigrant legislation promoted by the American Legislative Exchange Council (ALEC) and Federation of American Immigration Reform (FAIR), a group affiliated with Kris Kobach.[25]

In addition to the slew of conservative groups and activists that have found their home in Arizona, state politicians frequently appeal to rights movement opponents as they work to pass and implement laws that threaten minorities. Arizona houses several larger-than-life politicians who have backed laws that target minority communities by appealing to stereotypes based in the state's political ethos. Interviewees discussed several during the course of this study, most notably former state senator Russell Pearce, former governor Jan Brewer, and former Maricopa County sheriff Joe Arpaio. Pearce and Arpaio both won public support in Arizona and became leading figures within far-right national politics by fashioning themselves as modern-day John Wayne frontiersmen, protecting Anglo society from perceived undesirable minority elements who "invaded" Arizona through the southern border. Both were at the peak of their political power during the 2000s, when anti-immigrant fervor gripped the state anew. Pearce, a former chief deputy under Sheriff Arpaio, served in the state legislature from 2001 to 2011, and Arpaio served as the Maricopa County sheriff over six terms, from 1993 through 2016.[26] Both were defeated at the ballot box and unseated due to the mobilization that occurred in the aftermath of the SB 1070 rights episode.[27] The defeat of Pearce and Arpaio is also indicative of broader changes in the state, including a demographic shift that involves a younger, more diverse electorate. It is this shifting electorate that, along with post–SB 1070 movement mobilization, likely contributed to the election of Democrat Krysten Sinema to the US Senate during the 2018 midterm elections.

## A Defensive Rights Episode: Anti-Immigrant Fervor and the Formation of SB 1070 in Arizona

The 1990s were a relatively calm period for Arizona, likely due to the economic promises of the decade, which drove up the demand for labor nationwide. In response to this demand for labor, the migrant community in the US rapidly increased in the mid-to-late 1990s.[28] This increase was particularly stark in Arizona as a result of the federal programs enacted by President Clinton (Operation Hold the Line [1993] and Operation Gatekeeper [1994]), which increased the number of border patrol agents in other major border states, especially California and Texas, effectively funneling most migration from Mexico through Arizona's southern border, which was less heavily monitored.[29] At the time, the federal government, controlled by politicians in both political parties who wanted to minimize immigration into the US, believed that these programs would slow migrant traffic from Mexico into the US, as crossing through Arizona's desert was more treacherous.

However, the effort to stem immigration ultimately backfired, as those fleeing the economic violence and turmoil in Latin America, bolstered by Clinton-era globalization policies, continued to migrate to the US despite more dangerous and deadly border crossings. During the 1990s, the Latinx population in Arizona increased by about 215,000, 89 percent higher than the previous decade, and net migration soared 193 percent to about 392,000 people.[30] This spurred concern among many of Arizona's Anglo residents and politicians, especially as researchers reported that Arizona would soon become a majority-minority state.[31] In the aftermath of the 9/11 terrorist attacks in New York, Anglo politicians in Arizona heightened comparisons between the state's migrant population and "foreign terrorists." Within the state, growing concerns about rapidly changing demographics spilled over into debates about national security. These shifting external political events marked the onset of what would become a wave of anti-immigrant advocacy in Arizona, which would surpass and galvanize other counter–rights movement goals, such as anti-LGBTQ and anti-worker policies that were affiliated with the state's Southern traditionalist, frontier ethos. In the 2016 presidential election, the national government experienced an upsurge of anti-establishment, populist sentiment, that would bring President Donald Trump and other authoritarian figures into elected office. But in Arizona, this upsurge began more than fifteen years before the 2016 election. During the 2000s, Arizona became the testing ground for anti-immigrant advocacy that would soon overtake the US at the national level.

Figure 2.1 depicts how the SB 1070 rights episode emerged from networked political actions (i.e., litigation, legislation, ballot initiatives, and executive actions). This network was disrupted in 2010 when the economic recession and the departure of Governor Janet Napolitano to the Department of Homeland Security created a new opening for a massive anti-rights advocacy moment—the defensive rights episode SB 1070.

During the 2000s, well over one hundred anti-immigrant bills and ballot initiatives were filed in Arizona, which in turn triggered numerous court cases challenging the anti-immigrant laws when they passed. This onslaught of opponent advocacy makes it difficult to focus in on only a few rights advocacy moments as a means of analyzing how SB 1070 developed in the state. In Washington State, it is possible to analyze how the Referendum 74 campaign emerged out of a few prior episodic rights campaigns. In Arizona, however, the sheer number of campaigns complicates matters. In order to accurately delineate the climate out of which SB 1070 emerged, figure 2.1 and the next sections focus on those rights campaigns preceding SB 1070 that were of the greatest importance to the advocates, activists, community workers, and politicians who participated in this study. As figure 2.1 shows, the episodic moments that composed Arizona's political/legal network prior to SB 1070 included a number of anti-immigrant laws and lawsuits that challenged the constitutionality of these laws. These included Proposition 200, which denied a number of state social services to undocumented immigrants; the US Supreme Court

Prior Networked Political Actions (e.g., Proposition 200, *Arizona v. Inter Tribal Council of Arizona*, Proposition 300, 287(g) in Maricopa County)

New Action(s), Creating a Shift in the Political Network (Departure of Governor Napolitano to DHS, economic recession, and the rise of the Tea Party)

SB 1070 Defensive Rights Episode

Social Movement Expansion and Contraction

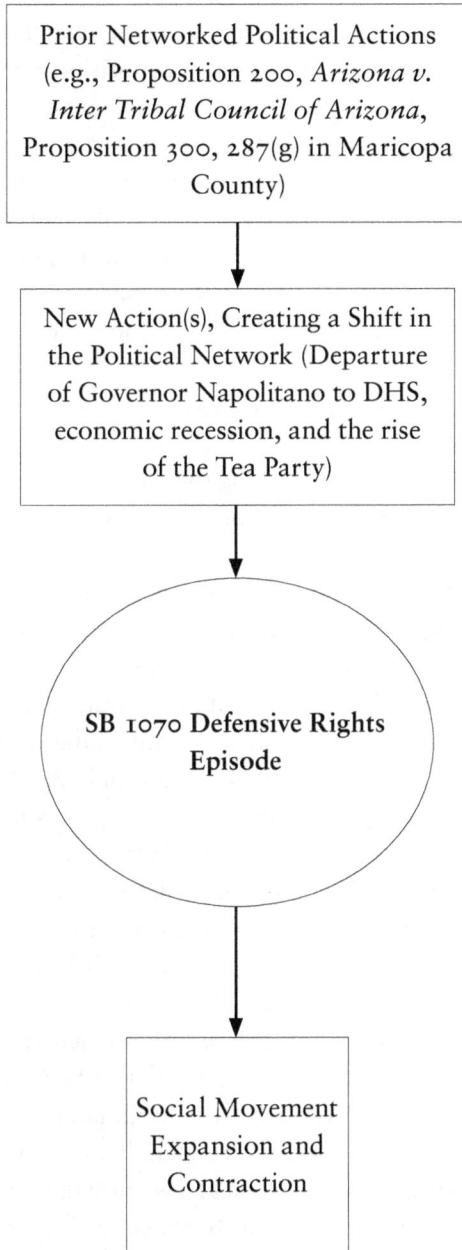

FIGURE 2.1. Formation of the SB 1070 Defensive Rights Episode

case *Arizona v. Inter Tribal Council of Arizona*, which held that part of Proposition 200 was unconstitutional; Proposition 300, which denied in-state college tuition to undocumented residents; and the extension of the Immigration and Nationality Act's section 287(g) over Maricopa County, which granted Sheriff Arpaio the authority to enforce federal immigration law. The following sections describe in greater detail how the defensive rights episode SB 1070 emerged in response to events that altered this political network, such as the departure of Democratic governor Jan Brewer, the 2008 financial crisis, and the rise of the Tea Party.

## A Growing Storm: Rights Episodes in Arizona before SB 1070

After major demographic shifts during the 1990s in Arizona and the 9/11 attacks, anti-immigrant organizations increased their advocacy work in the state with the help of local politicians and activists in the early 2000s. Arguably the first major anti-immigrant initiative of the decade was Proposition 203, which passed in 2000 by 63 percent.[32] Proposition 203, modeled after California's Proposition 227, eliminated bilingual education programs in Arizona. During the campaign, proponents used messaging that played on social fears about immigrants and Spanish-language speakers in Arizona, fears that were embedded in the racialized nativism that had developed in the state.[33] The proposition appeared on the ballot following a lawsuit over the initiative's language, which opponents contended misstated the bilingual education law and exaggerated the availability of alternative educational programs.[34] The same year that Proposition 203 appeared on the ballot, Russell Pearce was elected to the house of representatives.[35] Pearce's election began an era of anti-immigrant legislation in the state legislature that reached a crescendo with SB 1070, which Pearce introduced and helped author with the assistance of FAIR and Kris Kobach. Kris Kobach would later become the Kansas secretary of state and an affiliate of President Trump's administration.[36]

At first, bills introduced in Arizona's legislature that targeted the state's immigrant and Latinx population were considered radical and extreme, even by Arizona's standard. According to State Senator Gallardo, when anti-immigrant groups and legislators started pursuing legislation in the early 2000s, most legislators "would sit around and laugh" at the bills they introduced. In fact, in 2003, none of the anti-immigrant bills introduced by then representative Pearce even made it to a floor vote.[37] With not yet enough support in the legislature, anti-immigrant groups decided to pursue their goals at the ballot box. Together with Russell Pearce, they created Proposition 200, the Arizona Taxpayer and Citizen Protection Act, also known as the Protect Arizona Now initiative.[38] Proponents modeled Proposition 200 on California's Proposition 187, which passed by 60 percent in California in 1994.[39] Proposition 187 denied state services, such as education, health care, and social services, to undocumented immigrants; required local law enforcement and public workers to turn in undocumented immigrants to federal authorities; and made it a felony to create, sell, or use false identity documents.[40]

In California, Proposition 187 faced a legal quagmire, as at least eight lawsuits were filed by immigrant rights advocates, preventing its implementation.[41] Parts of Proposition 187 ran afoul of long-standing US Supreme Court precedents such as *Plyer v. Doe*, which acknowledged a basic right to education for undocumented immigrant children in 1982.[42] Other provisions of the propositions were preempted by the federal Priority Responsibility and Work Opportunity Reconciliation Act (PRWORA) and the Illegal Immigration Reform and Immigrant Responsibilities Act (IIRAIRA), which were passed in 1996. The acts created a comprehensive federal scheme for determining undocumented immigrants' eligibility for public benefits, and a federal immigration regulatory scheme, respectively. The PRWORA, IIRAIRA, and federal lawsuits ultimately voided the provisions of Proposition 187 that prohibited undocumented immigrants from accessing social services and required local police, social workers, and educational providers to turn undocumented immigrants over to state and federal authorities.[43]

## Proposition 200 and the First Major Immigrant Rights Threats

Anti-immigrant rights proponents of Proposition 200 in Arizona attempted to skirt the court cases and federal laws that negated most of Proposition 187 by constructing a more limited ballot initiative in the state that (1) denied state social services, but not educational services, to undocumented immigrants; (2) required proof of citizenship to register to vote; and (3) required photo identification in order to vote.[44] Proposition 200 passed by about 56 percent in Arizona in 2004.[45] As with Proposition 187 in California, immigrant rights movement actors swiftly challenged Proposition 200 in court and were largely successful at dismantling the new law.[46] In cases immediately filed after Proposition 200, the Ninth Circuit Court did determine that Proposition 200 was constitutional on its face. However, this is largely attributable to then attorney general Thomas Goddard (a Democrat), who held that the welfare provisions of Proposition 200 only applied to a small number of state programs, such as utility assistance and state programs providing cash assistance for disabled people, and not to broader public housing, food assistance, and employment programs that would have thrown the proposition's constitutionality into question.[47] The US Supreme Court in *Arizona v. Inter Tribal Council of Arizona* found that the part of the proposition that required proof of citizenship in order to register to vote violated federal law. In this ruling, the court held that Arizona could not require prospective voters to submit information, here proof of citizenship, because this additional information goes beyond what is required by the uniform federal form according to the National Voter Registration Act of 1993.[48]

The manner in which Proposition 200 played out would ultimately hold for true for much rights movement and counter–rights movement proposals enacted into law in Arizona. In the Proposition 200 campaign, anti-immigrant rights advocates were forced to focus on a ballot initiative campaign because this was the political tactic that presented the possibility for an opponent advance within Arizona's political advocacy network. However, the success of Proposition 200 was delimited by another political tactic: litigation. With little political power in Arizona, few allies, and minimal statewide coalitions, rights movement organizations and activists frequently filed lawsuits to curb harmful laws passed by opponents in the state's legislature and by Arizona's voters at the ballot box. Immigrant rights advocates resorted largely to court cases to stem the tide of anti-immigrant laws, not because of a grand strategy which determined that the courts were better vehicles for social change, but because they were entirely shut out of other political institutions. With anti-immigrant sentiment increasing in the aftermath of 9/11, there were few inter- and intra-movement partnerships capable of mobilizing to stop anti-immigrant measures in Arizona during the early 2000s.

Even Democrats were largely absent from progressive state-level advocacy at the time. Democrats, rather than launching statewide campaigns in the early 2000s to thwart anti-immigrant momentum, responded by criticizing state-based approaches and focusing their efforts on federal-level calls for Comprehensive Immigration Reform.[49] Furthermore, at the local level in Arizona, Democrats were not universally supportive of immigrant rights. Indeed, many of the bills Russell Pearce introduced after Proposition 200 were supported and signed into law by then governor Janet Napolitano, a Democrat. For instance, Governor Napolitano signed House Bill (HB) 2779 (the Legal Arizona Workers Act) into law in 2007. HB 2779 prohibited employers from hiring undocumented immigrants and made it a felony for people to work with fake identity documents. This law was forcefully implemented by Sheriff Arpaio in the late 2000s as he conducted raids of local businesses in search of undocumented immigrants after the Maricopa County Sheriff's Department was delegated the authority to enforce federal immigration law under Section 287(g) of the Immigration and Nationality Act. In one of these raids, Guadalupe García de Rayos was arrested and convicted of working with false identification under the 2007 law. As a convicted felon, García de Rayos was ultimately deported in 2017, one of the first high-profile deportations of the Trump administration.[50]

After Proposition 200, anti-immigrant organizations began to pass numerous propositions and bills in Arizona. Most of the propositions were initiated as legislative proposals that were passed by the Arizona State Senate and House of Representatives and vetoed by Governor Napolitano. Often, when a proposed bill was vetoed by Napolitano, it would reappear as a House Concurrent Resolution or a Senate Concurrent Resolution and get placed by the legislature on the ballot, where Arizona voters were likely to approve the legislature's proposal, thereby skirting the governor's veto. This happened with Proposition 300, which eliminated in-state tuition for undocumented students and passed by 71 percent of the vote in 2006.[51] The Arizona legislature sent Proposition 300 to the ballot by passing Senate Concurrent Resolution (SCR) 1031 in 2006 after Napolitano vetoed a version of the proposal in 2005.

## INTER- AND INTRA-MOVEMENT COALITION BUILDING IN THE 2000S

During the 2000s, coalition efforts to stem the tide of counter-movement advocacy were minimal. Indeed, when the Arizona legislature considered

SCR 1031, the proposal to eliminate in-state tuition for undocumented students, only a handful of faith groups and educational institutions opposed the measure at the legislature.[52] LGBTQ organizations did not come to the legislature to express support for immigrant rights advocates during key hearings. The only union that came to the legislature to oppose the legislation was the Arizona Federation of Teachers Union (AFT-AZ)). Local affiliates of United Food and Commercial Workers (UFCW), Service Employees International Union (SEIU), and the International Union of Painters and Allied Trades (IUPAT), unions that would eventually become major players in coalition building in Arizona, were not present at hearings to express opposition to the proposal to eliminate in-state tuition.

The lack of inter- and intra-movement coalition formation undoubtedly hindered immigrant rights advocates from effectively combating the influx of anti-immigrant movement momentum in Arizona. But immigrant rights advocates were not the only ones who suffered from the lack of cross-community alliances during this time. The alliance void also hindered the mobilization capacity of LGBTQ rights organizations in the state. In 2006, an alliance of conservative legislators and religious organizations, led by Cathi Herrod of the Center for Arizona Policy, successfully got a measure on the ballot to prohibit the legal recognition of all same-sex relationships, including civil unions and domestic partnerships. The 2006 attempt, Proposition 107, also known as the Protect Marriage Arizona initiative, ultimately failed by about 52 percent.[53] The failure of Proposition 107 marked one of the first same-sex marriage successes at the ballot box. However, the success was short lived when, in 2008, the same counter-movement coalition got a limited version of Proposition 107 on the ballot. The new initiative, Proposition 102, only prohibited same-sex marriage, but left open the possibility for the state to eventually recognize same-sex civil unions. Proposition 102 passed by 56 percent of the vote.[54] The coalition of inter- and intra-movement rights organizations that opposed both propositions included a range of LGBTQ groups, politicians, businesses, some faith groups, and unions. However, Latinx organizations, immigrant rights organizations, and other organizations that represent communities of color were notably absent from endorsement lists on LGBTQ advocacy campaign websites.[55]

Although inter- and intra-movement coalition work at this time in

Arizona was minimal in statewide rights campaigns, it was not entirely absent at the city level. For instance, in *Queer Migration Politics*, scholar Karma Chávez documents the long-standing alliance between two organizations: the Tucson-based LGBTQ organization Wingspan and the grassroots migrant rights and justice organization Coalición de Derechos Humanos. Following the 2004 election, after Arizona passed the anti-migrant Proposition 200 and when it became apparent that an initiative against same-sex marriage was certain, the two organizations issued a joint statement that appeared in the *Tucson Weekly*, arguing that both initiatives were part of the same opponent strategy.[56] Such an alliance is a clear indication of grassroots inter- and intra-movement coalition work despite a lack of unified cross-community support in many statewide coalition campaigns to stop harmful ballot initiatives and legislation.

Furthermore, many of the smaller defensive rights episodes that emerged in the 2000s were important activating moments for organizers, activists, and community workers who later became involved with inter- and intra-movement coalition building. In early 2006, as anti-immigrant bills and propositions began to pass with increasing frequency on the local and national levels, Somos America was founded—a statewide coalition of immigrant justice organizations.[57] During this time, many queer migrant youth who later became movement leaders and cross-community organizers were also activated. For example, Manuel, the leader of a queer migrant organization involved in coalition building, first started organizing in Arizona in response to Proposition 300:

> Manuel: In 2006, we start organizing because I had a full-ride scholarship to college and a presidential scholarship. *And then in 2006 we get hit with Proposition 300 that takes away any financial aid for undocumented students and then puts us at out-of-state tuition. So what that did is I started organizing with some local people.* [emphasis added]

In this interview excerpt, Manuel describes how undocumented youth were personally impacted by Proposition 300, as many lost access to in-state tuition once the proposition passed. This served as an important awakening moment for Manuel and others who experienced the negative fallout of the new law. Later in the interview, Manuel further argued that coalition work at the time was limited because immigrant organizing "spaces were mainly dominated by religion" and "old guard leaders" whose "views" were very "limited"—an indication that openly LGBTQ people were largely excluded from working within immigrant community organizing in the mid-2000s.

Like Manuel, Nicolas, another individual who later became active in coalition work, described how Proposition 300 activated immigrant youth as well:

> Nicolas: In 2006, Arizona voters passed Proposition 300, which is our immigration tuition law here in Arizona. And essentially Proposition 300, what it said is that if you're undocumented and you're a student you will have to pay out-of-state tuition; you don't qualify for public aid, scholarships, things like that. . . . [I]t wasn't really until Proposition 300 passed that we had more involvement by immigrant youth, more consistently. And so it was after that that I started to see more of my peers here really continue to want to be involved and kind of join the movement around issues of immigration.

According to Nicolas, a youth "movement around issues of immigration" began to emerge in Arizona during the 2000s. This was confirmed by another interviewee, who argued that most Latinx and immigrant community work in Arizona focused on health and human services rather than immigrant justice advocacy during this time. However, this began to shift around 2004 as the flurry of anti-immigrant laws picked up momentum. According to scholar Cristina Beltrán, 2004–2006 was also an important moment politically for Latinx and immigrant world building at the federal level.[58] In 2005, the US House of Representatives passed a harsh anti-immigrant bill that criminalized being undocumented and offering nonemergency aid to undocumented people. In response, hundreds of thousands of Latinxs, immigrants, and their allies protested the legislation in cities across the US.[59] This was the first time that many of them participated in a political protest. Beltrán argues that these protests served as "scenes of public disclosure and self-making," during which immigrants and their allies transformed themselves into public, political subjects.[60] It is likely not a coincidence that people in Arizona like Manuel and Nicolas began to see themselves as community workers who were part of a queer migrant movement during this time. This movement building increased in the latter half of the 2000s as progressively more destructive anti-immigrant and anti-LGBTQ laws passed in the state. Ultimately, this momentum would converge with an explosive force in 2010 when the Arizona legislature passed SB 1070.

### A Storm Hits Arizona: SB 1070 and Movement Re-Formation

During the 2000s, although some of State Senator Pearce's anti-immigrant proposals were signed into law or approved by a majority of the state's electorate at the ballot box, many others were vetoed by Democratic governor Janet Napolitano. This changed in 2008, when Governor Napolitano was nominated by President Obama to serve as the secretary of homeland security. Napolitano was succeeded by Arizona's Republican secretary of state, Jan Brewer, who was much more supportive of legislation backed by Pearce, FAIR, and other Republican leaders in the state, who were once considered the fringe of Arizona politics.[61] When Brewer became governor in 2009, proposed legislation that was vetoed by Napolitano suddenly had a realistic opportunity to pass in the legislature. Furthermore, during this time, far-right movement mobilization against the newly elected President Obama increased at the local level with the rise of the Tea Party, particularly in states like Arizona, which had a history of racialized nativism. Anti-immigrant sentiment was further bolstered by the onset of the financial crisis of 2007–2008 and the economic recession, which hit Arizona particularly hard as home sales plummeted and the state's tourism industry experienced major losses. In a state with a history of anti-immigrant fervor erupting in a new "hot moment" around a major economic decline, Arizona was ripe for the emergence of a massive defensive rights moment. As a result of the shift in Arizona's political network and the national economy, State Senator Pearce introduced SB 1070 in 2010, an omnibus bill composed of a variety of prior legislative proposals that had failed to pass under Napolitano's governorship.

Because SB 1070 was an omnibus bill, when it was passed it enacted an array of anti-immigrant proposals into law. This makes the net of issues covered by the bill much wider than those covered by single-issue bills, such as the marriage equality legislation in Washington State. Furthermore, SB 1070 provoked a defensive response from both the Latinx and migrant communities, the primary targets of the bill, placing responsibility for how movement advocacy emerged mostly on opponents rather than

on movement advocates, as was the case with the marriage equality legislation in Washington State. The wide net of issues covered by SB 1070
and the fact that the bill placed rights movement advocates in a defensive
position increased SB 1070's potential to expand rights movement mobilization to a larger degree than the marriage equality rights episode in
Washington State. Defensive actions tend to unify and expand movement
coalitions because they more forcefully highlight common opponents
and emphasize shared experiences of oppression. Offensive actions can
do this as well if they provoke enough concerted opponent response and
similarly encompass a wide range of issues. But rights movement actors,
who are locked in a perpetual struggle against power, rarely have the
political opening necessary to accomplish expansive political movement
mobilization through a created rights campaign.

The most controversial components of SB 1070 (1) create new state
crimes related to immigration (e.g., the law criminalized transporting and
harboring undocumented immigrants), (2) open cities and other localities
to lawsuits if they enact "sanctuary" laws designed to limit cooperation
between federal and local law enforcement on immigration law, and (3)
enact new local police powers to enforce federal immigration law.[62]

The portions of SB 1070 that criminalize and create penalties for
the harboring of undocumented immigrants were condemned by immigrant rights advocates, who expressed concern that they criminalized
mixed-status families. The crimes laid out in the bill also excluded most
businesses in the state and, instead, specifically targeted undocumented
immigrants, their families and friends, and individuals who hire them
for work from the roadside. Because the new crimes created in SB 1070
did not target businesses and because provisions of SB 1070 also created
an affirmative defense for entrapped employers, the Arizona Chamber of
Commerce and Industry remained neutral on the bill as it worked its way
through the legislature. This made it more difficult for immigrant rights
advocates to effectively argue to the legislature that the bill would harm
businesses in the state.[63]

At the legislature, proponents and opponents of the legislation referenced legal arguments and court cases in arguing for and against the law
during hearings on SB 1070. State Senator Pearce, the bill's prime spon-
sor, insisted that the bill respects the "constitutional right" of citizens to
expect the enforcement of immigration laws and facilitates the partnership

between the federal government and the states, which have an "inherent authority" to enforce immigration law. Pearce's arguments foreshadowed what would become a major court case that centered on state authority to enforce federal law under the federalism doctrine. Opponents of the bill, such as Jessica Allen, the executive director of the Border Action Network, argued that SB 1070 "would open up the state of Arizona to tremendous lawsuits" similar to lawsuits elsewhere that have required cities and states to pay millions of dollars in plaintiff fees for passing laws similar to SB 1070. John Thomas, a representative from the Arizona Association of Chiefs of Police, contended that the law would be particularly harmful in rural communities that "are going to have to pay outside counsel to come and defend them" in court as a result of the bill.[64] Despite the outcry against the bill, the firm support for the bill among anti-immigration advocates and legislators pushed SB 1070 swiftly through the legislature. In April 2010, Governor Brewer signed the bill into law—setting off a firestorm of political movement mobilization.

When SB 1070 passed, the bill had an immediate impact on everyday Latinx and low-income migrant workers, who suddenly faced the prospect of becoming the targets of law enforcement to a greater degree than in the past. This shocked and offended many members of minority communities in the state and, thus, ignited immigrant, Latinx, and labor rights movement mobilization throughout Arizona much more than did any of the legislation, ballot initiatives, court cases, or executive actions of the 2000s. Although SB 1070 was supported by much of the public,[65] thousands of people were mobilized by the law, and they poured into Phoenix to protest and be a part of the newly re-forming immigrant rights movement.[66] A coalition of worker, migrant, and Latinx rights organizations and individuals affiliated with the queer and trans migrant movement launched ¡Alto Arizona!, explicitly drawing parallels between Rosa Parks and the Montgomery bus boycott of the civil rights movement and the wave of anti-immigrant laws in Arizona.[67] The campaign called for a boycott of Arizona and for President Obama to intervene in the state to end both SB 1070 and the federal immigration programs his administration was conducting in the state, such as the 287(g) program, which granted Sheriff Arpaio's Maricopa County Sheriff's Office the authority to enforce federal immigration laws.[68]

### Inter- and Intra-Movement Coalition Expansion in the Aftermath of SB 1070

Defensive rights episodes, such as SB 1070, have greater mobilizing and activating potential because they occur as a result of opponent mobilization and thus—to a larger degree than offensive rights episodes—reinforce a shared political movement past, shared experiences of oppression, and a common core of opponents across multiple minority communities. Many interviewees discussed how mobilizing and activating the explosive SB 1070 defensive rights campaign was within immigrant and Latinx communities. During her interview, Diana, an organization leader with a marginalized group that primarily serves immigrants and communities of color and also partners with and supports local queer organizations, directly and eloquently emphasized how SB 1070 was an activating moment:

> Diana: A lot of it I think was fear and the anger . . . the fear that you were going to be separated from your family and the anger that someone had control over that. . . . Like they did the English-only law, Prop. 200, they did Prop. 300, they had been doing different laws that had affected our community, 287g, Secure Communities,[69] and it had been happening, but none of us had really noticed or really activated to it. But SB 1070 was so blatant, racist, that it shocked us. And it awoke us. I don't know, some people weren't shocked because they had seen it coming, but for a lot of us that were not involved, that were younger, [we] had no idea. . . . And they would talk about it, blatantly and loudly and say this is what we want—we want you to self-deport, we want you to leave, right? Russell Pearce, Joe Arpaio, talking about Tent City and that's like his concentration camp and . . . 2010 was a very loud year of them speaking. . . . 2010 provided that opportunity for us to make that choice, and we chose to fight. And here we are continuing that.

Diana's discussion of history as well as the fear and anger spurred by opponent activists like Russell Pearce and the infamously anti-immigrant Sheriff Arpaio reinforced a shared political movement past narrative that, in the aftermath of SB 1070, would ultimately enable many immigrant rights advocates in Arizona to build alliances with communities that faced similar counter-movement attacks.

In July 2010, shortly after SB 1070 passed, the US Department of

Justice filed *Arizona v. United States*, a lawsuit that challenged the constitutionality of SB 1070. The case would eventually reach the US Supreme Court. The federal government's lawsuit was one of several filed in the aftermath of SB 1070. The lawsuit challenged four provisions of the bill: (1) the section that made failure to comply with federal immigration requirements a state misdemeanor, (2) the section that made it a state misdemeanor for undocumented immigrants to work, (3) the section that allowed state law enforcement to arrest people who they have probable cause to believe are removable from the US, and (4) the infamous "show me your papers" provision.[70] In 2012, the Supreme Court held that federal law preempted all of the sections of SB 1070 challenged by the federal government, except the "show me your papers" provision. Although the federal lawsuit would eventually gut much of SB 1070, in 2010, as soon as the lawsuit was filed, it effectively raised the profile of SB 1070, both in Arizona and nationally, increasing media attention on the law and further mobilizing political movement advocates.

Once SB 1070 passed and activated members of minority communities, advocates in Arizona looked for ways to build political power within marginalized and mainstream movement organizations against the anti-rights forces responsible for the law. Organizers in the area realized that immigrant rights advocates needed to focus on civic engagement and create a broad inter- and intra-movement coalition to unite and coordinate the newly mobilized constituencies in the state. In the following interview excerpt, Louis, an organization leader who works with immigrant workers, describes how one of the largest and most sustained coalitions was created and why immigrant rights activists decided to devote significant resources to civic engagement:

> Louis: Seven of us went to the flagpole at the capital and did a press conference and kind of a vigil, kind of a prayer vigil, and asking the governor to veto 1070. That prayer vigil, we just had decided to stay the night. And then we never left for like 103 more days. And that grew to, we were over forty thousand [people] at one point. We had giant student walkouts. So this large, direct action, nonviolent direct action campaign on the literal grass of the state capitol, is really what launched [our civic engagement coalition] because inside of the vigil we were certainly having a lot of conversations . . . and many of us realized we needed to move into a civic

engagement phase because that would be the real way to defeat and move beyond the attacks and the defensive posture. And so we started civic engagement work really for the first time for most of us in the wake of 1070.

The civic engagement coalition described by Louis would eventually work with both mainstream and marginalized organizations, and continued to expand and mobilize in response to SB 1070. James, a union organizer in Arizona, explained during his interview why some unions started to work with immigrant and Latinx rights organizations following the passage of SB 1070. According to James, once SB 1070 "came down and drowned out everything," funders no longer wanted to support worker's rights and economic justice issues that the communities James organized cared about the most. Instead, all "anybody wanted to talk about was immigrant rights in Arizona and the fight against SB 1070." As a result, in order to stay alive in the expanding political movement in Arizona, James's labor organizers had to shift their priorities and more forcefully focus on the intersection between the immigrant rights and labor movements. They did this by joining the civic engagement coalition and participating in the struggle to build Latinx voting power in Arizona for long-term political movement ends similar to the economic justice goals James and Arizona workers' rights activists desired. Over time, this civic engagement coalition became a powerful grassroots advocacy network that mainstream organizations turned to in order to help elect supportive politicians. This, in turn, gave the marginalized organizations that composed the civic engagement coalition leverage over mainstream organizations as the newly activated political movement began to pursue policy solutions later in the 2010s.

In addition to the civic engagement coalition created out of SB 1070, the defensive rights episode also activated many Latinx and undocumented youth in the state. The Latinx and undocumented youth movement in Arizona became particularly important in local electoral races in Phoenix and in creating local inter- and intra-movement coalitions around policy proposals in the 2010s. For example, one group of Latinx youth activated by SB 1070 ultimately ran grassroots campaigns around a number of elections in the greater Phoenix area. In 2011, they knocked on seventy-two thousand doors in one district, increased Latinx voter turnout by 480 percent in the district, and helped elect Daniel Valenzuela to the Phoenix City Council in a seat never held by a Latinx person.[71]

Eventually, Latinx youth affiliated with this group would join other organizations and help build inter- and intra-movement partnerships in the emerging grassroots advocacy network. Some of the leaders of this group became part of a civic engagement coalition that formed after SB 1070 went into effect. This civic engagement coalition, which encompassed labor unions, immigrant rights organizations, queer migrant organizations, and a mainstream LGBTQ organization in 2016, ultimately began to push policy proposals in the state. One of these proposals was the ONE PHX ID campaign, which formed in order to support a municipal ID card that members argued would aid undocumented, disabled, trans, and homeless people in Phoenix. The emergence of local inter- and intra-movement coalitions like the civic engagement coalition is indicative of political movement expansion and the formation of an institutionalized grassroots advocacy network capable of mobilizing people from the ballot box to public policy campaigns in the aftermath of SB 1070.

Possibly one of the greatest electoral victories for movement actors was the defeat of State Senator Pearce. After passing SB 1070, Pearce introduced several anti-immigrant bills, including SB 1038, which sought to deny citizenship to children born to noncitizen parents, in violation of the Fourteenth Amendment. Although many of these bills ultimately failed, they underscored the extremism of anti–immigrant rights movement advocates like Pearce in Arizona. During this time, Arizona lost millions of dollars due to conference cancellations spurred by the Arizona boycott campaign that formed in response to SB 1070.[72] This shifted the political climate against Senator Pearce. According to Victor, one of the individuals who helped launch the effort to remove Pearce from office, after Pearce was appointed as the president of the state senate in 2010 and after the wave of anti-immigrant extremism, "People were like, this is too much." More specifically, many Republicans grew tired of the policies Pearce pushed in the state legislature. In 2011, a group of political movement activists collected enough signatures to trigger a recall election. The movement activists were not aided by the Democratic Party but by the Mormon Republicans who dominated Pearce's district. The Mormon Church, which was trying to reach out to Latinxs at the time, opposed SB 1070. Due to the Republican split in Pearce's district and an ethics scandal,[73] the legislator once considered the most powerful and invincible politician in Arizona was ultimately unseated by a moderate Republican.[74]

Following SB 1070, most organizations and individuals involved in coalitional advocacy were from the labor, Latinx, immigrant rights, and queer migrant communities in Arizona. Yet many interviewees indicated that broad support from mainstream LGBTQ organizations was lacking. Progressive LGBTQ people affiliated with these organizations often participated in protests and actions against SB 1070, but the mainstream organizations they were part of did not regularly do so. This started to shift in 2014, when conservative Christian activist Cathi Herrod, the president of the Center for Arizona Policy, worked with Republican legislators to craft SB 1062.[75] SB 1062 was a proposed expansion of the state's Religious Freedom Restoration Act (RFRA), which, if passed, would have allowed state businesses to refuse service to LGBTQ people. The bill passed in both the state house of representatives and the senate, but was ultimately vetoed by Governor Brewer, who was convinced by the public outcry, pressure from businesses that faced possible economic losses due to a new boycott-Arizona campaign, and the National Football League's threat to remove the 2015 Super Bowl from Arizona if the law passed.

Many interviewees compared SB 1062 and SB 1070 and explained that similarities between the dual defensive rights episodes were what led to the emergence of cross-community coalitions between immigrant rights and mainstream LGBTQ organizations in the 2010s. According to Clara, one of the Latinx youth activated in the wake of SB 1070, the anti-LGBTQ SB 1062 initiated a similarly vortex-like response in Arizona:

> Clara: That was an unexpected bill. . . . And that was crazy. It really was. It was the community that helped stop that. It truly was the community. Because for the first time you saw business leaders openly criticizing this. You saw people on both sides of the aisle criticizing this bill. And it's something that, *it was like wildfire, man, I mean it spread so fast and it spread throughout the whole state.* You started seeing "We are Open for Business for Everyone" signs everywhere. [emphasis added]

The "wildfire" sparked by SB 1062 activated a variety of rights movement organizations, including those that represented the Latinx, labor, and mainstream LGBTQ communities.

During his interview, State Senator Steve Gallardo discussed both how SB 1070 helped to create inter-movement coalitions and how the anti-immigrant SB 1070 and anti-LGBTQ SB 1062, which appeared in 2010 and 2014 respectively, mobilized inter-movement partnerships by emphasizing a shared movement past and common opponents. Gallardo explained that SB 1070 was an important mobilizing moment that helped activate, or "wake up," cross-community support for immigrant rights issues from groups that previously had not participated in attempts to thwart anti-immigrant laws. SB 1062, the next major defensive rights campaign after SB 1070, then helped create alliances between mainstream LGBTQ and immigrant rights groups by emphasizing how members of both communities shared the same opponents. According to Gallardo, the "same group of legislators," the same opponents or "enemies" who pushed anti-immigrant laws likewise targeted LGBTQ people when they tried to pass SB 1062 in 2014. The dual defensive rights campaigns contributed to the formation of inter-movement coalitions by reinforcing that both communities are subjected to the same "hate," the same "attacks."

LGBTQ community advocates also described how these dual bills (i.e., SB 1070 and SB 1062) assisted in the creation of inter-movement coalitions by emphasizing a shared political movement past that extended well beyond each rights campaign. For instance, Roger, an LGBTQ community advocate who works with mainstream LGBTQ organizations and marginalized organizations, supported efforts to stop SB 1070 and SB 1062. According to Roger, the common opponents who activate political movement organizations by passing or attempting to pass laws that target the communities these organizations serve are deeply rooted in an inter-movement past. SB 1070 was not an isolated attack on a single community. Instead, Roger described in his interview how activism around SB 1070, spurred by a common core of opponents, was reminiscent of the LGBTQ community's Marches on Washington, massive political rallies in Washington, DC conducted in the 1970s through the early 1990s in order to draw national attention to various forms of state violence directed at the LGBTQ community. Roger argued that at the state level, both SB 1070 and SB 1062 were "like the MLK holiday"—the political moment in the late 1980s and early 1990s when opponent groups in Arizona moved to prevent the state from adopting Martin Luther King Jr. Day as a state holiday. For Roger, these intense defensive moments were important mechanisms of both inter-movement and intra-movement mobilization. Thus Roger argued that ultimately "1062 was one of the best things that happened to us [the LGBTQ community] because it's that slap in the face, a slap in the face that any community needs to wake up the sleeping giant that is an otherwise unengaged electorate."

## THE LIMITS OF MOBILIZING THROUGH A DEFENSIVE RIGHTS EPISODE

The defensive rights episode that emerged in Arizona in 2010 did aid in the expansion of movement mobilization. Activists, community workers, organizers, and politicians interviewed for this study argued that SB 1070, in conjunction with future defensive moments such as the anti-LGBTQ SB 1062, activated new organizations and people and contributed to the construction of inter- and intra-movement coalitions over time. Interviewees demonstrated how these moments emphasized a shared political movement past and a common core of opponents who use the same messaging and tactics when advocating for laws that harm minority communities in the state. Yet despite the mobilizing, expansionist capacity that exists within defensive rights moments like SB 1070, these moments also simultaneously constrain movement mobilization. According to interviewees, defensive rights episodes constrain movement mobilization because they center thwarting a rights loss, because of their cyclical nature, and because they reinforce hierarchical exclusions across movements by centering the experiences of those movement constituents deemed most "acceptable" by mainstream society.

It is important to note that SB 1070 does appear to have expanded movement mobilization more than the offensive Referendum 74 campaign for marriage equality in Washington State. SB 1070 was likely more expansive because of its defensive nature, which sustained the movement actors longer than an electoral campaign or legislative session cycle and minimized coalition fragmentation, as the blame for the necessity of movement-based advocacy, and the trauma that this entails, was placed on opponents. However, the defensive rights moment still centered pushing back against a rights loss that many advocates felt solely impacted the migrant and Latinx communities, often at the expense of other communities. James, the union organizer quoted earlier, made this point in his interview. According to James, once SB 1070 exploded in Arizona, labor movement advocates lost much of their funding. James's "efforts to raise money and build interest in economic justice . . . fell on deaf ears because all any funders or anybody wanted to talk about was immigrants' rights in Arizona" in the aftermath of SB 1070. As a result, James had to shift his focus from workers' rights to immigrants' rights in order to maintain a place in the burgeoning immigrant rights–centered political movement in Arizona. James also explained that the boycott-Arizona campaign, one of the cross-community actions that emerged out of SB 1070, harmed union membership because it drove business out of the state, particularly those businesses that held conferences that rely on hospitality workers. He estimated that one union "would probably have 20 percent to 30 percent more members" had it not been for the boycott-Arizona campaign. This is an indication that SB 1070 narrowed the focus of movement mobilization onto a single community and onto rights issues that mattered to that community, while placing issues important to other coalitional constituencies at the margins—at least during the highest point in the defensive rights struggle.

Furthermore, Victor, one of the activists who worked to get Pearce removed from office, questioned the utility of the broad-based inter- and intra-movement partnerships that formed after SB 1070 because they often did not include Republicans. According to Victor, "If you really want to help immigrants [in Arizona], especially on a policy, you have to have Republicans." This is certainly true in a state political climate dominated by the Republican party. Without Republican support, political movement coalitions that formed in the aftermath of SB 1070 have still largely been unable to pass legislation in the Republican-controlled legislature. However, the coalitions have continued to expand in Arizona even though the momentum behind SB 1070 has largely waned. Coalition partners have been able to successfully thwart some anti-immigrant legislation in the state legislature and recently achieved important movement advances through the passage of Proposition 206, which increased the minimum wage in the state and through the electoral defeat of Sheriff Arpaio in 2016.

The SB 1070 defensive rights episode also marginalized some movement constituents and, in doing so, limited mobilization as well. Defensive rights campaigns can be traumatic moments that most negatively impact individuals who exist at the margins. In his interview, Nicolas, a former organization leader who has worked with mainstream immigrant rights organizations and marginalized migrant LGBTQ organizations in inter- and intra-movement coalitions, articulated how the trauma inflicted by laws like SB 1070 and the failure of the federal DREAM Act in 2010 disproportionately impacted those who are intersectionally marginalized.

> Nicolas: With the passage of SB 1070 in April 2010, it was a huge loss— the passage of SB 1070 in Arizona and then a bigger loss with the failure to pass the DREAM Act. . . . And I started to hear stories about friends who are gay and talking about their experiences during SB 1070, for example. One of the stories that impacted me the most was a story about a friend of mine after SB 1070 passed. . . . One of my friends said that right before it passed his parents found out that he was gay. When SB 1070 passed we had this mayhem here in Arizona where people were just leaving, and his parents and his family were one of those families that packed up and moved to Texas. And my friend said that when SB 1070 passed and they were getting ready to leave, essentially his parents told him that if he wanted to go with them that he couldn't be gay anymore. And for him, it was big because not only is he dealing with being undocumented in his family, but now on top of that he's being kind of alienated by his family because of his sexual orientation. . . .
>
> When he said that, I started to talk to other friends about how they also experienced being LGBT and in this movement. . . . During that time, I started, because I am gay myself, it's just not something that I put out as part of my immigrant story, so to speak. It was never something that we emphasized. So then, when I started sharing my story I started thinking about how do I highlight this aspect of my story and how do I draw these similarities between what's going on with immigration now and being gay and discrimination and things like that. So then I started talking to my friends about their interests and just expanding their stories and then eventually we decided to form [LGBTQ migrant group name redacted], and this was kind of in tandem with what my peers across the country were doing in bringing out this issue of LGBT immigrants more.

Nicolas relates how Latinx and queer youth in Arizona both initiated inter- and intra-movement mobilization in the aftermath of the 2010 defensive rights campaigns and were disproportionately harmed by these campaigns. Nicolas's friend experienced dual ostracism as his family was forced to flee Arizona in the wake of SB 1070 and also refused to take him with them unless he renounced his sexual orientation. Yet within this moment of social and familial trauma, Nicolas and other advocates also created an opportunity for inter- and intra-movement mobilization and organizing, creating new organizations in order to ensure that their interests were represented in mainstream LGBTQ and immigrant movement organizations that had previously failed to recognize those who are intersectionally marginalized. This simultaneous experience of trauma and opportunity illuminates the often paradoxical implications of rights episodes.

SB 1070 arose out of a state ethos based in Southern traditionalist, frontier, law-and-order values that enabled the development of a racialized nativism within Arizona's Anglo community. Immigrant rights advocates tried to stem the tide of anti-immigrant political advocacy through the courts and, in some instances, were successful at doing so. However, when Arizona's political environment shifted in 2009 as Democratic governor Janet Napolitano was selected by the Obama administration to lead the Department of Homeland Security, the Tea Party rose in response to the election of President Obama, and a major economic crisis fueled calls for harsh anti-immigrant laws, the state became fertile ground for the formation of a defensive immigrant rights episode that manifested in SB 1070.

There were key differences between the SB 1070 defensive rights episode and Washington State's created marriage equality rights episode. In the two rights episodes, the blame for marginalization fell on different parties. In the marriage equality rights episode, mainstream movement organizations were responsible for the formation of the episode and were criticized by movement actors for the marginalization and exclusion of certain people and organizations. This criticism was exacerbated in a rights campaign composed mostly of organizations that tend not to think strategically about movements beyond single campaign cycles. In the SB 1070 defensive rights episode, mainstream movement actors still faced some of the blame for marginalizing certain movement constituents; however, most of the blame was placed on the opponents responsible for the formation of the episodic rights campaign. This minimized coalition fragmentation in the aftermath of the rights episode.

The SB 1070 defensive rights episode both expanded and constrained movement mobilization. SB 1070 activated new organizations and individuals and expanded movement mobilization by emphasizing a common core of cross-community opponents, a shared political movement past, and shared experiences of oppression across different communities. At the same time, SB 1070 also paradoxically contained movement mobilization because it centered issues that most impacted the state's immigrant communities while marginalizing issues that mattered to other minority communities. The next chapter will delve into the factors associated with coalition expansion and contraction in greater detail by further analyzing in-depth interviews conducted with organization leaders, advocates, and community workers in each state.

Chapter 3

_____

# UNITY AND DIVISION

Paradoxes in the Formation of Political Movement Coalitions

Interviewer: When these bills started to emerge [and] when propositions started to emerge, particularly anti-immigrant ones, would you see any support for stopping them from LGBT community organizations—

State Senator Gallardo (AZ): *(interrupting)* No . . . no. And not to single out the LGBT community; I mean, keep in mind that in the early 2000s, we didn't have support from the labor community. Organized labor was not very supportive, was not opposed to these bills. . . . I think it took a while for us to realize that we couldn't fight these battles alone, that we needed, at least as Latinos, we needed to build relationships.

Political movement coalitions do not arise naturally or easily. They have to be constructed through the hard work and ingenuity of advocates and community workers. I argue that movement constituents formed inter- and intra-movement coalitions in Washington and Arizona by constructing narratives and building relationships around the idea that individuals and groups involved in these coalitions were part of one community that shared a common political movement past, or civil rights past, and the same opponents or "enemies." This enabled the new relationships built within and across disparate political movements to last beyond episodic rights campaign by contributing to movement expansion and mobilization over time.

However, the construction of these new inter- and intra-movement alliances come at a cost. Political movement formation and expansion in both state contexts also simultaneously divided movement constituents based on power. According to interviewees, coalitions that formed were often fragile, superficial, and quickly fractured. Interviewees argued, first, that division occurred because a disproportionately large amount of funding went to mainstream organizations that claimed responsibility for successes at the expense of marginalized groups. Second, interviewees argued that coalitions were frequently fragile because the rights episodes that initiated coalition formation also involved the tokenization of marginalized constituencies within movements. Finally, interviewees contended that the new coalitions were often superficial because the groups that composed them had different policy and issue preferences, with mainstream organizations primarily concerned with the achievement of rights wins and marginalized groups concerned with uprooting institutionalized power in the long term in ways that mainstream groups sometimes felt were at odds with their interests.[1]

### One Community: Factors That Contribute to Coalition Unity

In Washington and Arizona, the emergence of inter- and intra-movement coalitions coincided with the development of collective political movement narratives. In both states, movement actors formed a collective understanding of their connection to a shared past, which involved relationship building that emphasized how movements composed of seemingly disparate subject positions were part of one community through the construction of civil rights and other political movement narratives. Coalitions also formed through the recognition of shared opponents or "enemies." These shared opponents encompassed specific individuals, including politicians; leaders of interest groups; and law enforcement officials who targeted and attacked minority populations over prolonged periods of time. However, opposition was also constructed as a more generalizable fear of community ostracism as a result of one's subject position—for example, as an LGBTQ person or undocumented immigrant. Seemingly divergent organizations form a collective civil rights past narrative when they recognize that the same messages, attacks, and fears experienced as a result of their own members' subject positions also apply to other minority subject positions.[2]

For instance, the experience of "coming out" as LGBTQ is a collective understanding of past that applies to LGBTQ people and involves considerable fear of community ostracism or "othering" by those who do not hold this subject position. My research finds that organization leaders and advocates who represent undocumented LGBTQ people were able to initiate the formation of common civil rights past narratives between queer migrant and lesbian and gay organizations within the LGBTQ rights movement. They did this in limited circumstances by holding such events as Double Coming Out forums and through direct conversations with other minority community organizations and individuals. During these events and through these conversations, interviewees emphasized the similarity between "coming out as LGBTQ" and "coming out of the shadows" as undocumented—a similar collective past experience that involves fear of community isolation for both. In recognizing the similarities between experiences of coming out, members from divergent groups were able to form a collective understanding of past, based on generalizable opponents, that aided in the formation of intra-movement coalitions between queer migrant organizations and LGBTQ organizations that had historically de-emphasized or ignored queer migrant constituents in Washington State and Arizona.

SHARING STORY AND CONSTRUCTING A COMMON PAST

In both state contexts, interviewees identified the importance of relationship building in the creation of expansive political movement coalitions. This was particularly apparent among LGBTQ undocumented immigrant youth in Washington and Arizona, who integrated into their respective communities by emphasizing similarities between the narrative of "coming out" as LGBTQ and the narrative of "coming out of the shadows" as undocumented. Interviewees described how they would highlight these similarities when talking with the broader community and with LGBTQ and immigrant rights organizations in order to expand the political movements to which these groups belonged. For example, Emilio, an organization advocate who works with a group that represents LGBTQ people and undocumented immigrants in Washington State, described these coming out similarities and how they bridge multiple movements. According to Emilio, the coming-out narrative is "a similar scenario" with "parallels" between the LGBTQ and immigrant rights movements. Emilio and other leaders in organizations that represent undocumented LGBTQ people highlighted these similar stories in order to create community within and across different minority populations. These dual coming out narratives often enabled the formation of inter- and intra-movement coalitions because they allowed LGBTQ people to see how their community related to the undocumented immigrant community and vice versa. In this way, Emilio and other advocates helped construct a narrative that illuminated how the LGBTQ and undocumented immigrant communities were actually one common political movement rather than only distinct communities with different movement trajectories.

Interviewees argued that forms of relationship building such as sharing dual coming out narratives were crucial for expanding movement mobilization for this reason. Indeed, sharing story was a prominent factor that interviewees identified in expanding beyond single subject position constructions within individual movement organizations, across political movements, and in the broader community. For example, Sarah, the leader of a small LGBTQ organization in Arizona, described sharing story as one of the principal tactics used by activists who participated in a marriage equality action that involved a walk across the state. The walk was a campaign led by Sarah's organization, in which members walked 660 miles across the state of Arizona and visited 114 cities in order to share their stories with rural Arizona residents. In the excerpt here, Sarah describes sharing story as a movement tactic:

> Sarah: [The walk action was] . . . done in July and August, so it was very hot and the point was to be dramatic. . . . When we started doing it, it was definitely, "I've never met a gay person," and by the end it was a very different dynamic, and people wanted the trainings. . . . *And it was really about storytelling and about, you know, once you hear someone's story you can never un-hear it.* Their viewpoint might not change that day, but you've definitely planted that seed. . . . We set meetings for people along the way, whether they were government officials or everyday people or schoolteachers or whoever they were, we tried to set meetings in each town. But then we also just talked to people on the street, and we had some really difficult conversations, but *they always seemed to go pretty well because it was just a human dialogue.* [emphasis added]

For Sarah and the walk participants, sharing story enabled relationships to grow between rural residents and LGBTQ people. This, in turn, destigmatized LGBTQ status among some rural residents. It also allowed participants in the action and people they encountered to see how they were all part of one community. For the LGBTQ, labor, and immigrant communities, sharing story served the same function in the creation of inter- and intra-movement coalitions. The more that groups and individuals saw themselves as part of the same community, the more sustainable these coalitions were in the long term.

Manuel, a leader of a queer migrant organization in Arizona, even more concretely related how sharing story was an important component of enabling coalitions to form between immigrant and LGBTQ communities. In the excerpt here, Manuel describes dual coming-out stories and how sharing them became an important way for groups to empathize with one another and work together in coalition:

> Manuel: I think for me, what made me come out and, like, the feelings, was Prop 300 [an anti-immigrant law that ended in-state tuition for undocumented students]. I was dedicated to school, and I understood that that was what I wanted to do. But then I also understood that I needed to share my story. I remember the first time I spoke on stage and talked about my story and coming out, I had these butterflies in my stomach, right, just nervous feeling and this sense that everybody was going to know my status and the police were going to come to my house and deport all of us, and I felt like maybe I was going to walk down the street and people were going to throw things at me or maybe I was going to be called illegal. And that didn't feel good. . . .
>
> And then I came out in 2009. And I had the same feeling of losing friends, but this time it was like the feeling of losing my family, right? Coming out and really, really feeling alone and like I wasn't going to have any support system was scary. Also feeling like I was going to get gay-bashed or something like that. It's the same feelings that I was going to get things thrown at me while I was walking down the street. They were very similar. And I think this is why the LGBT community was able to connect and we were able to bring membership in when [our local queer migrant organization] started because we were able to connect the same feelings and the feelings were very in line.

Manuel discusses two coming-out narratives here. First, he talks about what it felt like to come out as undocumented in the aftermath of Proposition 300.[3] Manuel then describes how similar this experience was to coming out as a queer person. In recalling these coming out stories, Manuel also relates an experience of significant risk when describing what it means to come out and identify as part of an emerging group. Because Manuel's dual coming out stories related to the stories of risk associated with owning a stigmatized status for other groups, people who heard Manuel's stories more easily understood how their own past struggles overlapped. Manuel argues that this ultimately helped queer and migrant groups relate to one another and work together in inter- and intra-movement coalitions.

Sharing story is not a new tactic or something that is specific to solidifying alliances alone. Labor movement organizers have long used their personal narratives as a means of organizing new members and building power. Indeed, many union organizing materials stress the importance of personal, one-on-one conversations for recruiting new union members and building political capacity.[4] It is interesting that interviewees from across the LGBTQ, labor, and immigrant movements identified a common union organizing tactic as one of the most effective means of creating coalitions and mobilizing movements. Interviewees who were also involved in the labor movement often used the union organizing, "one-on-one" language to describe what other interviewees identified as "sharing story," "storytelling," or "relationship building."

Louis, who works with an immigrant worker advocacy group and with local unions that have been involved in the creation of inter-movement coalitions between LGBTQ, labor, and immigrant communities, described how one-on-one, grassroots conversations were central to all of his organization's civic engagement. These conversations were a way "to tell your story" and "to connect in a personal way . . . so it becomes not about politics, not about, you know, this party or that party, but about, my life and the challenges that I face and why I'm out here talking to you." For example, during get-out-the-vote campaigns, canvassers with Louis's organization would tell their own unique stories in order to convey to people why voting on a given issue was so important. One of these original narratives involved DREAMers coming out to voters as undocumented and telling voters that they needed to "to be a voice that speaks for me because I'm not able to vote in this election" due to their immigration status.[5] Canvassers used their DREAMer narratives during issue-driven campaigns, such as the successful effort to pass Proposition 104, in order to convince citizens to vote. Proposition 104 was a Phoenix ballot initiative that passed in 2015. The proposition increased the city's sales tax to fund expansion of light rail. It was supported by a bipartisan coalition that included LGBTQ and labor movement organizations.[6] According to Louis, these one-on-one conversations, or sharing of personal stories, about how policies impact individual lives were one of the best ways to build political power for oppressed minority groups such as low-income workers and undocumented people.

In the formation of inter- and intra-movement coalitions, sharing story also involved the construction of common movement and civil rights past narratives. Movement narratives were often used to illustrate how the missions of LGBTQ and immigrant organizations were connected to one another. In her interview, Sage, an advocate in Washington State who conducted outreach with organizations in building coalitions around LGBTQ movement issues, discussed the utility of political movement narratives for inter-movement coalitions. When Sage would reach out to organizations to convince them to join Washington's Referendum 74 campaign for marriage equality in 2012, talking about "our long civil rights history" was one of the major tactics she employed. Sage's group also convinced community of color organizations to join the coalition by "getting very highly visible people to support the campaign" who would then talk with others about how marriage equality "is a civil rights issue." In this way, Sage was able to get organizations to join the coalition that otherwise might not have because they believed that LGBTQ issues were "outside of our mission." These "highly visible people" were minority leaders who highlighted that "there are LGBT members of communities of color." They did so during one-on-one conversations with their communities and other organizations. Ultimately, these conversations drove up support for marriage equality during the rights episode, expanding the cross-community coalition.

The construction of shared political movement narratives helped interviewees like Sage convey to different political movement groups that minority communities are connected, creating the possibility for long-term coalition relationships. Rachel, who worked for a marginalized organization, also clearly articulated the importance of creating a common political movement past for promoting coalition unity. Rachel conducted workshops with mainstream organizations to encourage the formation of inter-movement coalitions. During her interview, Rachel described how the recognition of a common civil rights past unites organizations in this manner:

> Rachel: We generally start off [our workshops], so an organization like [mainstream progressive women's rights group] or unions that are predominately white that have done strategic partnerships with us, they bring together their staff, their board, and their core leaders. And we need to build collectively a shared understanding of our history that weaves all of our movements together, so the civil rights, the immigrant rights, the LGBTQ justice, the labor unions. You need to be able to see the timeline of where our work has both been intersected and also been siloed. And then, I think, just walking through that timeline. People kind of see we are facing the same opposition, we are facing the same kinds of attacks, the messaging that they use against our communities is fairly consistent across different communities, whether it's because you're abnormal, or immoral, or criminal, or a threat to the American way of life, right? So those kinds of messagings are fairly consistent across our marginalized communities.

According to Rachel, the development of a common civil rights past narrative can be the basis for a long-term inter-movement alliance. It builds strength between groups by calling out common opponents in movement struggles and illuminating how these opponents strive to divide marginalized communities. Furthermore, Rachel describes how inter-movement coalitions can form through building a "shared understanding of our history that weaves all our movements together." For Rachel, the creation of a common political movement narrative that incorporates the LGBTQ movement with the immigrant rights movement, labor movement, and civil rights movement contributes to coalition formation.

Rachel's organization encountered groups that were opposed to marriage equality and initially hesitated to join the Referendum 74 marriage equality coalition. After Rachel's group worked with some of these organizations, through what Rachel called in her interview a process of "deep storytelling" and "a lot of one-on-ones with folks who were very religious and opposed to this," several of these hostile organizations ultimately ended up endorsing and joining the Washington State coalition that formed around the marriage equality rights episode. For Rachel and other interviewees involved in the construction of movement coalitions like the Referendum 74 campaign for marriage equality, sharing story and the construction of a common political movement or civil rights past were crucial movement unifying tactics. Through sharing story, movement actors emphasized similar experiences across the LGBTQ, immigrant, and other minority and under-represented communities. In doing so, movement advocates and community workers illustrated how struggles that impacted one minority community were intertwined with the struggles of others. This de-othered individual experiences and created a collective understanding that unified seemingly different communities.

Unity in Opponents and Political Threats

Not all interviewees used civil rights narratives to assist in the formation of cross-community coalitions in both state contexts. Indeed, many marginalized groups reject civil rights narratives that they argue do not uproot institutional oppression. These groups argue that civil rights narratives enable people to resign themselves to state-supported "equality" that does not combat state power structures premised on police violence, racism, and economic hardship. For marginalized groups that reject civil rights narratives, formal legal change, such as expanding anti-discrimination laws to encompass more minority communities, falls short because it both fails to combat and helps uphold systemic power-laden race, gender, and class hierarchies. Therefore, rather than employing civil rights narratives, many interviewees constructed political movement past narratives in describing their coalition work, drawing on common opponents.

These interviewees referenced shared struggles or attacks when describing how their own communities related to others and, thus, why it is important to work together in coalition. In Arizona, it was common for interviewees to discuss SB 1070 and SB 1062 as cross-community attacks that demonstrated how seemingly divergent minority communities share common movement histories. Recall from chapter 2 that SB 1070 (the Support Our Law Enforcement and Safe Neighborhoods Act) was the virulently anti-immigrant law, passed by the Arizona legislature in 2010, that enabled local law enforcement officers to check immigration documents when they have a reasonable suspicion that a person is undocumented.[7] SB 1062, also described in detail in chapter 2, was a proposed state religious freedom bill in 2014 that, had it passed, would have allowed businesses to discriminate on the basis of LGBTQ status.[8] During her interview, Valeria, an advocate who works on immigration and LGBTQ movement issues, described how SB 1070 made her "more understanding and sensitive of everybody's issues and how they are all related" and led her to believe that "just because something is the law doesn't mean that it's right and doesn't mean that it's good." According to Valeria, post–SB 1070 laws that targeted other groups, such as SB 1062, were examples of "the same thing happening" across seemingly different under-represented populations. This pattern of harmful laws directed at minority communities convinced Valeria to expand her advocacy beyond immigrant rights to include other targeted community issues, such as "LGBT rights, police accountability, . . . women's reproductive rights." For Valeria, SB 1070 represented an attack on one community that is connected to similar legal attacks on the LGBTQ community, people of color, and women that collectively create a common political movement past. The extremism that characterized SB 1070 made her realize that the attacks on each of these communities do not occur in isolation; rather, they demonstrate that these communities are engaged in the same political movement struggle.

Interviewees argued that when SB 1062 emerged in 2014, alliances that were barely forming between LGBTQ and immigrant rights movement groups in the aftermath of SB 1070 grew stronger. In the following excerpt, Arizona state senator Martín Quezada[9] describes how SB 1062 strengthened cross-movement coalitions because it emphasized how these two communities shared the same opponents:

> State Senator Quezada: I think those alliances have gotten stronger since [SB 1062]. And a lot of that happened when . . . Senate Bill 1062 was here. We started to see the same thing that happened to us as immigrants, as an immigrant community back when Senate Bill 1070 was happening to the LGBT community this year in Senate Bill 1062. And so, as Latino and immigrant, immigrant rights kind of activists, we rose to the occasion, fought that just as hard. And we came to the aid, I think, of the LGBT community. And it became a bigger issue. It started to become a bigger issue, I think, because of those alliances and because people started to see the impact it had on our economy.

Other interviewees corroborated the strengthening of inter- and intra-movement coalitions around SB 1062 as well. In response to SB 1062, Latinx, labor, and immigrant community leaders and organizations held press conferences in support of the LGBTQ community and appeared at rallies and protests opposing the proposed legislation.

In addition to shared legislative attacks, interviewees identified other forms of opposition that strengthened inter- and intra-movement coalition alignment. In the following exchange, Harry, the former leader of a mainstream LGBTQ organization in Washington who identifies as white and gay, discussed how shared opponents eventually helped in the formation of an inter-movement coalition by shifting labor organizations in Washington toward greater acceptance of lesbian and gay rights:

> Harry: That was a big shift also from 2004. In 2004, I was working on a campaign for [a Democratic party candidate], and the labor groups were not on board on what they call the 3Gs: Guns, God, and Gays. . . . The first thing they said is we like you [candidate's name], . . . but you're not good on this. Our members care about Guns, God, and Gays. . . . But that was showing that the conversation was not there yet within the labor organizations, and that shifted a lot over the last ten years from 2004 to 2012.
>
> Interviewer: What do you think shifted it?
>
> Harry: I think it was things like Ref 71 [the passage of the "everything but marriage" domestic partnership law]. You know, *they saw the right people turn out to support it.* I also think that [my organization] had been part of the social justice conversation because of our alliance with [another progressive organization], and that the candidates that we were supporting were the candidates they were supporting. *We have the same opponents. You know, the enemy of my enemy is my friend.* [emphasis added]

Harry argues that lesbian and gay organizations' support of the same candidates and opposition to the same candidates as labor organizations ultimately helped shift labor organizations' position on lesbian and gay rights issues. By supporting crosscutting issues central to the labor movement, his organization became a part of the long-term "social justice conversation." This commitment to other groups' causes and goals, combined with the presence of the same core opponents, helped over time solidify the understanding that organizations serving divergent communities were part of the same movement.

Sometimes interviewees described how specific opponents or "enemies" aided the formation of inter- and intra-movement coalitions. For example, Tom, an LGBTQ person of color and the former leader of a mainstream LGBTQ organization, discussed how a common core of opponents helped unify LGBTQ and immigrant rights organizations in an inter-movement coalition in 2009, during the "everything but marriage" campaign, which legalized domestic partnerships for same-sex couples in the state:

> Tom: If you care about more revenue for programs that serve low-income communities, the people who are trying to oppose this are some of the same people who are trying to oppose marriage equality and a lot of all the other socioeconomic issues that we care about. We were able to kind of quietly make the argument to [groups that advocated for socioeconomic issues and communities of color] that our opposition is trying to divide us and that we need to stick together because that is the only chance that we have to win.
>
> Interviewer: So identifying common opponents was a big component in terms of getting people to agree?
>
> Tom: Yes, and obviously the big boogeyman that we could point to was Tim Eyman, who was behind a ton of it. You know he was obviously the first one to move on I-200 [the statewide affirmative action ban]; he was the genesis behind it and played a significant role in a number of the anti-LGBT measures as well. So it wasn't like we were making stuff up. It was like this is clearly, if you are paying any attention at all, you know that this is part of some plan by our opposition to divide us. So I think that we were able to make that argument quietly to our various coalition partners to get on board and do what they could to support these issues.

Tom describes in this exchange how the presence of a common group of opponents helped unite coalition partners that cared about socioeconomic issues, including immigrant rights organizations, in Washington State. Notably, Tom points to Tim Eyman as a key unifying resource for intersectional coalition alignments. Eyman is a conservative political activist in Washington State who frequently pushes statewide ballot measures designed to limit the rights of racial and LGBTQ minorities and to reinforce "small government" by making it more difficult for the state legislature to raise taxes.

Interviewees involved in coalition building in Arizona similarly described how specific opponents would contribute to the formation of inter- and intra-movement coalitions. Nicolas, one of the founders of an undocumented immigrant advocacy coalition in Arizona, explained how partnerships emerged between his group and a local LGBTQ group when the two realized that they were simultaneously protesting outside Arizona senator John McCain's office:

> Nicolas: Going back to 2010, one of the big actions that we had here in Phoenix was called DREAM Army, where we spent weeks outside of Senator McCain's office to try to get him to support the DREAM Act and focusing in on the stories of DREAMers who wanted to go to the army. And, of course, thinking of the senator as a veteran, we hoped that he would listen to those stories.
>
> But I remember that one time we were out there protesting Senator McCain on the DREAM Act . . . and on the other side of the street on the other corner on 16th street here in Phoenix, there was a group of LGBT folks . . . that was protesting outside because of Don't Ask Don't Tell. . . .
>
> I think something that kind of worked against us but also for us eventually was the political alignment, again, just the fact that we had similar targets. Like Senator John McCain, for example, with the LGBT community, it was, it was just a given. After that we were more intentional in reaching out to LGBT groups to see how we could support each other's actions or strategies and how to expand our stories.

After 2010, Nicolas worked in grassroots advocacy efforts with the local LGBTQ organization discussed in the previous interview excerpt. Interviewees in Arizona likewise argued that former Maricopa County sheriff Joe Arpaio, former governor Jan Brewer, and former state senator Russell Pearce were opposition leaders who served as shared opponents.[10] These individuals and others supported actions and legislation that LGBTQ, labor, and immigrant organizations viewed as forms of hate legislation—for example, SB 1070 and SB 1062, which ostracized and targeted immigrants, workers, and LGBTQ people. Many interviewees argued that having these people as cross-community opponents enabled LGBTQ and immigrant rights groups that were the subjects of opponent attacks to relate to one another as oppressed communities with shared political movement struggles.

### Fragile Unions: Factors That Contribute to Coalition Fracture

As discussed in the previous section, there are a number of factors that interviewees argued were crucial to the formation of inter- and intra-movement coalitions among the LGBTQ and immigrant communities in Washington State and Arizona. These factors included sharing stories that emphasized how movement constituents were all part of one community, the construction of political movement and civil rights past narratives, and the recognition that communities shared common opponents. Partnerships did begin to emerge in Washington State and Arizona, according to interviewees. However, interviewees were also quick to argue that coalitions, when they did form, were often superficial, easily divided, and fragile. Interviewees contended that these newly formed unions were fragile because a disproportionate amount of funding went to larger, mainstream groups; because coalitions involved the tokenization of marginalized people, especially those who were intersectionally marginalized; and because mainstream and marginalized groups within these coalitions often disagreed with one another as to which policies to pursue (rights-based issues versus structural change) and which political tactics were most effective.

#### "Money and Power"

David is the former leader of a group that represents LGBTQ people of color in Washington State. He has long been a member of the collective of political movement organizations that started forming coalitions in the 2010s. In 2012, when mainstream LGBTQ groups and other groups that are part of Washington State's political movement community formed the Referendum 74 campaign for marriage equality, David's group was quick to join:

> David: At that time we were interested in building our capacity for community mobilizing and engagement, so we already had the interests. And then it was in all the papers [laughs]. I mean everyone was just jumping on that bandwagon.

When I asked David to describe his experiences with the Referendum 74 campaign and whether he saw the marriage equality rights episode as something that would specifically help the community his organization served, he was quick to point out that it would not, because people his organization served "are worried about having a job, making money, paying the rent, et cetera, not getting deported, and marriage is not necessarily at the top of their list." David did point out some important benefits that he felt his organization acquired from participating in the coalition, but these benefits were tempered by the bad experience his organization had with the campaign overall:

> David: Yeah, so it did help us to build capacity. We had some of our folks get media training. A couple of our staff were actually featured in the marketing pieces. We went around and gave presentations; it helped us to deepen our relationships with some of the . . . organizations in the community like [names of organizations that represent immigrants and communities of color redacted], those folks. It gave us a way to cement those relationships more. It actually raised our profile within the community. A lot more people heard of us who hadn't heard about us before during the campaign, so that had a lasting effect. After the campaign, people still remembered who we are. And that was a result, I think, of our participation in the campaign.
>
> What was not so great about it is that it was the people who were sitting around the big table—so there was a big table and there was a little table. And we were not at the big table. The big table was all a pay-as-you-play or whatever they call it—a pay-to-play type of deal. There was a small number of organizations that each brought a large sum of money to the table, and they sort of were able to pay to be the big decision-makers. . . .
>
> *But you know, overall, I had a bad, that was not a good experience.* I mean it was good in the sense that I described earlier in terms of capacity building for us. What I thought was this, that the marriage equality campaign was an opportunity for movement building. . . . It was an opportunity for movement building, and that opportunity was not taken. I don't think they were interested in that. And actually, you know [a local mainstream LGBTQ group leader] kind of warned me, well it wasn't a warning, he just told me at the very, very beginning before any of the

work started, very, very early in the whole process, he says, "Look, this is going to be a campaign, and in campaigns the only thing anybody cares about is winning, and everything else is not important."

And that's how it played out. You know they calculated what's it going to take to win and that came I think at the expense, I think, of communities like ours and organizations like ours, and that was very unfortunate. But it was also a valuable learning for me because I guess that's kind of how liberals behave in a situation like this. [emphasis added]

David argues that his organization's experience in the Referendum 74 campaign coalition was a bad one overall. His group was asked to participate, but it was treated as an afterthought group that was not essential to the coalition. Furthermore, the group was relegated to the smaller, "lower-tier" table. The community of color and immigrant groups that were part of the smaller table were also given less money than the larger mainstream advocacy groups and wealthy funders who ran the "big table." This solidified the perception that the campaign coalition was not devoted to or concerned with maintaining ties with marginalized groups once the campaign ended. Consequently, David argued that the coalition was "an opportunity for movement building that was not taken."

This wealth and power separation between mainstream and marginalized groups was discussed by multiple interviewees when referencing the Referendum 74 campaign. Emma, an advocate with a mainstream organization in Washington, corroborated David's argument that outreach to communities of color was an afterthought in the Referendum 74 campaign. Emma delineated in more detail how the marginalization of communities of color in the marriage equality coalition was one example of the historical exclusion of people of color in progressive organizing in Washington State:

> Emma: While most of us who worked on the POC [people of color coalition] found our work to be important, I don't think that as a whole the campaign leadership viewed it as important. I felt like some of the campaign leadership was quote-unquote "allowing us" to do the work. You know, versus proactively saying, "OK, we really need to get this work done in communities of color. How can you help us make that happen?" . . . You know, I would say, in general, in Washington, unless it's an immigrant-rights issue, POC work is always an add-on. . . .

Interviewer: Why do you think that is?

Emma: I think Washingtonians, and this is just my own analysis. I think Washingtonians, particularly those in Western Washington, especially those in Seattle, view themselves as, "Well I'm liberal and progressive. Of course I'm always thinking of communities of color." But really, when a campaign plan or a work plan is put forth, to me it's obvious that communities of color are not part of the foundation of whatever they're working on. It's always an add-on. . . .

Interviewer: What do you think that does to relationship building between organizations?

Emma: I think it's hurtful. I mean, it doesn't necessarily prevent that relationship from happening, but I think that, you know, even here at [mainstream organization name redacted], I think there are some organizations that are very suspicious of us and will still work with us, but it's kind of like they are resigned to knowing what we are.

Like David, Emma argues that issues for communities of color are considered an afterthought or "add-on" in Washington State in all campaigns, both legislative and electoral. She also elaborates more on what treating communities of color as mere "add-ons" does for progressive organizing. According to Emma, this leaves all campaign coalitions between mainstream and marginalized groups fragile. Marginalized groups are hurt by this exclusive form of coalition building that leaves forgotten the issues that matter to their communities. They are always "suspicious" of mainstream groups that receive most of the funding whenever these groups reach out and ask them to join their coalitions. Emma argues that the relationships between mainstream and marginalized groups still develop, but these relationships are unstable and superficial.

Some interviewees angrily argued that coalitions are exclusive because of the disproportionate funding that is funneled into mainstream groups during campaigns. Priya, for example, is an advocate who worked with both mainstream and marginalized groups during the Referendum 74 campaign. She ultimately left the advocacy arena in Washington as a result of her experience with coalition partners. During her interview, Priya argued that the historic division between mainstream and marginalized organizations, a division that prevents the creation of a long-term movement, is really about "money and power":

> Priya: The thing about Washington State, I think we won marriage not
> because we have a movement, like a real queer movement; it's because we
> have *money and power*, and that will get you a victory as well. [emphasis
> added]

For Priya and other interviewees who work on coalition building in Washington State, inclusion and exclusion in policymaking campaigns are dictated by large funders who capitalize on opportune moments in order to display their "progressivism" and attract business for their companies. This was particularly apparent during the Referendum 74 campaign for marriage equality, which brought in massive donations from wealthy donors such as Jeff Bezos of Amazon and Bill Gates of Microsoft. Many argue that the inclusion of funding from these businesses is necessary to fund statewide advocacy campaigns and the massive coalition that emerged in support of the referendum. However, the inclusion of wealthy funders also likely contributed to the creation of a coalition that centered "money and power" and facilitated the further marginalization of immigrant and community of color groups that did not have the funding necessary to be included at the "big table."

## TOKENIZATION

In Arizona, advocates and organization leaders also criticized inter- and intra-movement coalitions that disproportionately assisted bigger, mainstream organizations that are better situated to capitalize on the money that flows into immigrant and LGBTQ communities from national organizations and foundations interested in thwarting opponent advocacy. This disproportionate distribution tears away at the recognition of collective struggles. For example, Manuel, the leader of a queer migrant organization in Arizona, argued that in the aftermath of SB 1070, as queer migrants started sharing their stories that aided the formation of alliances, other organizations took advantage of the new popularity of queer migrant narratives:

> Manuel: It started to become trendy to have UndocuQueers in your or-
> ganization. We'd see a lot of our people have an exodus I guess of our

membership and then funnel into these organizations that at first weren't accepting but now, because they need the funding and because it's sexy to do this kind of work, now have undocumented or UndocuQueer people in their organizations. . . . I think that the biggest problem we see locally is that a lot of the time, they failed to mention how these opportunities were created. So what we see is that, although we've been organizing for four years, because a lot of the curriculum we've done has been locally and we haven't got a lot of attention, a lot of the bigger organizations take advantage of the fact that nobody has heard and then they start getting the funding.

For Manuel, the "biggest problem" within local movement building occurred as attention and funding shifted toward mainstream organizations that, he argued, "took advantage" of the sudden interest in his community, tokenizing queer migrant community members and swallowing all funding opportunities. Manuel later called this tokenization of intersectionally marginalized people "the Nonprofit Industrial Complex." The term *Nonprofit Industrial Complex* is a queer, trans, and critical race critique of nonprofit funding of political movements that privileges social service and pro-state reform policies over policies proposed by marginalized community advocates like Manuel that focus on undoing state violence (e.g., combating police brutality and the carceral state).[11] Tokenizing occurs when larger mainstream organizations invite the participation of marginalized community members without placing them in leadership roles or broadly tackling issues that disproportionately impact these individuals, such as immigration detention, economic security, and health care. Jasbir Puar and other scholars recognize tokenizing in this form as a "gestural intersectionality" where the mere presence of the intersectional subject is used by organizations to show "intersectionality," despite the fact that mainstream organization agendas remain unchanged.[12]

Other interviewees described how the tokenization of LGBTQ people of color is a form of racism within mainstream LGBTQ organizing, which fragments partnerships between mainstream and marginalized people. In the excerpt here, Mateo describes why he stopped working with mainstream LGBTQ organizations in Arizona as a result of tokenization:

Mateo: Going back to when I was more involved with LGBT advocacy.

One of the reasons I left the board of [a local mainstream LGBTQ organization] was it just felt like they didn't get it. . . . *So I was involved in several things and then just stopped because I was really frankly annoyed with leadership of the LGBT community. They just really seemed to be speaking to middle, upper class, and affluent white men.* On the board of [a local mainstream LGBTQ organization], I complained about lack of representation. I was the only minority board member. It was a fairly big board, I think about fifteen or sixteen people. I was one of the only ones who wasn't rich and I was the youngest board member as well, so there was a lot of issues.

But like everything you would see coming out, the *Echo* magazine used to have more of a role in terms of informing the gay community about issues and organizing people for events and causes; it still exists, but it's much more diminished with the rise of online stuff, people stop picking up magazines. So *Echo* magazine was one of the big, big, kind of distributors of information [for local mainstream LGBTQ organizations] that would have events and publicize things, and print things. Any images you saw are always beautiful, young, healthy white men, mostly in skimpy attire. . . . *There rarely, there might be a black person. Very incidental, very token-ey. But not meaningful representation of poor LGBT people or minorities, disabled, elderly, any of those things.* And so this is just kind of my ongoing annoyance with these, the way these organizations did business. *They were telling the rest of the community that they weren't, I mean, by what they did, how they operated, how they spoke, what they put out there in the community. It made the rest of the community feel irrelevant.* And so, I just kind of got tired of waving that flag for a long time, and just had of step back, honestly, to this day. [emphasis added]

Here, Mateo describes the frustration he experienced as an LGBTQ person of color working with local mainstream organizations. Mateo argues that rather than fully including working-class people and people of color, many of the organizations he was a part of only included people who did not fit a wealthy, white, slim, and abled ideal as "tokens." There was no "meaningful representation of poor LGBT people or minorities, disabled, elderly." This left Mateo extremely aggravated with mainstream organizations because he felt that they were isolationist and exclusive. After relating his experience on the board of a mainstream LGBTQ organization, Mateo later became more hopeful because of what he sees as a "great new leadership emerging" that is more diverse and more fully inclusive. This is a reference to the leaders in Arizona who have facilitated the new inter- and intra-movement coalitions in the state in recent years. However, Mateo also makes it clear that the history of exclusion and the tokenization of LGBTQ people of color and low-income people are continual barriers to inter- and intra-community relationship building.

In Washington State, some of the activists interviewed, particularly those with marginalized subject positions, talked about how the tokenization of their identities in coalitions prompted them to leave the advocacy arena altogether and to regret their participation in episodic rights campaigns. For instance, Priya is a queer person of color who worked with both mainstream lesbian and gay organizations and religious institutions during the marriage equality campaign. She decided to leave mainstream advocacy as a result of the ostracization of the interests of communities of color that she witnessed after participating in the marriage equality coalition. Priya described her experience with mainstream coalition building in Washington in this way:

> Priya: [The marriage equality campaign] was an experience. I came out of it being like I never want to do political organizing again. The kind of urgency and also just the nature of the campaign, the urgency behind everything is like, I need this today, I need a million dollars by the end of the week, I need a couple from Vancouver, Washington, and then their picture by 3 p.m. today and a quote, *and let's put this brown face in and that brown face in just so we have brown faces.* . . .
>
> And afterward the relationships you are building in order to get support from communities of color to really stand up in front of their community and say I vote for this, I want this, you know? And after the campaign what's the plan? Are you going to keep, are you going to continue this relationship? No. *You just want to be able to take a picture of this brown person speaking in front of a brown audience, voting for marriage equality.* [emphasis added]

Priya vehemently argues that the mainstream marriage equality coalition in Washington failed to build lasting, genuine relationships between most organizations involved in advocacy. According to Priya, most of the relationships were superficial and also harmful because they involved the tokenization of communities of color. What Priya calls the "urgency" behind the rights episode made her feel exploited by, rather than genuinely supported by, the organizations involved in the campaign. This significantly harmed her relationship with the organizations. In this way, coalitions can function as a double-edged sword—both expanding movements and crippling their formation by simultaneously reinforcing hierarchical exclusion.

Issue Fracture
In addition to coalition fissures due to funding discrepancies and tokenization, interviewees argued that genuine policy and political differences divided inter- and intra-movement coalitions. Issue fracture occurs when mainstream and marginalized organizations are involved in different political projects that do not align unless they are forced to by the onset of an explosive rights advocacy moment or a rights episode. Some mainstream groups are primarily concerned with obtaining rights associated with state recognition of minority subject positions such as marriage equality, a pathway to citizenship for some undocumented immigrants, and other discrete rights outcomes that are easily translatable to prospective funders. If these organizations do support policies designed to combat police brutality, economic inequality, or immigration detention, these are often framed as secondary concerns or are discussed generally in ways that marginalized organizations feel are not clearly connected to advocacy. Many marginalized organizations, by contrast, are primarily focused on eradicating immigration detention, prison abolition, police brutality, and income inequality. Marginalized organizations can engage in political advocacy around these issues in ways that are perceived as disruptive by some mainstream organizations and those who fund mainstream advocacy efforts.

The political divisions between mainstream and marginalized groups can create tensions between organizations that are a part of inter- and intra-movement coalitions. Amanda is a leader who works primarily with mainstream organizations in Arizona. In the exchange here, she describes how tension emerged between mainstream and marginalized groups as a result of this political division over the 2013 Comprehensive Immigration

Reform (CIR) effort at the federal level[13] and delayed executive action during the 2014 get-out-the-vote effort:

> Amanda: [A marginalized migrant community organization] ran a Boycott the Vote campaign last year, and that caused a lot of angst. Yeah. I mean I can understand where they're coming from, but it definitely caused a little bit of a blowup.
>
> Interviewer: What was the Boycott the Vote campaign?
>
> Amanda: Well, they just, you know, they were telling their members and sending out emails like "Don't vote," "Show Democrats what," you know. Because Obama had promised executive action and didn't do executive action before the election I think in his attempt to sort of save the Senate, which was misguided. And there was this sort of national idea that Latinos should not vote in 2014 so that Democrats would see that you have to, we're not just going to continue to vote for you when you do nothing for us. . . . And we're like OK we can understand the argument; however, we've been working for decades to try to engage these people. We've been working our asses off. and this is about local and state-level elections; it's not about Obama. You know, it's not even a presidential election year and you're telling people to stay home when we're busting our asses to get people to come out. And so there was the tension there.

By 2014, marginalized organizations that represented Arizona's immigrant and Latinx community were angered at the lack of movement at the federal level on immigration reform and the continued detention and deportation of undocumented people despite a flurry of pro-immigrant organizing at the local level in Arizona. As a result, one marginalized organization in Arizona, in coalition with other grassroots organizations across the US, called for a boycott of the vote in 2014. The following is a statement, included in a coalition press release, from one of the leaders in Arizona who supported the boycott campaign:

> Obama's latest political game demonstrates clearly that the Democratic Party is choosing to fight for another potentially fruitless term in office at the expense of our lives and families. In Arizona, we have learned that our community's bravery far surpasses that of any elected official. With the announcement of the President's cowardly delay on immigration relief, our support for the Democratic Party cannot be taken for granted. With-

out affirmative relief for our families, we are calling for a boycott of the vote. We cannot support a party that is destroying our families.[14]

In late November 2014, shortly after the 2014 election and the Boycott the Vote campaign described in the press release here, the Obama administration issued executive orders that expanded the Deferred Action for Child Arrivals (DACA+) programs and created the Deferred Action for Parents of Americans and Lawful Permanent Residents (DAPA) program. Once again, marginalized migrant and LGBTQ organizations quickly criticized both executive actions, which implemented some of the measures promised by the failed CIR bill. Organizations that were part of the marginalized coalition argued that the executive actions failed to cover queer families, immigrants without children, and immigrants with criminal records. The text of the DACA+ and DAPA executive orders broadly interpreted what qualified as a criminal offense and included those charged with misdemeanors such as DUIs.[15] This is indicative of a continued divide between marginalized and mainstream groups over both immigration policy and the political tactics necessary to accomplish movement goals. Ultimately, the DAPA and DACA+ programs were never implemented because a federal lawsuit prevented Obama from doing so before he left office.[16]

In Washington State, interviewees described how partnerships between mainstream and marginalized organizations fractured over CIR as well. In the following excerpt, Camila, an advocate with the coalition of marginalized organizations that opposed CIR, describes this division. In explaining how mainstream and marginalized groups can divide, Camila references the Nonprofit Industrial Complex critique of mainstream organizations and Democratic Party–backed coalitions that she argues exclude input from marginalized communities:

> Camila: I learned because I worked with different community organizations, nonprofits, and I learned how they are funded, and I learned that the main foundations that actually had the money to pay for these were actually working really closely with the Democratic Party, so that's why I understood that when a bill came down, they had already been in agreement with the Democrats to do it the way Democrats wanted the bill, not the other way around—you know, having organizations have a say on exactly how the bill should be.

Democrats would bring a bill just saying, OK we have stakeholders here, they agree, let's go with the bill. And people, undocumented people were never considered to give any input. *We were told to be quiet, to hide, to never reveal our identities.* So we didn't for the longest time, we didn't. Until we saw more and more of these bills that never made it, but every time they were introduced again they were getting worse. *It was not about recognizing people's lives; it was more about businesses.* . . . So that's why, by 2010, I set up [local marginalized migrant organization], and I started helping with other communities, and we built another campaign besides comprehensive immigration reform, they call it CIR. [emphasis added]

In this interview excerpt, Camila criticizes mainstream organizations for operating in a top-down manner. According to Camila, these groups are not connected with marginalized communities. They do not form policies that are driven by the experiences of those who are most impacted by the outdated immigration system that exists in the US.

Camila and other interviewees argued that the decision to depart from mainstream organizations over CIR was driven by a desire to create bottom-up immigration reform in the US, where undocumented immigrants and the organizations they are part of are included as the leaders of immigration policymaking rather than as token constituents used to support policies created by elites. For leaders and advocates who work with marginalized communities, the exclusion of the people most impacted by policy is part of the Nonprofit Industrial Complex, in which wealthy funders take the lead and create policies that never challenge systemic inequities. Mainstream organizations that are part of the Nonprofit Industrial Complex receive funding from wealthy donors and push policy proposals that come from elites who hold political power, while smaller, marginalized organizations that are excluded from this system and the policymaking decisions produced through it receive funding from community members and push policy proposals that come from engaged organization members. The division between marginalized and mainstream organizations over Comprehensive Immigration Reform is an indication that these organizations are often working on divergent political projects that tear away at coalition development or result in the creation of superficial coalitions between the mainstream and marginalized at opportune episodic rights moments.

In addition to divisions between mainstream and marginalized organizations over policies and political preferences such as CIR, interviewees also discussed coalition fissures between LGBTQ and immigrant organizations over group priorities. Although there were some rights-based issues—for example, marriage equality in Washington State and the successful campaign to stop SB 1062 in Arizona—that resulted in large inter- and intra-community coalitions, there were also issues that did not involve large cross-community coalitions because movement organizations did not see them as overlapping issues that are part of the same struggle. Interviewees in Arizona, for instance, argued that one of the issues over which LGBTQ and immigrant communities divided was support for combating human rights abuses carried out by Maricopa County sheriff Joe Arpaio. Interviewees said that although some individuals within LGBTQ organizations supported efforts to thwart Arpaio, widespread support within these organizations was lacking. In the interview excerpt here, State Senator Steve Gallardo describes the absence of LGBTQ organizations in immigrant community efforts to undermine Arpaio:

> Interviewer: Have you seen any LGBT support, with that, with the various legal actions against him and protests?
>
> State Senator Gallardo: They're very silent [said quietly] . . . None. . . . In terms of the LGBT community? Publicly no. I think if you, if you talk to many within the LGBT community, many of the more progressive side, I mean they would agree that Sheriff Joe Arpaio has to go. Cause his time is done, and it's time to change, and they probably don't agree with his policies, but in the greater LGBT community, it's not being discussed.
>
> Interviewer: Why don't you think that is?
>
> Senator Gallardo: I think the focus in the LGBT community has been predominantly marriage. And it looks like that is, hopefully, a fight in the past and we can move on to other challenges, but that's been the focus of the LGBT community. It really has. . . . Let me put it this way: The LGBT community is going through the same growing pains as the Latino community has gone through, in terms of understanding the importance of coalition building. It took us a while before we said, "You know what, we can't fight these fights alone. We can't win these battles. We need to bring other people under our umbrella and work with others to defeat. . . ."
>
> And I think the LGBT community is kind of going through the same

growing pains [now]; they can't fight alone. They can't, or it's difficult to win on the issue of equality without having other people with you and fighting for it.

Senator Gallardo is in a unique position to understand the complexities of inter- and intra-movement coalition building in Arizona. He has been an advocate for the Latinx, immigrant, and labor communities for over fifteen years. In 2014, during the height of the campaign to stop SB 1062 (the state-based religious freedom bill that would have allowed businesses to refuse to serve LGBTQ people), Gallardo came out as gay. This placed him in direct conversation with LGBTQ, labor, and immigrant organizations involved in coalition building in Arizona. Gallardo argued in his interview that LGBTQ organizations have been largely absent in efforts to fight Arpaio. Other interviewees described this absence as the by-product of the historical exclusion of LGBTQ people of color from organizational spaces that are controlled predominately by white cisgender gay men who have narrow political movement visions that do not encompass anti-racist organizing or issues. This is indicative of a fragile coalition, one in which groups align for strategic political reasons rather than because they see other community issues as intertwined with their own. However, Senator Gallardo also contended that this environment is shifting, in large part because of new political threats to the LGBTQ community in the aftermath of the legalization of marriage equality across the US.

The lack of a cross-community coalition around struggles to thwart Sheriff Arpaio is an example of the continued exclusion of LGBTQ people of color and immigrants within LGBTQ organization spaces. In his interview, Alejandro, an LGBTQ immigrant who is active in an organization that led the struggle against Arpaio, corroborated this continued exclusion. Alejandro argued that there is "apathy" toward issues that matter to people of color within many LGBTQ spaces. This is an indication of continued divisions between some LGBTQ and immigrant groups on core issues, even in the aftermath of the coalition formation that occurred around marriage equality. There continues to be tension when it comes mobilizing organizations in support of issues that impact those at the margins of their communities, whose issues are often excluded in the service of narrow organizational visions that center on more advantaged community members.[17]

Inter- and intra-movement coalitions both build and fracture movement mobilization. In Washington State and Arizona, LGBTQ and immigrant movement coalitions often grew through the construction of a collective narrative. Advocates accomplished this by sharing their personal stories through in-depth conversations with organizations and people who became coalition partners; by constructing a common cross-community political movement past; and by calling attention to common opponents and political threats. However, the coalitions that formed were also often fragile, superficial, and easily divided because the factors that contributed to their formation existed in the same space as factors that drove the coalitions apart. At the same time that coalitions united, they divided as funding disproportionately went to mainstream organizations; as marginalized organizations and their members were tokenized in the service of coalition goals; and as coalition partners disagreed over policy preferences that were indicative of communities engaged in divergent political projects.

Because coalitions grow and fracture at the same time, those people who have expansionist understandings of political movements are important. These individuals work within both mainstream and marginalized organization spaces and help expand organizational missions to better encompass intersectionally marginalized people. They can sometimes help cross-community groups see how they relate to other minority communities and communicate why it is strategically important for seemingly divergent communities to work together in inter- and intra-movement coalitions. In this way, people who communicate an expansionist view of political movement can operate as translators within and across disparate communities, thwarting the containing effects of movement building. The next chapter describes the importance of these intersectional translators in the formation of coalitions.

Chapter 4

# THWARTING DIVISION THROUGH INTERSECTIONAL TRANSLATION

Tom (in Washington): I feel like there are a certain number of people . . . who feel it all the way personally on a very pure social justice belief that they are all intertwined. But I would say that they are the minority and that a lot of people who lead organizations don't share the same broad perspective of social justice, but know they want to win, and in order to do so they have to build relationships with coalition partners, and some of that requires going outside of their comfort zone to support issues that may not fit exactly, squarely within their worldview.

Tom is the former leader of a mainstream LGBTQ organization in Washington State. During his interview, Tom mentioned several organization leaders in Washington who straddled the line between mainstream and marginalized movement communities and played an important role in thwarting the paradoxical effects of political movement formation. Tom felt that these people "saw the connections" between different political movements and helped form sustained coalitions by demonstrating why it was strategically important to create and maintain expansionist alliances across divergent minority communities. For Tom, these individuals were tactically important because they helped coalition partners understand why committing to the movement is in their interests. In this chapter, I develop the concept of *intersectional translators* to explain how certain leaders pushed back against the containing effects of political movement formation in some circumstances in Washington State and Arizona. Multiple interviewees described important leaders who demonstrated for mainstream and marginalized coalition partners how adopting an expansionist view of movement was in their strategic interests. Mainstream and marginalized organizations adopt this expansionist view when they realize that it is strategically necessary to do so in order to be prepared for new and unforeseen short-term political threats and opportunities; to build a pool of leaders over time; and to sustain and strengthen coalitions that aid individual organizations and other coalition partners in achieving political movement advances that matter to the communities they serve and to funders. In this way, an expansionist view is not in tension with pragmatic decisions, but rather involves organizational preparation for new political threats. Intersectional translators help organizations adopt an expansionist view by encouraging them to make short-term decisions with an eye toward movement expansion and by pointing out how some seemingly egalitarian short-term choices can be harmful for organizational and coalitional longevity.

My understanding of intersectional translators draws from Sally Merry's use of translation in *Human Rights and Gender Violence*, which describes how human rights are adopted in local, grassroots contexts.[1] Merry argues that certain people function as "translators" in rights advocacy. These people translate grievances into a rights language based on frameworks constructed by transnational elites (such as women's right to inherit), which translators then teach local actors to use when speaking with reporters and in advocating to end collective grievances. Like the translators in Merry's study, the intersectional translators I interviewed for this project would translate a boundary-pushing framework across the organizations and individuals involved in political movement coalition building. In doing so, intersectional translators sometimes helped thwart coalition fragmentation and movement contraction after discrete campaigns. Intersectional translators did this by explaining to coalition partners why adopting an expansionist view of political movement was strategically important. This expansionist re-imagining of movement formation centers long-term and broader political goals, such as the abolition of immigration detention. Organizations that adopt an expansionist view understand discrete rights wins as smaller, short-term advances rather than as final ends or goals that define a movement.

Merry uses the concept of translation to describe how grievances are represented within movements composed of "a coalition of groups" with different social layers ranging from "poor to rich, lower class to social elite, rooted to transnationally mobile, minority to dominant group, and uneducated to educated."[2] Like Merry's, this study is similarly concerned with layered coalitional dynamics (i.e., inter- and intra-movement coalitions) that are inclusive of a broad spread of individuals: from mainstream to marginalized, wealthy to working class, heterosexual and cisgender to LGBTQ, and citizen to undocumented. For Merry, translators are people who help those who are part of one social layer frame their collective grievances in the language of others so that the multiple layers of groups that compose a movement can understand one another's perspectives.[3] This concept is also similar to *norm brokerage*, a term used by transnational movement scholars to describe how movement advocates mediate between international and domestic norms, as, for example, domestic LGBTQ groups do when working with international organizations and actors to advocate for LGBTQ issues in hostile domestic environments.[4]

In LGBTQ and immigrant coalition construction in Washington State, there were certain people who, like Merry's translators, went between mainstream and marginalized organizations, explaining why it was in the interest of each organization and in the interest of the movements they cared about to work together in coalitions and to adopt an expansionist understanding of movement while strategically engaging in short-term campaigns. In some cases, these translators expanded the array of issues that movement organizations advocated for, expanded partnerships, and ultimately facilitated the expansion of political movements. In doing so, translators created opportunities for individuals and groups to see how their own struggles against state violence and state power are intertwined. The intersectional translators whom I met during my fieldwork pushed back against movement contraction in three ways: (1) through participating in and intentionally using mainstream rights campaigns as short-term advances that serve expansionist goals; (2) through the construction of new groups and subgroups that highlight the tactical importance of intersectionally marginalized people within existing movement communities; and (3) through educational outreach and in-depth conversations between translators and various mainstream and marginalized organizations.

## Understanding Intersectionality as Practice
## in the Struggle for Legal Rights Advances

In examining how intersectional translators can thwart the containing effects of movement formation, I draw from intersectionality theory. At its core, intersectionality theory exposes how "single axis thinking undermines legal thinking, disciplinary knowledge production, and struggles for social justice."[5] Intersectionality as a concept has multiple meanings. Many scholars have used it in order to make visible the struggles of those who are intersectionally marginalized and to reveal how grassroots organizations adopt strategies that transcend unidimensional struggles for change.[6] Intersectionality scholars also are often critical of institutional legal strategies for social change. These scholars argue that struggles for legal rights can force groups into individualistic identities that reify rather than challenge institutional inequalities and contribute to the systematic deployment of state violence against people who hold identities that are legally constructed as "undeserving."[7] Many contemporary critical race, queer studies, and feminist scholars who employ intersectionality argue that the pursuit of legal rights as isolated wins marginalizes the interests of bisexual individuals, people of color, and queer and trans people by limiting the imaginations of those who advocate for social change within these communities.[8]

Intersectionality also describes how intersecting structural hierarchies constrain the formation of political movements. In the Washington State and Arizona political networks described in detail in chapters 1 and 2, intersecting structural hierarchies delimited the set of opportunities available for movement actors at any given time. For instance, in Arizona, political institutions are largely controlled by politicians who view undocumented people and queer and trans people as social "outsiders" who are part of underclasses. Their view is reinforced by the state's Southern traditionalist, law-and-order political ethos. Within this context, politicians passed laws designed to target these communities, such as SB 1070, which increased the policing of undocumented immigrant communities in the state, and SB 1396, which prohibited public schools from teaching non-heterosexuality in the classroom. In the Arizona political network, these laws created intersecting structural hierarchies that limited political opportunities for movement organizations by making it politically impractical to pursue broader policies designed to aid undocumented immigrant and trans and queer communities, such as the elimination of immigration detention. For this reason, minority communities have formed a political movement in the state largely by focusing first on combating harmful laws and pursuing smaller advances, such as passing a municipal ID for undocumented immigrants in Phoenix or a statewide ballot initiative that mandates paid sick leave. Movement advocates do not understand these short-term strategies as being in tension with broader policy goals. Instead, they understand these short-term strategies as part of an iterated process of building an expansionist movement that may be able to achieve broader goals, such as the elimination of immigration detention, in the future.

The understanding of intersectionality that I adopt recognizes both that intersectionally marginalized communities are often excluded from rights advocacy, and that intersecting structural hierarchies determine the boundaries of movement formation. Building off of this understanding of intersectionality, I examine the experiences of certain movement actors who act as intersectional translators by communicating to mainstream and marginalized organizations how they can strategically and pragmatically build expansionist movements within the intersecting structural hierarchies that exist in a given state context. In doing so, intersectional translators engage in "intersectionality as practice" by pushing back against the ossification and fragmentation that often occurs in the aftermath of rights episodes.

Studying intersectionality as practice is difficult because there continues to be a divide between academic and activist understandings of what intersectionality is and whether it can be effectively utilized by political movements. Because of the divide between intersectionality as an abstract ideal versus intersectionality as a practical part of the subject positions and structural constraints that characterize on-the-ground movement formation, some intersectionality theorists contend that intersectionality can never be fully employed in real-world political movement settings. For these scholars, the concept is often diluted in meaning when used by advocates who understand intersectionality through representation alone rather than through the practice of building movements. Some scholars further argue that there is value in keeping intersectionality as an abstract ideal within the "politics of not yet" or the politics of "just out of reach."[9] Indeed, for many movement advocates, intersectionality has become a meaningless buzzword that is limited to calls for broader representation in marginalized organizations. Movement actors who use the term *intersectionality* in this way often use it as a replacement for *diversity* or *multiculturalism* and argue that intersectionality is achieved whenever people who have been historically intersectionally marginalized are represented on organization boards, in tasks forces, and in coalitions. This understanding diverges significantly from the way that many mainstream and marginalized movement actors I interviewed employed the idea of intersectionality as a practice while translating pragmatic strategies within intersecting structural hierarchies.

Despite the difficulties associated with using intersectionality to understand political movements, some scholars are beginning to actively engage with real-world applications of intersectionality.[10] However, most of this scholarship still studies intersectionality at an abstract level rather than through the lens of actual political movement actors who grapple with intersectionality as practice in their advocacy and political movement organizing. I situate the practice of intersectionality within the real experiences of people who enact it in political movement formation. In doing so, I move beyond the identity critique focus of many intersectionality scholars. Instead, I examine the extent to which the organization leaders and advocates in this study employ intersectional translation within political movement coalitions to thwart movement fragmentation.

## Barriers That Inhibit the Adoption of Expansionist Movement Formation

The barriers to the practice of intersectionality that make the formation of expansionist political movements difficult are interrelated and intertwined. There are two primary barriers that appeared over the course of my interviews and participant observations: (1) limitations derived from interpreting organizational missions in narrow ways, and (2) the historical exclusion of what political scientist Dara Strolovitch calls "intersectionally disadvantaged subgroups" within movement organizations.[11] Disadvantaged subgroups are composed of intersectionally marginalized people who hold intersectional subject positions within organizations. For example, people who engage in advocacy as LGBTQ, undocumented, and Latinx are members of a disadvantaged subgroup as compared to people who engage in advocacy as LGBTQ but not otherwise as members of another minority community. Understanding these barriers within and across mainstream and marginalized organizations helps us understand the limits of coalition politics. According to previous studies on coalition politics, "when organizations work together on policy issues, many of the challenges and dynamics within individual organizations that engender low levels of activity on intersectionally disadvantaged issues are replicated within the coalition."[12] As a result, coalitions often divide and fracture due to the same barriers to intersectionality as practice that plague movement organizations.

How organizational structures and missions are interpreted can serve as a barrier for expansionist movement building. According to many interviewees, a large number of organizations operate in a top-down manner in which decisions about what issues to focus on are made by a small board of directors without input from membership.[13] These organizations may distribute surveys and ask members on email listservs to identify which issues matter the most to them, but there are rarely opportunities for members to help shape what appears on a survey or in plans to fight for issues. This top-down structure can exist within both mainstream and marginalized organizations.

Movement contraction often occurs when an organization's mission is interpreted by leaders in a way that allows the organization to refuse to engage in coalition formation with other minority communities. This happens, for example, when LGBTQ organizations advocate for marriage equality, expanding anti-discrimination protections, or trans inclusive health care, but refuse to participate in immigration reform campaigns, or when immigrant rights groups advocate for Comprehensive Immigration Reform, but refrain from participating in what they see as campaign coalitions specific to the LGBTQ community. Intersectional translators combat movement contraction by explaining to an organization that does not see the utility of working with other minority communities that doing so can help the organization achieve its own goals and better serve community members. When organizations refuse to work with other minority communities, organization leadership and the issues that organizations advocate on behalf of are often reflective of the most advantaged members.[14] Intersectional translators interviewed for this study described this barrier by referencing the "limited" organization leaders who would not join some rights campaign coalitions that centered what these leaders perceived as issues that mattered to other minority communities alone.

In recent years, many organizations have faced community-led critiques for their continued exclusion of intersectionally marginalized subgroups. For example, activists and academics have long criticized many national LGBTQ organizations for centering the interests of white cisgender gay men and lesbians and ignoring those of trans and queer people of color.[15] In 2015, the national LGBTQ organization Human Rights Campaign (HRC) made news headlines when an internal report conducted by the Pipeline Project found that the group was a "judgmental," "exclusionary," "sexist," and "homogenous" "white men's club."[16] In the report, individuals interviewed argued that "people of color, transgender people, and lower-socioeconomic people face institutionalized discrimination" within the HRC that results in lower salaries and lack of promotion into leadership roles.[17]

When a national LGBTQ organization like the HRC earns a reputation as an exclusive entity, this reputation shapes how community members perceive local affiliate organizations. As a result, some interviewees who participated in this study used national examples to describe continued exclusion at the local level, and other interviewees recalled direct experiences of discrimination within local groups that solidified the perception that such groups were most concerned with more advantaged community members. For instance, in 2013, the national HRC, in coalition with national mainstream LGBTQ organizations and civil rights organizations, held a rally on the steps of the Supreme Court building in Washington, DC when the court considered the first two marriage equality cases of the 2010s, *Hollingsworth v. Perry* and *United States v. Windsor*. A press release about the event focused on the representation of a diverse array of labor, civil rights, women's, and immigrant community speakers in addition to LGBTQ community speakers at the rally. Despite the diverse array of participants, however, undocumented immigrant speakers were told to edit their speeches to eliminate any reference to their documentation status or be removed from the speaker roster, and trans attendees were asked to lower the trans pride flag so that it was out of the view of television cameras. The HRC ultimately issued an apology for editing the speeches and telling trans attendees to lower the trans pride flag.[18] The event was supposed to be a moment when mainstream and marginalized

LGBTQ groups worked in coalition to advance marriage equality. Instead, for some interviewees in this study it became another example of the historical exclusion of intersectionally marginalized subgroups within LGBTQ organization spaces.

Nicolas, an advocate in Arizona who works with the LGBTQ undocumented community, remembered the incident years later and described how it harmed cross-community coalition building at the local level. During our interview, Nicholas recalled how "the national HRC held an event in DC" that included members of the national Queer Undocumented Immigrant Project (QUIP). Nicholas described how "a lot of the local groups started to turn away from the establishment LGBT groups" after members of QUIP were "cut off" and told "that they were not going to be speaking anymore." Nicolas's experience with the national HRC is an example of how the historical exclusion of intersectionally marginalized subgroups within movement organizations serves as a barrier to the realization of expansionist movement formation. HRC and mainstream LGBTQ groups had already earned a reputation for centering the interests of white gay men by the time they held the marriage equality rally on the steps of the Supreme Court in 2013. Likely in response to criticisms that the organization was exclusive, HRC and other national LGBTQ groups invited other minority communities to participate in the marriage equality rally. However, the history of organizational exclusion and marginalization plagued the event as HRC staff went around to the diverse array of groups represented and told them to eliminate speech and symbols that HRC staff felt deviated from the purpose of the event. This exclusion, in turn, had a ripple effect on local advocacy, solidifying the perception among queer and trans migrant community organizations that they were not welcome in many LGBTQ movement campaigns, and hindering future coalitions between LGBTQ groups and immigrant groups.

The exclusion of intersectionally marginalized subgroups within movement organizations is not limited to LGBTQ organizations. Interviewees in Arizona and Washington discussed similar experiences of organizational exclusion of LGBTQ people within immigrant organizations, labor unions, and organizations that represent communities of color. These individuals related homophobic experiences they had had in immigrant, labor, and community of color organizing spaces and described how these experiences were indicative of organizations that were not committed to forming an expansionist political movement. Organizational exclusion is something that exists within all communities across mainstream and marginalized organizing spaces and continues to be a barrier that reinforces movement contraction. For example, during her interview, Olivia, the leader of a mainstream LGBTQ organization in Washington State, described how "siloed" conversations are on police brutality and hate crimes within organizations that represent communities of color and LGBTQ people. For Olivia, the lack of cross-community outreach on these issues stemmed from "barriers from within the LGBT community for understanding racism" and what she perceived as the lack of "comfortability" that many communities of color have working with the LGBTQ community. The coalition fragmentation that results from the inability to communicate across subject positions harms movement building both in communities of color and in LGBTQ communities because it hinders the realization of both long- and short-term goals, such as creating solutions that account for the intersectional array of experiences of violent hate crimes and police brutality.

## The Strategic Importance of Intersectional Translation

Intersectional translation is strategically important in political movement formation because it can help minimize barriers that exacerbate movement contraction. Translators create the opportunity for intersectionality as practice by preventing political movements from ossifying around discrete rights-based issues. When translators intervene, they demonstrate to movement organizations and individuals why it is strategically important to re-imagine wins as short-term advances. This, in turn, creates an opportunity for movement organizations and coalitions to form around new causes in the future and helps prevent coalition fragmentation. The intersectional translators I interviewed used three mechanisms to convey the strategic importance of adopting an expansionist view of the movement: (1) the tactical use of rights campaigns as resources or tools, (2) the creation of new groups and subgroups for intersectionally marginalized people, and (3) education campaigns (led by intersectional translators) such as Double Coming Out forums and other LGBTQ community of color events.

## PARTICIPATING IN RIGHTS CAMPAIGNS

Strategically participating in short-term rights campaigns was one of the most controversial mechanisms intersectional translators used to communicate the tactical importance of adopting an expansionist view of movement formation within the layers of LGBTQ, immigrant, and community of color organizations that make up inter- and intra-movement coalitions. Interviewees were sometimes divided over the utility of working within rights campaigns. Some interviewees argued that rights campaigns did not assist in the formation of expansionist movements because rights campaigns form around discrete advocacy moments that ossify around a win and then dissipate. Translators strategically participated in rights campaigns in order to build relationships with communities that would later partner with them on political projects and, in doing so, instilled an expansionist view within the various movement organizations that participated in rights campaigns with them.

In my interviews, some of the best examples of intentional participation in a mainstream rights campaign came from those intersectional translators who worked on the Referendum 74 campaign for marriage equality. Interestingly, some translators argued that they enabled the formation of cross-community partnerships by de-emphasizing civil rights narratives. Instead, these translators used their personal stories to demonstrate how LGBTQ people were part of communities of color, and, as a result, helped destigmatize LGBTQ status, enabling communities of color and other coalition partners to see LGBTQ people as members of their own communities. For example, during his interview, Steven, an LGBTQ person of color who worked for the people of color coalition within the Referendum 74 campaign for marriage equality, explained how personal narratives contributed to the formation of cross-community partnerships. According to Steven, alliances formed more easily by "getting away from the civil rights issue and actually stressing the personal part" or otherwise de-emphasizing rights during outreach with people and with organizations that represent communities of color. Instead, Steven highlighted his personal relationships and experiences, which included raising a child with his same-sex partner. Steven argued that by "stressing the personal part" and talking about "personal feelings," supporting marriage equality became less about an issue and more about supporting another person who was part of your community and who shared your values. In this way, he helped the communities he worked with form partnerships through personal conversations that could last beyond a discrete advocacy moment. Steven is one of the interviewees discussed in chapter 3, who advanced a shared understanding of political movement past based on common community experiences and shared opponents rather than civil rights narratives. Steven enabled the construction of inter- and intra-movement coalitions by helping form partnerships that could last beyond the marriage equality rights episode.

For Steven, marriage equality was an issue that personally impacted his life. However, other intersectional translators argued that they participated in the marriage equality campaign even though they did not personally believe in marriage as an institution. Rodrigo works with an organization that represents LGBTQ people of color. He participated with the Referendum 74 campaign for marriage equality on behalf of the organization and appeared in advertisements supporting marriage equality. During his interview, he explained that he personally did not "believe in marriage" because he found the institution oppressive, especially for women. However, participating in the campaign brought Rodrigo's organization partnerships with other groups, including "sponsors," that lasted beyond the marriage equality rights episode. After the campaign, Rodrigo's organization had new partnerships that they could call on while "doing politics in Olympia" (Washington's state capital). Rodrigo also described how—together with organizations with which his group had solidified partnerships through the marriage equality campaign—his group worked on an advocacy day in Olympia that called for legislation to assist in the eradication of HIV/AIDS, a disease that disproportionately impacts the LGBTQ communities of color Rodrigo works with.

In his interview, Rodrigo described how his organization strategically used the marriage equality campaign as a resource for furthering expansionist movement formation. Camila also worked on the marriage equality campaign with the coalition of communities of color. Like Rodrigo, Camila was skeptical of marriage equality, which her community saw as a very white LGBTQ issue. However, through the campaign, intersectional translators such as Camila formed new relationships with other groups that represent communities of color, as Camila explains here:

Camila: We did the marriage equality campaign, and I really like the process that the [LGBTQ Latinx organization I worked with] did, because they first surveyed the community. They asked the community, "What are your top priorities?" And immigration came as the top priority. And we had listed marriage equality and some of them said, well unless I can marry my partner and get papers [laughter], but otherwise I don't see how marriage equality is going to help me, right? So we identified marriage equality as really a very white LGBT issue. But then we had a conversation where we figured, well we can push it, so it's a step towards on a federal level, immigration recognizes those marriages, and then people can be in the process of being a legal permanent resident. *But also it builds our work with other LGBTQ groups, so we did it intentionally to join the marriage equality [campaign] because we wanted to connect with other people of color LGBTQ groups.* [emphasis added]

Camila points out that "nothing really grew of the marriage equality campaign" for the communities her organization represents. However, because her organization participated in the campaign very intentionally and used it as a means of building relationships with other organizations and demonstrating the utility of engaging in expansionist movement formation, her organization was able to begin new partnerships with other groups. Camila's organization later used these partnerships when new political threats manifested in Washington. After the campaign, these partnerships continued and grew through other campaigns that focused on community-driven political projects. For instance, during her interview, Camila discussed the People's Movement Assembly that a collective of local organizations in Washington created to challenge the legitimacy of immigration detention. The assembly took place at the Northwest Detention Center in Tacoma, Washington, and is part of a broader movement against immigration detention that Camila's organization has helped build from the bottom up in the Pacific Northwest. For Camila, the marriage equality campaign was problematic and exclusive, but she participated nevertheless, and used that participation as a tactic for building a more expansive movement.

Other interviewees also described how they persuaded coalition partners who held different subject positions than their own to join short-term campaigns in order to cultivate relationships they could later call on as new political threats arose and as new political opportunities developed.

Tom is an LGBTQ person of color and was a leader of a mainstream LGBTQ organization in Washington State. During his interview, Tom explained how he worked as an intersectional translator within his organization by showing other leaders why it was strategically in their interests to participate in campaigns led by communities of color:

> Tom: I think that what was more challenging frankly was conversations on the board level. . . . One particular board member [name redacted] was very adamant that we were an explicitly anti-racist organization. And, personally, I was very much in favor, but knowing that [it was] a majority-white board who didn't necessarily see eye to eye on racial justice issues, I thought it was going to be very difficult. So there was a movement by I think [mainstream civil rights organization] and a few other people of color–led organizations who wanted to push a resolution or a bill, to reestablish state-based affirmative action programs, which had been taken away by . . . [searches for name of initiative]
>
> Interviewer: Initiative 200.
>
> Tom: Yes, exactly, and so we had a really divisive discussion about whether or not we should sign on as a supporter of affirmative action and [sighs in frustration] very disappointingly, one person who had been working in politics for quite some time said, "You know I worked as an organizer on that campaign and now I've come around to think that it's a matter of fairness, so everyone should be treated equally." And I was like, crap. She came out opposed to this resolution. And I was like, this is just terrible.
>
> We ended up at that point feeling gridlocked, so I made the pitch, "You may not agree personally with this, but we need coalition partners. So, if you're willing to do just what you can for the sake of getting our agenda passed, sign onto this because otherwise we are going to lose support in communities of color." So that at least, that argument, and that relates to one of your questions here, *sometimes it's not based completely on the merits, but based on a political calculation to get people on board with something that they otherwise wouldn't necessarily support.* So that was definitely a learning moment where, so we don't all agree on this issue, but we agree on our goals, and this is necessary to achieve our goals. . . . [emphasis added]

In this excerpt, Tom acted as an intersectional translator when one leader argued against the coalition. According to Tom, sometimes getting leaders to understand why they should expand movement coalitions is "based on a political calculation." In persuading leaders, Tom played into their desire to win LGBTQ rights. It was strategically important to join the coalition to build relationships that the LGBTQ organization could turn to in future campaigns, regardless of what organization leaders thought about the "merits" of the issue being advanced by the community of color–led coalition. Tom acted as an intersectional translator by communicating to other organization leaders in a language they understand why it was tactically important to support issues that "may not fit exactly, squarely within their worldview." Tom persuaded other leaders that committing to expansionist movement formation was necessary to build relationships with other communities that could later be called on to support the LGBTQ organization's interests.

## Constructing New Groups and Subgroups

Throughout the interviews, intersectional translators described how experiences with homophobia or racism within movement organizations sometimes became awakening moments that "fueled" the creation of new spaces for intersectionally marginalized people. These spaces ultimately became important organizing venues where intersectional translators communicated why committing to expansionist political movement formation was strategically important for social movement actors across mainstream and marginalized organizations. For example, Juan helped found one of the first queer migrant organizations that formed in Phoenix, Arizona, in the aftermath of SB 1070. The organization was created in order to bring attention to the "intersectionalities between being queer and migrant" within the state's progressive movement. Early organizing efforts were very effective. According to Juan, the space he and others created ended up "rippl[ing] into all these other organizing spaces as well," resulting in the "birth of queer migrant organizing" across a multiplicity of political movement organizations. The year 2010 was a pivotal one for political movement organizing in Arizona. It was the year that the Arizona legislature passed SB 1070, a law that increased racial profiling during police stops and, consequently, contributed to the formation of a defensive rights episode that targeted Arizona's Latinx, migrant, and queer and trans communities. SB 1070 was a moment that touched off a new era of intense immigrant movement organizing. Juan had previously been a part of immigrant organizations in Arizona. However, Juan also argued that, at the same time, he was "pushed out" of some immigrant organizations in Arizona due to homophobia. Juan explained that this "offered fuel to the fire" and encouraged him to "step out of that space and create another space," forcing conversations around queer and trans migrant experiences within a movement community that had shunned them. Juan and other interviewees described how queer migrant spaces "flourished" in the face of the double trauma of SB 1070 and exclusion due to homophobia. This flourishing occurred as many people who were part of the queer migrant community in Arizona started interacting with mainstream and marginalized organizations and people, forcing space for the practice of intersectionality.

Like Juan, Samuel is an intersectional translator who began a new queer migrant organization in Arizona in the 2010s. Both Juan and Samuel created space for queer migrant "voices" and "stories" that they argued were excluded from immigrant narratives produced by previous rights movement organizations and coalitions. Through these spaces, community organizers planned educational forums and events designed to persuade mainstream and marginalized organizations to adopt an expansionist view of movement formation that incorporated intersectionally marginalized people and their stories. One of the strategies adopted in these spaces was an educational model that members of the queer migrant movement used to demonstrate how emphasizing heteronormative family narratives harmed expansionist movement building. These critiques of who constituted a "good" or "deserving" immigrant regularly appeared in interviews with intersectional translators within their descriptions of how they conveyed the tactical importance of forming new coalition partnerships within and across mainstream and marginalized movement organizations. Samuel describes how new queer migrant groups challenged the construction of who constitutes a "good" immigrant, and, in doing so, advanced an expansionist view of the movement:

> Samuel: As queer and trans community, we often are estranged to our families, particularly the people in [immigration] detention. . . . They don't have a single person in the country who knows where they are or

in the world who actually knows that they're in that [immigration deten-
tion] center. People who have been here for ten years, twenty years, when
they come out they may lose their home and they lose contact with their
family. . . . So, we realized that step one was really making sure that we
identified and found people in detention and then advocated for them
based on their work as humans. We recognize that a lot of the storytelling
we've done as an immigrant rights movement has been *around families
and the value of people for being good citizens and community members.*

Which always leads to the question, well, what about people who are
bad people and bad citizens and bad community members? Do they deserve human rights? *And who is good and who is bad? A lot of times it's
queer and trans people. We are default bad. We're stigmatized.* We don't
have wholesome church relationships or ten children to stand for our, you
know, the breadth of our heart.

We're just people who are here, working and being part of community and city and the world. We set out to find our people and also to
tell the story about why our community has value. Beyond family, beyond church, beyond wholesomeness and goodness, why we have value as
human beings and why we don't just deserve, but we own human rights.
[emphasis added]

Samuel describes how queer migrant organizations created space for
new stories and narratives that were later communicated to other mainstream and marginalized movement organizations. According to Samuel, queer migrant community building is committed to expansionist
political movement formation because it disrupts the notion of who is
considered "bad" in narratives adopted during rights campaign advocacy. Queer and trans people who do not have families are constructed
as "bad" or "undeserving" immigrants, excluded from the rights-based
policies that emerged out of some mainstream organizing. For example,
in November 2014, President Obama attempted to expand the existing DACA program and create a new DAPA program that would have
granted work authorization rights and relief from deportation for some
migrants who were part of heteronormative families. The programs covered only a limited number of people who migrated to the US without
documentation as children and their parents, and, thus, did not include
queer migrants without traditional, nuclear family ties.[19] Many LGBTQ

families were excluded from the executive actions because they either did not have legally recognized relationships with their children or were part of non-biological kinship networks that exist outside of state-recognized nuclear family structures.[20] Some of the queer and trans people Samuel's organization served were among those excluded from the executive actions. By sharing stories that emphasized the "value" queer and trans migrants have as human beings, Samuel's organization directly challenged the utility of exclusionary, heteronormative-family-based policies, urging immigrant organizations to adopt new understandings of who belongs.

Queer migrant stories also demonstrate how movement building around policies based on heteronormative families without considering the experiences of intersectionally marginalized people is tactically short-sighted because it limits organizations' ability to form partnerships with people who are in non-heteronormative kinship networks. By emphasizing non-heteronormative stories, queer migrant organizing promotes the development of expansionist political movement capacities beyond dual, static categories—"good" versus "bad," "deserving" versus "undeserving," "family" versus "single," and so on. Samuel's queer migrant organization challenged other groups to adopt intersectionality as practice by perpetually rethinking and re-imagining how binary, static narratives constrain political movements, limiting partnerships with groups that can serve as important allies.

As in Arizona, intersectional translators in Washington State also created new groups and subgroups within movement organizations that opened opportunities for advancing a commitment to expansionist movement formation. In Washington State, in the aftermath of the marriage equality campaign, a new trans-focused advocacy group emerged. The group ultimately became a strategically important component of political movement organizing in Washington because it created an organizing space for marginalized trans and gender nonconforming people who then partnered with mainstream and marginalized organizations in statewide campaigns. In the following interview excerpt, Bianca, one of the leaders of this organization, describes how an experience of exclusion fueled her desire to form the trans organizing space:

Bianca: What I noticed as an external observer of the marriage equality movement was that there was a lot of money and organizational effort, a coalition. Organizations said, "Hey, we're going to directly benefit from this work, and so we're going to put money in it. It's an investment in our future and our community's future, and so we're going to invest and we're going to pump a lot of energy and life into this." And because there was not a diversification of causes and issues that were being addressed, when marriage equality effectively passed, or was certainly slated to pass, I remember being in a space, pretty much on the eve of the election and asking someone involved with the campaign and saying, "So what's next for some of these organizations that are super giant [that were behind the marriage equality campaign in Washington]?"

And it's like, "Well, this person's going off to do that, we're effectively going to become smaller. We don't have any other funding. We don't even know officially what we are going to be doing." And they said, "Maybe we're going to be focusing on homeless issues or the elderly."

And it was a singular moment for me. You know, sometimes you have those moments? And this was a moment where I felt like, here I am talking to not just a certain person, but to the marriage equality movement as a whole. And I had been told repeatedly in blog posts and from leaders and experts that, hey, *we're dealing with marriage equality first and then we are going to move onto those trans issues because those are super important.* And here I was being told by somebody who was getting their paycheck from the marriage equality movement that, "Well, I don't know what we're going to deal with next." [emphasis added]

In this excerpt, Bianca relates her frustration with the marriage equality movement and LGBTQ organizations in Washington State. Many members of Washington's trans community decided to participate in the campaign for marriage equality because they were told that the LGBTQ movement would address trans issues after the campaign. After the campaign, however, much of the funding disappeared, and LGBTQ leaders appeared unsure of which issues or communities they should start mobilizing around next. Problems were exacerbated further when movement opponents started to push anti-trans legislation and ballot initiatives in Washington State in 2016 that directly targeted trans people. Many trans community advocates like Bianca were disillusioned by mainstream LGBTQ advocacy in Washington, which supported and funded the marriage equality campaign but then dissipated at the moment when trans people across the state faced escalating threats. Out of a deep frustration with the continued marginalization of the trans community, trans organizers and advocates in Washington created their own organization. Bianca's organization, like the queer migrant organizations in Arizona, activated and organized trans and gender nonconforming people, developing a new pool of community members and leaders who later partnered with mainstream and marginalized organizations in statewide coalitions where they seized on new opportunities to convey why trans people were strategic allies in the movement. Through creating a new organization, the trans community became a key player within political movement building in Washington in the LGBTQ policy vacuum that emerged after the marriage equality campaign. As other LGBTQ organizations lost their funding and active members, the new trans community organization filled in the organizing gap and earned the support of more advantaged LGBTQ organizations by reminding them of promises they had made to the trans community in past rights campaigns. The trans community's strategic importance to the formation of an expansionist political movement in Washington accelerated as they partnered with other movement organizations in campaign coalitions.

In addition to the formation of the new organization in Washington State that bolstered the strategic importance of the state's trans community in coalition building, new subgroups sometimes emerged within long-standing organizations and expanded organizational commitments to marginalized communities. For instance, three interviewees described how an organizational space was re-imagined through the creation of a support group for trans people of color in one local organization in Washington. Jesse, one of the organization's leaders, created a people of color (POC) subgroup within the organization, which ultimately helped expand the group's mission. The subgroup was created in direct response to an experience with racism. This painful moment ultimately became a mechanism for rethinking how the organization could better serve the needs of trans people of color. After what Jesse described as "race-related" statements were made during a group meeting, Jesse went to leaders of the organization and convinced them to support a trans POC subgroup and to conduct anti-racism education within the organization to better serve marginalized people who were already part of the group. In order to facilitate this, the organization sent Jesse to a conference to learn "the language to describe racism [and] explain it to other people." During our conversation, Jesse described the process of becoming an intersectional translator. At the conference, Jesse learned how to "contextualize structural racism and state racism" and how to communicate this to both leaders and members of the organization.

Jesse became an intersectional translator within the organization, fostering new dialogue and new opportunities for expanding the array of perspectives within the organization. In this way, Jesse also became part of a new pool of leaders committed to expansionist political movement formation. Jesse enabled the adoption of anti-racist community-building strategies. As an intersectional translator, Jesse intervened not only to ensure the representation of trans people of color within the group but also to foster anti-racist organizational restructuring through new staff training and partnerships with other organizations that represent marginalized people across the country. Jesse helped instill an expansionist understanding of the community, one that incorporated intersectionally marginalized people, within the organization. Jesse translated for the group why it was strategically important to expand capacity and how this expansion served the organization's existing mission. In doing so, Jesse constructed an opportunity for expansionist community building and the incorporation of intersectionally marginalized people within the organization.

ORGANIZING THROUGH EDUCATION

In addition to creating new subgroups and organizations, intersectional translators led educational forums within LGBTQ and immigrant community organizations. These forums provided an opportunity for communicating—to both mainstream and marginalized coalition partners—the strategic importance of committing to expansionist movement formation. The educational forums were spaces for recognizing the similarities and differences between intersectionally marginalized people and the movement organizations that primarily centered more advantaged subject positions (e.g., LGBTQ groups *or* immigrant community groups).

Intersectional translators described an array of educational forums and activities that they conducted to translate how expansionist movement building that incorporated intersectionally marginalized people served the interests of all coalition partners. Double Coming Out forums were perhaps one of the most powerful educational forums that translators discussed during interviews. In the 2010s, queer migrant organization leaders, advocates, and community workers conducted Double Coming Out forums in Arizona. In these forums, translators would share with mainstream LGBTQ groups the similarities and differences between "coming out of the closet" as LGBTQ and "coming out of the shadows" as undocumented, and expand coalition partnerships in doing so. For example, Manuel, a leader with an organization that represented the queer, trans, and Latinx migrant communities, explained that these forums helped "build bridges between the LGBT and undocumented community." During our conversation, Manuel explained that the forums started because queer and trans migrants "understood that the same fears that we felt when we were coming out of the shadows as undocumented were the same fears that we felt when we were coming out of the closet."

For Manuel, the Double Coming Out forums underscored that seemingly dissimilar identities can have a shared past, emphasizing one of the factors associated with constructing expansionist coalitions discussed in chapter 3. Within the LGBTQ community, coming out of the closet, with the accompanying fear surrounding potential community ostracism as a result of articulating one's identity, is a unifying community narrative. Similarly, coming out of the shadows as undocumented involves a considerable fear of community ostracism that supports a collective community narrative. Manuel described how the Double Coming Out forums would highlight these shared experiences of fear around recognition in order to create a collective past or a narrative in terms through which forum attendees could relate, understand their shared experiences, and "build a powerful movement" composed of communities that also constantly "push each other." Manuel's use of the phrase "push each other," which highlights an emphasis on difference, is particularly telling. For Manuel, the Double Coming Out forums were an educational space used to convey that intersectionally marginalized people are part of existing political movements by emphasizing how the narratives of divergent minority communities (here LGBTQ people and migrants) overlapped. At the same time, the forums conveyed difference, compelling movement organizations to evaluate campaign advances based on the extent to which they serve expansionist goals that incorporate marginalized communities. The forums "pushed" attendees to imagine a community that formed the building blocks of a more expansive movement.

During our conversation, Manuel further described serving as an intersectional translator within migrant community spaces in addition to within mainstream LGBTQ spaces. Manuel intervened in migrant community spaces by using drag as a mechanism for educating the community about gender. In the excerpt here, Manuel explains breaking down gender norms in the migrant community through drag:

> Manuel: When we started doing the Double Coming Out forums, far more than that what really helped was the fact that I would go to different spaces in the migrant community and then perform as Alexandra and then I would start talking about LGBT issues. And I would get parents and people just come and talk to me and be like, so you are a woman? You want to be a woman? And I would tell them what drag was, I would break it down for them right, gender, and they would be like "that's fascinating." And we would invite them back to our meetings, and we started building membership like that, through my drag. . . .
>
> So that's how I started. I keep saying my LGBT advocacy was successful because I was able to use drag as a vehicle, as a tool, to bring communities together.

According to Manuel, drag served as an additional vehicle for educating the migrant community about gender. Through drag, Manuel again pushed the boundaries of acceptability within a community space—here, the boundaries of gender norms within migrant community spaces. In doing so, Manuel communicated how LGBTQ people who have nonnormative genders are part of migrant communities. Through drag and Double Coming Out forums, Manuel built membership and brought communities together that previously existed in separate spaces. Manuel used the educational forums to highlight how queer and trans migrants are part of minority communities and to convey the strategic importance of intersectionally marginalized people in connecting overlapping experiences and aiding coalition partnerships in struggles for social change.

For intersectional translators like Manuel, education served as one of the most successful mechanisms for conveying the importance of queer migrant experiences to coalition partners. Juan is another intersectional translator who held queer history and educational workshops along with Manuel in Arizona. Juan helped form queer and trans migrant spaces in Arizona in the aftermath of SB 1070 in response to experiences of exclusion in migrant and immigrant organizing. According to Juan, "education and organizing" are the best tactics for accomplishing social change. During our interview, Juan argued that building community through education was an important tool for translating experiences across communities because it helps "create a base" for a movement with broad coalition partnerships and helps an "idea to grow" and take root. Through educational forums and workshops, people like Juan translated for others how to form communities around ideas that could grow into expansive movements.

In addition to holding educational forums, intersectional translators would educate those involved in political movement struggles about how to strategically develop messaging that incorporated other minority populations that they saw as potential coalition partners. For example, Diana is a translator who works with a marginalized organization that has formed LGBTQ, labor, and immigrant coalitions around local issues. During our interview, she discussed how she once pointed out flawed LGBTQ movement messaging and, in doing so, helped local LGBTQ movement organizations create new messaging that did not alienate coalition partners. According to Diana, during a media training on messaging for campaigns led by LGBTQ organizations, mainstream LGBTQ organizations were encouraging training attendees to explain to others that, under some circumstances, refusing service to LGBTQ people and same-sex couples violates the law. Diana found the use of the phrase "the law is the law" in the training to be particularly problematic for undocumented people because "'the law is the law' has been the way that they've marginalized and oppressed us." Diana explained that she understood that the phrase for LGBTQ people emphasized how their community was "finally validated" and "humanized." However, she translated the limits of this talking point by explaining that the phrase didn't "resonate good with us [immigrants] as a community" because "those words exactly have been used to continue to oppress us and marginalize us and dehumanize us." Diana pointed out that this messaging threatened LGBTQ organizations' ability to form partnerships with members of the immigrant community because this is the same language that anti-immigrant groups use to dehumanize undocumented immigrants. By educating LGBTQ organizations about the limits of their messaging tactics and the ways in which these tactics stigmatized immigrant communities, Diana helped the LGBTQ community form messaging strategies that were better suited for the development of partnerships that could aid in the advancement of collective LGBTQ and immigrant rights movement goals. This, in turn, underscored the importance of committing to expansionist movement formation that incorporated people like Diana among local LGBTQ organizations in Arizona—people who could help LGBTQ organizations become better allies in the movement.

Intersectional translators in Washington State also held educational forums designed to initiate conversations between LGBTQ and other minority communities in the state. For instance, translators within Washington's LGBTQ and Asian and Pacific Islander (API) communities held an educational event in 2015 that was designed to foster a space for people in the state who identified as members of the LGBTQ and API communities. During her interview, Rebecca, one of the event organizers, described how the event was created and its intended goals. Rebecca explained that the event was created because of experiences of exclusion or lack of support among the LGBTQ/API community. According to Rebecca, a lot of LGBTQ/API "people don't receive the support that they need growing up and a lot of Asian American families" where being LGBTQ "becomes this thing where you're just silent about it." Rebecca and others who were part of organizations that represent the LGBTQ and API communities in Washington State organized the event "to make sure that people know that there's a place for them and that there are advocates and there are organizations that support them." The purpose of the event was to create a place for intersectionally marginalized people and to educate the broader API and LGBTQ communities about what it means to exist at the intersection of these populations. The event also nurtured the formation of a broad coalition of support organizations that came together to assist API and LGBTQ people. The event aided in the construction of new partnerships across organizations. Like the Double Coming Out forums in Arizona, the event in Washington pushed the boundaries of accepted norms within divergent minority populations and contributed to the formation of an expansionist political movement that incorporated intersectionally marginalized communities.

Although Double Coming Out forums and other educational workshops create opportunities for expansionist movement, intersectional translators argued that they were also limited by the surface-level understanding of diversity that exists within many movement organization spaces. For this reason, educational events like the Double Coming Out forums did not always convince coalition partners of the strategic importance of seeing small rights wins as advances or resources in the formation of an expansionist political movement. Problems persist for the realization of intersectionality as practice and expansive re-imaginings of movement because, of necessity, navigating between different spaces involves continually hitting up against the constraints placed on movements by intersecting structural hierarchies—such as the historical exclusion of intersectionally marginalized people in movement organizing spaces. However, as this chapter argues, by intentionally using rights campaigns as resources, creating new organizations, and conducting educational forums, intersectional translators can demonstrate why it is strategically important for mainstream and marginalized organizations to commit to the formation of expansionist political movements. Through the mechanisms described here, intersectional translators aided in expansionist movement formation within and across mainstream and marginalized organizations by convincing these organizations that expansionist movement building helps them all.

Intersectional translators communicated how expansionist movement formation helps organizations prepare for future political threats and opportunities (such as future attacks on migrants and queer and trans people). Translators like Jesse, who helped expand one organization's capacity to serve the community, show how expansionist movements can cultivate a pool of leaders. Some intersectional translators communicated how expansionist commitments can strengthen coalition partnerships. For instance, Tom emphasized the importance of movement expansion and helped form an inter-movement alliance when he convinced his LGBTQ organization to commit to affirmative action policy in order to build a partnership that could aid in the advancement of LGBTQ policies in the future. By exposing limits and later forging new political projects within the intersecting structural hierarchies that characterize political networks, intersectional translators were able to create opportunities for the formation of expansionist movements in Washington State and Arizona.

Conclusion

# PARADOXES OF POWER

Viewing political movements as coalitions uncovers how conflict and unity can exist within the same space. In the preceding chapters, advocates described their own experiences of empowerment, activation, and mobilization that contributed to the formation of political movement coalitions in a series of frenzied bursts around rights episodes. At the same time, these moments of mass movement created a sense of heightened urgency that contributed to marginalization, tokenization, and, in some cases, exploitation in each state context. Rights function in paradoxical ways within movements because they facilitate both movement expansion and contraction. Hierarchical power dynamics embedded in our society are present in internal struggles within political movements, even when these movements form around the most egalitarian aims.

This tension persisted throughout the rights episodes in both state cases analyzed in this book as certain understandings of movement surpassed others, creating coalition unity across a field of fragmentation. This fragmentation has lasting impacts that can complicate future movement re-formations, and was especially apparent after same-sex marriage was legalized in Washington State when opponents started to organize around eliminating trans rights. During the marriage equality campaign in Washington State, as in many other states, campaign materials centered gay and lesbian couples who wanted to marry, while queer and trans community members who were not married or coupled were largely not depicted. Although lesbians and gay men of color appeared on some campaign materials, interviewees in Washington State said that there was significantly less money devoted to inclusion of communities of color in the campaign. One interviewee argued that the community of color coalition was late to get onto the campaign website, and felt that leaders with many LGBTQ organizations considered outreach to communities of color an "add-on" rather than central to the campaign. Most advertisements featured white lesbian and gay couples, church leaders, and moderate and conservative community members who described their personal experiences with same-sex marriage.

As a result, most of the public education conducted through the marriage equality rights episode did not challenge gender norms. This meant that the marriage equality movement in Washington State involved almost no public education on gender identity and expression. When opponents later started to mobilize behind limiting access to public facilities for trans people, these historically marginalized community members were suddenly at the center of renewed attacks. Trans and gender nonconforming people found themselves doubly marginalized, both through exclusion from the LGBTQ movement's marriage equality campaigns and through opponent counter-mobilization in Washington State. Worse still, the funding behind marriage equality had evaporated, leaving LGBTQ organizations not as prepared to continue fighting for movement issues as many advocates who had fought for marriage equality had hoped. With discrimination and suicide rates among the trans community, particularly trans people of color, much higher than the national average, the renewed counter-mobilization targeting this community presented an especially tragic threat. The marriage equality rights episode in Washington State both encompassed a movement advance and complicated the political environment in ways that exacerbated harms experienced by marginalized communities within the movement.

Is movement contraction always a necessary component of political movement formation? Are there ways that progressive movement actors might limit or thwart tendencies toward exclusion and marginalization?

## Building Expansionist Alliances

I argue that there are four ways that political movement actors can minimize coalition fragmentation and exclusion: (1) by constructing a shared movement past and highlighting common opponents both during and after rights campaigns; (2) by devoting more resources to marginalized groups and individuals and providing opportunities for them to lead coalition organizing; (3) by adopting an expansionist commitment to movement formation through a politics of solidarity, and strategically using rights episodes to further this commitment; and (4) by forming nonpartisan institutionalized grassroots advocacy networks that exist in separate spaces than Democratic or Republican party politics. These suggestions are difficult to attain in all settings and contexts. Nevertheless, they serve as important aspirational guidelines for pushing back against the hierarchical power dynamics that exist in our society and frequently manifest in political movement organizing.

### CONSTRUCTING A SHARED MOVEMENT PAST AND HIGHLIGHTING COMMON OPPONENTS

Cross-community coalitions formed in Washington and Arizona through the construction of a shared movement past and a common core of opponents. Many interviewees emphasized how creating a shared civil rights past enabled different movement constituents to recognize how their movements overlapped. For example, some interviewees from Washington State who helped build coalitions between mainstream and marginalized organizations during the marriage equality campaign argued that emphasizing "a long civil rights history" helped divergent organizations see how the communities they serve are intertwined. Other interviewees constructed a common movement past by sharing collective experiences of discrimination and trauma that spanned multiple minority populations. By constructing a common past, individual communities perceived themselves as part of a larger, inclusive political movement, which often enabled these communities to work together in coalitions.

Highlighting common opponents was also a crucial mechanism that interviewees in both states used to aid in the formation of cross-community coalitions. Internalizing "the enemy of my enemy is my friend" and emphasizing how divergent minority populations faced "the same kinds of attacks" helped mainstream and marginalized organization leaders and members understand how their struggles were intertwined with the struggles of other communities in Arizona and Washington. Through recognizing shared opponents, different community members understood that it was strategically important to engage in the campaigns of others. This suggests that constructing a common past and underscoring shared opponents can aid in the formation of expansionist movements by growing cross-community coalitions that encompass long-term relationship building.

Enabling Historically Marginalized Groups to Lead
Incorporating historically marginalized groups and leaders in political movements is often difficult. This has a lot do with how funding is funneled into mainstream organizations. In her interview, Sage, one of the individuals who worked with mainstream organizers and the people of color coalition in the Referendum 74 campaign, described why it is challenging to enable historically marginalized organizations and people to lead political movement formation in Washington State. Sage explained that the funding in statewide campaigns frequently goes to "those organizations [that] have proven they can deliver." This means that organizations that rack up a series of small, short-term wins are often the most financially stable because they consistently attract funders during each political cycle. The Referendum 74 campaign attempted to combat this tendency by "casting a wide net," according to Sage, and reaching into communities that movement actors had not reached in the past on LGBTQ issues: communities of color in Washington State. The campaign was somewhat successful at accomplishing this goal; however, resources were still limited, which prevented the coalition from going "deeper" by siphoning more funding into these communities and building more genuine, lasting relationships. As in other interviews conducted for this study, Sage expressed her frustration with a coalition that began to reach out to historically marginalized organizations and people, but did not do enough to construct long-term relationships. Underneath Sage's frustration is an understanding that incorporating historically marginalized people in coalitions and allowing them to lead can be strategically important in movement building—for both mainstream and marginalized organizations.

Enabling historically marginalized people and groups to lead political movement coalitions is tactically important because the issues that impact them the most, such as ending immigration detention and police brutality, are broader movement goals that can sustain movement organizations beyond discrete rights episodes. Yet it can be difficult for coalition partners to understand why it is in their interests to construct rights campaigns as means rather than ends. This is the reason why intersectional translators were important in creating expansionist alliances. Intersectional translators helped thwart the paradoxes of power in movement building by showing mainstream and marginalized organizations in each state why adopting an expansionist commitment to movement formation was in their interests. Educational events such as Double Coming Out forums in Arizona expanded partnerships within coalitions beyond individual communities. Through these events, intersectional translators convinced coalition partners that committing solely to discrete rights campaigns is strategically shortsighted because these campaigns, when conducted in ways that do not consider long-term goals, can drain resources and collapse organizations. Interviewees described these educational events as tools "to bring communities together" by "pushing each other" to think beyond short-term wins and individual subject positions. Intersectional translators thus assisted in the formation of expansionist movements by persuading organizations to center historically marginalized groups.

## Adopting an Expansionist Commitment to Political Movement Formation

Enabling historically marginalized groups to lead is strategically important because these groups assist in the adoption of an expansionist commitment to movement formation over cyclical campaign wins. An expansionist commitment to movement entails centering long-term goals such as undoing systemic oppression through creating universal health care and child care, ending immigration detention, eliminating police brutality, and uprooting the carceral state. Adopting an expansionist commitment is often difficult to realize because it requires political movement actors to always think beyond campaign cycles in contexts where opponents often set political movement agendas. For this reason, movement actors should not ignore cyclical campaigns but, rather, think about them as tools that serve expansionist ends.

Movement actors can sometimes move beyond a focus on cyclical campaign wins and toward organizing around shared, expansionist ends by engaging in solidarity politics. *Solidarity politics* encompasses engaging with the practice of intersectionality in the real world without being torn apart by difference.[1] According to political scientist Ange-Marie Hancock, we can avoid being torn apart by difference by engaging in a "deep political solidarity" that goes beyond mere tolerance through a "cohesive ethic of equity, interdependence, and communal sharing" that is based in empathy, common values, and a shared sociopolitical past.[2] Many interviewees engaged in solidarity politics by committing to the campaign struggles of others in the service of expansionist movement formation. Solidarity politics also often involves "partial situated knowledge" in which each group within a coalition sees its own political movement narrative as partial or "unfinished" and thus remains open to hearing and learning from other groups' experiences.[3] Through solidarity politics, divergent movement communities can create a cohesive organizing ethic that values open dialogue with others by simultaneously recognizing similarity (i.e., shared values and a shared past) and difference (i.e., the ways in which one's own narrative and experiences are unfinished). Thinking about group formation as unfinished, yet also connected with others through common sociopolitical pasts, pushes back against the idea that justice can be universally attained through discrete rights wins. In solidarity politics, wins are advances in an incomplete journey toward the realization of a collection of shared interests.

## Creating Institutionalized Grassroots Advocacy Networks

In Washington State and Arizona, the LGBTQ and immigrant rights movements achieved wins in states with different political climates because cross-community political movement organizations began forming inter- and intra-movement coalitions, or institutionalized grassroots advocacy networks, in the late 2000s and 2010s. These networks were largely nonpartisan. They occurred across nonprofit and political organizations that were devoted to serving the needs of minority communities and workers rather than the needs of political parties. Because these advocacy networks were nonpartisan, they worked to get candidates elected who promised to serve minority communities, and engaged in advocacy after an election to hold the winning candidates accountable.

Nonpartisan, institutionalized progressive grassroots advocacy networks are not present in every state. In rural areas with high Republican constituencies, institutionalized conservative advocacy networks comprising such organizations as the National Rifle Association and those affiliated with the Christian right are often more common.[4] Advocacy networks like these can be less common in progressive political movements because minority populations lack the institutionalized power and resources that characterize opponent movements. However, in order to build a sustainable grassroots movement, political movement organizations can create similar institutionalized advocacy networks through the formation of inter- and intra-movement coalitions. In some areas, this means that coalitions may encompass mainstream organizations considered more moderate or conservative. For example, the Arizona coalitions were not always solely composed of progressive movement organizations. The coalition that defeated Sheriff Joe Arpaio won in Arizona both because of its powerful grassroots advocacy network and because it appealed to fiscal conservatives in the region who were angered over the mounting cost of Arpaio's various civil rights violations. Similarly, the coalition that defeated State Senator Russell Pearce in Arizona encompassed both progressive advocates and more religiously conservative Mormons who had grown uncomfortable with Pearce's tough stance on immigration, which they believed violated church teachings.

## Thwarting Movement Contraction: Applications

The suggestions described here for thwarting tendencies within movement formation toward containment are often difficult to implement. Hegemonic power dynamics reinforce the centering of dominant narratives at the expense of marginalized ways of being in all aspects of our social and political lives. Uprooting systems of oppression will always be extremely difficult because these systems form the bedrock of our own relationships with institutions, organizations, and individuals. For this reason, it may never be possible to form an expansionist political movement that eliminates marginalization and exclusion. However, my research uncovered inter- and intra-movement coalitions that embody some of the suggestions described here; in doing so, they might have greater expansionist potential than coalitions of the past.

THE SAFE ALLIANCE AND WASHINGTON WON'T DISCRIMINATE: FIGHTING FOR TRANS JUSTICE IN WASHINGTON STATE

After the marriage equality campaign in Washington State, the LGBTQ movement largely demobilized. In many ways, the community struggled to come to terms with how it should define itself once it achieved a large rights win that was unimaginable less than a decade earlier. This left many within the state's trans and queer communities dismayed. As Bianca described in her interview (see chapter 5), throughout the marriage equality campaign, trans community members were told, "We're dealing with marriage equality first and then we are going to move onto those trans issues because those are super important." Yet once the campaign ended, the movement seemed directionless, and the coalition largely dissolved. Trans advocates in Washington responded by organizing the trans and queer communities and their allies to build the political power necessary to persuade other political movement organizations in the state to incorporate trans justice. In doing so, trans advocates in Washington leveraged the promises made to their community during past LGBTQ rights campaign struggles. For example, trans advocates in Washington directly reached out to the local community and sought to develop and maintain active members by organizing the first Trans Pride Seattle in 2013. The event, which brings in nationally and internationally renowned queer and trans speakers each June, would draw between three thousand and five thousand people by 2016.

The organizers of Trans Pride Seattle, along with other local trans advocates, acted as intersectional translators, navigating the historical cleavages across Washington's mainstream and marginalized organizations by convincing coalition partners of the strategic importance of including trans justice within political movement campaigns through the use of educational outreach. In the 2010s, as a result of their efforts, a new set of grassroots public policy and educational coalitions formed in Washington State that centered trans community interests and needs. One of their first coalitions was the Coalition for Inclusive Healthcare—a network of LGBTQ and civil rights organizations and health care providers who sought to end discrimination based on gender identity and expression in public and private health care plans that operated in Washington State. The coalition achieved significant policy advances in 2014 and 2015 as trans advocates with the coalition shared their personal experiences of discrimination with state agencies and health care providers and, in the process, emphasized through educational outreach how they were part of the broader political movement community in Washington. In 2014, the Washington State insurance commissioner formally announced that health insurance policies sold in Washington could not discriminate on the basis of gender identity and expression.[5] In 2015, the state's Health Care Authority issued for the first time a set of rules providing inclusive coverage for transition-related care under the state's Medicaid program.[6]

As the Coalition for Inclusive Healthcare achieved important health care advances for trans Washingtonians, LGBTQ movement opponents were counter-organizing under the leadership of the national Family Research Council and the state-based Family Policy Institute of Washington. After experiencing marriage equality as an advocacy loss, religious right organizations like these began targeting the movement for trans justice. In a policy paper released by the Family Research Council in June 2015, leaders argued against what they perceived as "the third wave assault on the sexes": government recognition of trans and gender nonconforming people and the inclusion of gender identity and expression in nondiscrimination laws, or what they termed "bathroom bills."[7] LGBTQ rights opponents supported by these organizations began to mobilize in Washington State when the state's Human Rights Commission passed a rule in 2015 clarifying that the 2006 Anderson-Murray Anti-Discrimination Act, which prohibited discrimination based on sexual orientation and gender identity and expression, allowed trans people to use bathrooms and public facilities consistent with their gender identity.[8] After the Human Rights Commission's rule went into effect, local organizations affiliated with the religious right worked with conservative legislators to introduce six bills in the state legislature targeting the inclusion of gender identity and expression in state anti-discrimination law.[9]

In response to these newly activated opponents—the same group of "enemies" that has targeted the state's minority populations for decades—a new inter- and intra-movement coalition formed: the Washington Safety & Access for Everyone (SAFE) Alliance. The Washington SAFE Alliance was much larger than the Coalition for Inclusive Healthcare, likely both because of the prior outreach work initiated by the Coalition for Inclusive Healthcare and because of the grave threat posed by legislation introduced through opponent mobilization. In 2016, the Washington SAFE Alliance encompassed more than 160 LGBTQ, domestic violence, civil rights, and immigrant justice groups and labor unions devoted to educating the public about trans and gender nonconforming people. However, the coalition was still much smaller than the inter- and intra-movement coalition that formed during the marriage equality rights episode in 2012 (which included over five hundred organizations) and did not encompass as many immigrant or community of color organizations. It is unclear why the coalition was smaller, but it is possible that the smaller scope stemmed from the lack of educational outreach on gender identity and expression within immigrant communities and communities of color during and before the marriage equality rights episode. It is also possible that some immigrant and community of color organizations became wary of joining coalitions with LGBTQ movement organizations after experiencing tokenization and marginalization during the marriage equality campaign. It is further possible that, due to funding decreases in the aftermath of the marriage equality campaign, the organizations at the center of the new trans coalitions just did not have the resources to conduct as much organizational outreach as they did during the Referendum 74 campaign. Regardless of the reason, the smaller trans coalitions are indicative of both movement expansion and contraction in the aftermath of the marriage equality rights episode.

When the anti-trans bills were introduced in early 2016, coalition partners worked to educate state legislators about trans and gender nonconforming people. Coalition leaders helped prepare people to testify at the state capitol against the bills, meet with their legislators, and protest at the state capitol.[10] Organizations affiliated with the SAFE Alliance also encouraged supporters to attend hearings related to the anti-trans bills. At the hearings, advocates shared experiences of discrimination, drawing parallels among the multiple minority communities that composed the coalition. Ultimately, the SAFE Alliance stopped the anti-trans momentum in dramatic fashion in the state senate after persuading moderate Republican senators to oppose all six bills and educating Democratic legislators about trans justice.[11] During floor debate on one of the bills, legislators' speeches underscored how effective the coalition's educational outreach and testimony were at constructing a common movement past around shared opponents, and at leveraging the trans community as part of a broader political movement. For example, then state senator Pramila

Jayapal emphasized how "the history of civil rights in this country is that it has always been based on fear, it has always been based on otherizing."[12]

Despite thwarting the counter-mobilization and stopping the progress of the anti-trans bills in 2016, the state's trans community experienced an enormous degree of trauma when opponents spread falsehoods in the legislative campaigns, which compared trans people to pedophiles and sexually abusive people who preyed on women and children. High-profile threats to legal protections for trans people, such as those in Washington State, correlated with an increase in calls to national trans suicide hotlines.[13]

Opponent organizations are largely composed of white, middle-to-upper-middle-class people who have the resources to continue organizing against the state's trans community beyond a single campaign cycle. This was particularly apparent in the immediate aftermath of failed anti-trans bills at the state capitol in 2016. After the bills were killed, opponents mobilized behind a ballot initiative campaign (Initiative 1515). In response, LGBTQ organizations, civil rights organizations, labor unions, and local businesses formed the Washington Won't Discriminate campaign.[14] Shortly after Washington Won't Discriminate formed, trans leaders and state affiliates of the trans justice coalitions also launched the Transform Washington public education campaign, which featured a wide range of stories from trans Washingtonians. Members of the public education campaign's advisory committee included trans community leaders and trans and queer people of color. Washington Won't Discriminate also hired local UndocuQueer activist Carlos Padilla to serve as the organizing director for the political campaign. The inclusion of historically marginalized groups as leaders within Washington Won't Discriminate is an indication that at least some within the coalition were interested in using the campaign to assist with political movement expansion. This is also an opportunity for intersectional translation to enable the growth of political movement formation in Washington State among mainstream LGBTQ, queer and trans, and immigrant rights organizations. Thanks in large part to this mobilization, Initiative 1515 failed to make it onto the general election ballot in 2016.

Opponents quickly mobilized again behind a second anti-trans ballot initiative campaign (Initiative 1552) in 2017, but that effort also failed.[15] The continued attempts to bring anti-trans initiatives onto the general election ballot and to pass anti-trans bills in the legislature suggest that opponents will be mobilizing against the trans community for some time. However, because common opponents can activate and mobilize coalitions (as shown in the previous chapters), the presence of activated cross-community opponents may sustain and help expand the new inter- and intra-movement coalitions building in Washington around trans justice as well.[16] Indeed, the presence of these coalitions and their success at thwarting ballot initiatives and legislation have likely contributed to a shift in tactics among opponent groups. As of 2019, opponent groups are mobilizing through the courts and the federal administration to target trans people because of the greater support for anti-trans efforts among conservatives who control these institutions.

Washington SAFE Alliance and Washington Won't Discriminate formed in an attempt to revive the inter- and intra-movement coalitions of the past in response to new threats driven by the same core of opponents. The new coalitions paralleled past alliances that had thwarted the effort to place the state's LGBTQ-inclusive anti-discrimination law on the ballot in 2006 and passed marriage equality in 2012. Washington Won't Discriminate was even the same name that leaders used for the 2006 coalition. However, the new coalitions also appear to be more expansionist than past coalitions in some ways. For example, both Washington Won't Discriminate and the Washington SAFE Alliance included leaders from historically marginalized populations and organizations, enabling opportunities for intersectional translation. Advocates also actively emphasized a common political movement or civil rights past when conducting outreach with politicians and potential allies.

Yet these new coalitions are still limited. Some of the organizations affiliated with the coalitions have centered issues that matter to intersectionally marginalized people. However, because the coalitions formed in response to opponent counter-mobilization, they are primarily concerned with thwarting issues designed by opponents. This means that they are limited in their ability to support other issues that impact intersectionally marginalized people. Because the campaign issues that they are concerned with are led by opponents and intersecting structural hierarchies that enable the targeting of trans communities in Washington, the coalitions primarily engage in a politics of inclusion aimed at mainstreaming subject positions through public education.[17] This is entirely understandable given the extreme strain that opponent counter-mobilization has placed on trans and gender nonconforming people in Washington. It is possible that, when the opponent threat subsides, the coalitions will re-form around more intersectionally inclusive issues. But in a heightened moment of political threat, where opponents hold considerable power in the US, the future is deeply uncertain.

ONE PHX ID: COALITION BUILDING AROUND A MUNICIPAL IDENTIFICATION CARD IN ARIZONA

Washington's trans justice coalitions may mark the beginning of an expansionist cross-community political movement in Washington State; however, the extent to which these coalitions will expand beyond campaigns driven by opponent threats is unclear. By contrast, the coalitions that formed in Arizona in the aftermath of SB 1070 show more promise. As described in chapter 2, SB 1070 activated a new generation of community organizers in Arizona. Over time and through various campaigns in the early 2010s, these organizers formed an institutionalized grassroots advocacy network composed of immigrants, people of color, low-wage workers, and members of the queer and trans migrant community. This grassroots advocacy network grew, according to some interviewees, when the devastating impact of SB 1070 persuaded local organizations that the only way to stop attacks from collective opponents, such as State Senator Russell Pearce and Sheriff Joe Arpaio, was to build political power by expanding local alliances. One of the organizations that grew during this time was the Center for Neighborhood Leadership (CNL). CNL trained, mentored, and activated community leaders at the grass roots, predominately through outreach to students enrolled in local schools.

CNL is one of several organizations in Arizona that is committed to member-led grassroots change. Other organizations include Puente Arizona (a migrant advocacy organization), local labor unions, and Latinx community organizations. These organizations have spearheaded the formation of public policy and civic engagement alliances in the state in the aftermath of SB 1070. One of the new coalitions with the greatest expansive potential is One Arizona, the civic engagement coalition that formed through advocacy in response to the SB 1070 rights episode. One Arizona intentionally centers historically marginalized people, with its mission statement emphasizing "immigrant rights, voting rights, education equity, racial, economic, and restorative justice and climate justice" in solidarity with "women, workers, immigrants, and the LGBTQ community."[18]

The incorporation of historically marginalized people is even more apparent in the public policy campaigns that the One Arizona coalition has facilitated. These policy campaigns include the successful effort to pass Proposition 206 in 2016, which increased the minimum hourly wage in Arizona to $12 and required employers to provide paid sick leave, and the ONE PHX ID coalition, an effort to create a municipal identification card in the city of Phoenix. Both public policy campaigns illustrate the growth of cross-community movement mobilization in Arizona in the face of strong opponents. The ONE PHX ID coalition is especially intriguing because it was somewhat successful at thwarting anti-immigrant activists. The ONE PHX ID coalition's member organizations represented a broad spread of minority communities in Arizona, including the LGBTQ, immigrant, Latinx, and labor communities. Coalition member organizations included CNL, Equality Arizona, Arcoíris Liberation Team, Living United for Change Arizona (LUCHA), Puente Movement, the Service Employees International Union (SEIU), United Food and Commercial Workers (UFCW), and the International Union of Painters and Allied Trades (IUPAT). The coalition also included retired Phoenix police officer Paul Penzone, who successfully unseated Sheriff Arpaio in 2016.

In advocating for the municipal ID in Phoenix, coalition members frequently referred to the range of intersecting communities that the ID was designed to assist, from undocumented immigrants to trans people to people with disabilities to people who are homeless. In doing so, the coalition internalized a shared movement past that spanned each of these communities. The ONE PHX ID coalition organized a broad spread of individuals to testify in support of the municipal ID at the Phoenix City Council.[19] Through the voices of individuals represented in public testimony and interviewed by the local press, coalition leaders advanced the municipal ID proposal while, at the same time, incorporating the narratives of intersectionally marginalized people. Individuals who spoke at the city council meeting also argued that they felt compelled to speak in support of the ID in order to hold city council members accountable after having volunteered to turn out the vote to help elect council members who promised to represent their communities. The presence of individuals at the hearing who both participated in electoral efforts to vote supportive city council members into office and then opted to hold council members accountable through a community-led public policy proposal signifies the formation of an institutionalized grassroots advocacy network in Arizona that can mobilize local advocates from the ballot box through the legislative process.

The Phoenix City Council formally approved a municipal ID proposal in a narrow 5–4 vote in August 2016.[20] However, the struggle to adopt a municipal ID was complicated by nearly two years of opponent attempts to derail the proposal. During this time, State Senator John Kavanagh, one of the primary sponsors of SB 1070, and other anti-immigrant legislators in Arizona attempted to pass legislation that would ban municipalities from adopting local ID cards.[21] By orchestrating testimony against the legislative proposals and protesting at the state capitol, leaders of the ONE PHX ID coalition successfully fended off many attempts to stop municipal IDs. A bipartisan alliance of Republicans and Democrats in the state senate killed some legislation designed to prevent local ID programs in 2016. In an interview with a local news outlet, Viridiana Hernandez, the executive director of CNL, speculated that the bipartisan alliance formed because ONE PHX ID coalition advocacy persuaded legislators "that this was an anti-immigrant bill," and, after the negative press and economic hardship SB 1070 brought to Arizona, "some legislators on both sides are just tired of that."[22]

Throughout the coalition's short tenure, the organizations that composed ONE PHX ID demonstrated a commitment to all four suggestions for building an expansionist movement. First, core partner organizations such as CNL and the One Arizona coalition built alliances by internalizing a common movement past and emphasizing shared opponents. The Arizona coalitions were committed to grassroots community-led policies that centered economic, race, gender, and immigration justice, and they pushed policies that most benefited disadvantaged subgroups, such as a municipal ID program and a statewide ballot initiative that raised the minimum wage. Second, the new Arizona coalitions incorporated leaders and organizations from historically marginalized communities. The core organizations represented undocumented immigrants, low-wage workers, and members of Arizona's LGBTQ migrant community. These leaders were strategically chosen in order to underscore the coalitions' commitment to multiple communities and to increase the political capital of minority communities in the state. Third, the Arizona coalitions formed an institutionalized grassroots advocacy network composed of member-led organizations that create policy solutions from the bottom up. There are also indications that this network is able to mobilize people across multiple political venues, from the ballot box to the city council to the state legislature.

Finally, the Arizona coalitions described here incorporated an expansionist commitment to political movement formation through a politics of solidarity. The municipal ID effort ultimately stalled in 2018 because, according to Phoenix city officials, the contractor selected to provide the municipal ID cards said that it could no longer do so at no cost to the city.[23] However, before the municipal ID effort stalled, the ONE PHX ID coalition had tempered its support of the ID because the program threatened the safety of undocumented immigrants. Coalition leaders, concerned that the city might share information about undocumented immigrants collected through the program with federal immigration authorities who would deport them, made their support conditional on a written guarantee from the city that cardholder data would not be turned over to federal immigration authorities.[24] Ultimately, coalition leaders decided that it was strategically important to withdraw their support because the municipal ID program might harm undocumented immigrant coalition partners, who were coalition leaders and some of the most effective local organizers. This tactical decision to make support for the ID program conditional enabled coalition partners to maintain relationships with marginalized communities after the life span of a single political campaign. By tempering support, the coalition prioritized the interests of marginalized communities and the organizations that represent them over a campaign win. The decision to maintain and strengthen partnerships with marginalized communities is indicative of a grassroots advocacy network that is more committed to long-term political movement expansion than to short-term rights wins that are potentially harmful.

There is some evidence that the groups and people that were part of the ONE PHX ID coalition have, indeed, moved beyond the discrete rights campaign and on to new policy advances—an indication of movement expansion. In 2016, Puente Movement, CNL, and LUCHA (grassroots organizations in Arizona that are part of the One Arizona and ONE PHX ID coalitions) formed People United for Justice, a political organization devoted to bringing "together communities most impacted by racism and xenophobia to fight against criminalization and police violence." In 2016, while the nation was captivated by one of the most heated and politically volatile presidential campaigns in modern history, People United for Justice formed the Bazta Arpaio campaign in Maricopa County, Arizona. A play on the Spanish word for enough (¡Basta!) and the initials for the state of Arizona (AZ), the Bazta Arpaio campaign sought to remove Sheriff Joe Arpaio from office and elect Democrat Paul Penzone (one of the members of the ONE PHX ID coalition) as the new sheriff of Maricopa County.

Although many of the individuals who participated in the campaign were part of organizations that formed in the aftermath of SB 1070 in 2010, others had organized against Arpaio well before 2010, working with local attorneys to help collect the evidence to take Arpaio to court for violating the civil rights of Latinx and immigrant residents. Arpaio's abusive practices had taken a severe toll on these communities through heightened policing. According to many interviewees, community members joined organizations like Puente Movement out of necessity in order to organize for their own survival. These organizations helped stop many anti-immigrant laws at the state legislature and gathered the evidence necessary to prove that Arpaio's sheriff's department engaged in racial profiling and unlawful traffic stops. For example, Puente Movement created an interactive website timeline to document dozens of the abuses that members of the Latinx and migrant communities faced during Arpaio's tenure. The timeline includes both stories of police abuse, such as the time that Arpaio forced Alma Chacon to give birth while shackled to her hospital bed, and stories of community empowerment, such as the hundred-thousand-person march against SB 1070 in May 2010.[25] After Arpaio had wasted millions of taxpayer dollars on civil rights lawsuits, local organizers were able to persuade some conservative and moderate voters that Arpaio was economically harming the state—cutting against the "cheap and harsh punishment" political ethos internalized in Arizona. It finally seemed possible for Arpaio to lose an election, and the grassroots movement in Arizona, following years of smaller electoral and public policy advances, was ready to usher him out of office.

With an old school bus painted red and a large blow-up figure of

Sheriff Arpaio in handcuffs and a prison uniform, the Bazta Arpaio campaign tirelessly worked to get out the vote for the November 2016 general election.[26] In one memorable campaign tactic, Jerssay Arredondo and members of the Bazta Arpaio campaign and the local queer migrant community produced a music video remake of Selena Quintanilla's "Baila Esta Cumbia" with Arredondo, who goes by the stage name FreeDa Put@, in Selena drag.[27] The 2016 presidential election was a historic win for the Republican party, with candidate Donald Trump winning large segments of the American electorate through a campaign that centered the same anti-immigrant rhetoric of Sheriff Arpaio. But in Maricopa County, despite the nationwide surge in pro-Trump voters, Arpaio, a cross-community opponent, lost his election. Sheriff Arpaio's loss, ushered in by inter- and intra-movement coalition formation in Arizona, shows that political movement expansion is possible despite losses imposed by counter-movements, and despite intersecting structural hierarchies that delimit the opportunities available for movement advocates.

## Beyond Washington and Arizona

This book has focused on Washington State and Arizona in order to understand how political movements organize around rights, uncovering local coalition dynamics that drive movement expansion and contraction along the way. Although the preceding pages are concerned with coalition dynamics in two state cases, the findings discussed also apply to other political movement contexts. Since I completed my fieldwork, the potential for the formation of expansive political movements has emerged in numerous local settings. Some of the most obvious examples include larger, national movements, such as #MeToo and #BlackLivesMatter. These movements incorporate an array of cross-community groups and intersectionally marginalized people in the coalitions they've formed and issues they have embraced, which center systemic change, or the expansive view of political movement described in this book. Yet there are a growing number of cross-community, grassroots coalitions that embody the potential for expansionist political movement formation as well. For instance, there are indications that a movement for public safety and gun control is developing as students who are victims of mass shootings mobilize. The February 2018 school shooting in Parkland, Florida, is one concrete example of a rights episode that may activate expansionist possibilities. Like SB 1070 in Arizona, the Parkland massacre occurred around a traumatic moment that galvanized multiple communities into action, this time led by high school student survivors. My research shows that political movements can form when a series of traumatic episodes activate those affected by the events, who then form grassroots coalitions with other communities in response.

The newly activated Parkland survivors have begun reaching out to other communities who are impacted by gun violence, incorporating the experiences of marginalized people. In the aftermath of the shooting, several Parkland students formed a national gun control coalition and actively sought to incorporate cross-community experiences of gun violence. The students traveled to Chicago to meet with black youth whose urban communities experience chronic gun violence that differs from the suburban episodic mass shootings that occur at schools like Marjorie Stoneman Douglas High School in Parkland.[28] Furthermore, there are indications that the Parkland survivors' coalition is becoming a nonpartisan, grassroots advocacy network—in accordance with one of the four suggestions described in this chapter for thwarting movement contraction. After the Parkland tragedy, student survivors met with legislators, orchestrated a nationwide student walkout, and engaged in a media campaign in order to push legislators to pass gun control measures.[29] Their grassroots advocacy successfully convinced Florida legislators to pass a law that raised the minimum age to purchase any firearm in the state from eighteen to twenty-one, created a three-day waiting period for most long gun purchases, and banned the possession of bump stocks.[30]

Following its success in Florida, the Parkland students' group launched a national coalition in Chicago in order to highlight shared cross-community experiences of traumatic events that threaten people's right to live safe and secure lives. The event was partially designed to help construct a common cross-community past. In addition, the coalition has helped highlight important differences designed to expand the newly forming political movement. Leaders have expressed a desire to incorporate experiences of chronic gun violence in poor, inner-city communities in order to expand the array of gun violence issues embraced by the coalition beyond gun control, which is primarily aimed at stopping episodic shootings in mostly white, suburban settings.[31] It is unclear how the new coalition will evolve and whether the issues that emerge will be expansive, fully incorporating the policy priorities of urban communities, such as opportunities for youth employment and public school funding, which are aimed at eradicating the poverty in these communities that manifests in experiences of social inequality such as chronic gun violence. Initial attempts to create a cross-community coalition that highlights shared and dissimilar experiences foreshadow the possibility of expansive political movement formation.

In addition to the coalition of student groups and organizations that have formed around threats to young people's rights to public safety and security, the potential for political movement expansion around threats to rights and opportunities to advance rights exists in other contexts throughout the US as well. For example, the North Carolina Moral Monday protest movement first emerged in 2013 and has continued to organize protests at the state's capitol whenever lawmakers pass legislation that threatens minority rights in the state. The protest movement has held rallies that call attention to an array of rights threats, from threats to voting rights to threats to trans rights, such as the North Carolina legislature's HB2, which prevented cities in the state from passing ordinances that prohibit discrimination on the basis of gender identity and expression and has since been partially repealed.[32] The Moral Monday movement's embrace of cross-community groups and their priorities is indicative of the formation of an expansive movement at the local level in North Carolina.

Other political movements that have formed in response to rights threats and opportunities include the #RedForEd teacher protest movements, which have advocated for increased public school funding in many red (Republican-controlled) states where attempts to bolster the right to public education have long been stalled. #RedForEd catapulted into local communities across the US after teachers in West Virginia engaged in a nine-day strike that successfully garnered a 5 percent pay increase.[33] The statewide teacher walkouts, which occurred in a diverse array of states, including Oklahoma, Kentucky, Colorado, and Arizona, were run by grassroots networks organized by the teachers themselves. Mobilization occurred through social media, including Facebook and Twitter, in "right to work" states where teachers' unions held little political power and striking was illegal.[34]

Like the national #MeToo and #BlackLivesMatter movements, these grassroots teachers' coalitions used social media to great effect, building both local and national support for education funding. Even after the strikes ended, many teachers remained activated. In Arizona, the #Red-ForEd teacher activism helped engage a wave of teacher candidates for political office, including Kathy Hoffman, who went on to win the state-wide race for superintendent of public instruction in November 2018.[35] In West Virginia, organized teachers have continued to be a political force in the state. During the 2019 legislative session in West Virginia, teachers held a second walkout in response to a proposed bill that would have created charter schools in the state and allowed tax dollars to cover private tuition.[36] In response to the new mobilization, the bill failed to move through the state legislature. The teacher walkouts have become a bright spot for labor organizing in states that have passed laws designed to weaken labor unions. The teacher activism has been successful in part because of the formation of nonpartisan, grassroots networks that can be called on in response to community threats, including political threats to the right to public education.

How rights function in movements for social change is complex. Much of the scholarship on law and social change has tended toward either-or explanations of how rights impact movements. For most scholars, rights either fragment and individualize problems or serve as important resources for resolving long-standing inequalities. The interview analyses presented in this book emphasize, by contrast, that rights episodes are paradoxical. They have both harmful and beneficial effects in political movements for social change. To understand the multidimensional and paradoxical ways that rights operate within movements, scholars should focus on the formation of coalitions within and across movements rather than only on a small set of organizations that claim to represent an entire movement.

We often think about movements as entities that represent the interests of one community or population; however, to form a powerful expansion-ist political movement, communities must mobilize beyond individual subject positions and form genuine alliances among groups that hold seemingly conflicting interests. This book has begun to illuminate how analyzing the formation of coalitions across and within organizations that represent the LGBTQ and immigrant communities can reveal the para-doxical components of political movement advocacy. In doing so, it has shown that movements are best understood not as unitary, homogenous entities that represent only one community but, rather, as dynamic, multifaceted entities that form in response to tensions related to what goals a movement should pursue, what values and stories should compose the narratives at a movement's core, and whom a movement should represent.

In examining movement formation, I have centered the experiences of local organization leaders and community workers. This has allowed me to engage in an empirical study of the dynamics that shape grassroots inter- and intra-movement coalitions in two state settings, settings with the combination of similarity and variance necessary to form a generalizable theory about the role of rights advocacy in grassroots political movements in some local settings in the US. However, the process of engaging in a contextualized examination of grassroots movement building has revealed that movements differ tremendously depending on the local political network. Although I have highlighted some factors that contribute to movement expansion and contraction, this is not meant to be a comprehensive study of grassroots movements in all settings. Instead, my goal is to call attention to the need to study movements in local settings (rather than national settings alone) across intersectionally divergent communities, and to reflect on and elevate the voices of grassroots actors who are engaged in community building, rather than organizational elites who are not embedded in the local communities that they claim to represent. It is my hope that this book will encourage future research into grassroots movement building that is based in the experiences of intersectionally marginalized people. Future scholars can accomplish this through reflexive research that gives back to marginalized communities when they are the subject of study, while centering their narratives in theorizing political movements for social change from the bottom up.

Appendix 1

# TERMINOLOGY: DESCRIBING MULTIPLE SUBJECT
# POSITIONS IN SHIFTING COALITIONS


Subject positions in political movements are in a constant state of flux. This is especially true of the LGBTQ (lesbian, gay, bisexual, trans, and queer) movement, which challenges socially acceptable conceptualizations of sexuality and gender. The political labels that movement actors use in advocacy have altered dramatically over the past sixty years. For example, the term *homosexual*, which was often used in describing members of the LGBTQ movement in the 1960s and 1970s, is considered overly medicalized and a relic of mid-twentieth-century stigma. Similarly, the term *queer*, which was once an epithet for people perceived as LGBTQ, has been reclaimed by members of the LGBTQ community and is now used by mainstream and marginalized organizations alike. Many of the LGBTQ organizations discussed in this project do not use the same acronym or terminology when engaging in advocacy around sexual orientation and gender identity. This is a reflection of broad debate and community tensions over language and terminology. In order to best achieve clarity and inclusiveness, and because this project concerns inter- and intra-movement coalitions, I use the term *LGBTQ* to broadly refer to the organizing of mainstream groups that focus on such issues as expanding anti-discrimination laws and workplace protections as well as marginalized queer and trans groups that focus on issues such as trans inclusive health care. I use this term because it was the one most often employed by members of both communities during my fieldwork. Stated differently, I use *LGBTQ* when discussing the political movement as a whole. I use the terms *lesbian and gay* and *mainstream LGBTQ* to refer to mainstream organizations that have primarily focused on achieving discrete rights-based goals and formal legal equality. I use the terms *queer, transgender, trans,* and *gender nonconforming* to refer to marginalized organizations that are committed to economic, racial, and gender justice issues that are broadly aimed at contesting systemic oppression.

The subject positions adopted by members of the immigrant rights movement have, similarly, shifted over the past few years and are contested. Recognizing this, I use *immigrant* to describe those who engage in advocacy around Comprehensive Immigration Reform and those who advocate for more community-based alternatives that reject what they see as harmful compromises when it comes to the militarization of the border and immigration detention. I use *migrant* to describe those organizations that advocate on behalf of seasonal migrant workers in the US. Finally, use of the label *Latinx* started to surge among student, activist, and community-building groups in 2015, including groups that advocate for migrant justice and are a part of this study. Advocates started adopting *Latinx* as a gender inclusive term to describe the range of gender identities present in Latino community organizing spaces.[1] The term is still deeply contested within movement spaces as of this writing; however, I use it in this project because it was used by an array of study participants in describing their advocacy.

Appendix 2

# METHODOLOGY: STUDYING INTER- AND
# INTRA-MOVEMENT COALITIONS

The research presented in this book is based on a multimethod study conducted between December 2014 and October 2015 that encompassed semi-structured, in-depth interviews; participant observations; and archival research. I conducted fifty-one interviews in total—twenty-six in Arizona and twenty-five in Washington State. I interviewed organization leaders, advocates, community workers, and politicians who were active in and supportive of the campaigns associated with cross-community coalitions in Washington and Arizona and those who, though involved in interest group advocacy, chose not to engage in key campaigns. I also interviewed individuals who later came to regret or doubt their involvement in some campaigns, or questioned the utility of coalitions in movement mobilization. Many of the individuals interviewed who chose not to engage in some campaigns, who expressed regret over their participation, or who viewed alignments with mainstream organizations with speculation, hold either intersecting identities (e.g., identify as immigrants, persons of color, and/or LGBTQ) or more marginalized identities within these communities (e.g., are trans, gender nonconforming, or undocumented people).

Interviewees were given one of two interview protocols, one for organization leaders and one for advocates, community workers, and politicians. These protocols were designed as a loose guide for the interviews in order to allow interviewees the freedom to construct their own personal advocacy stories. I have included both interview protocols in appendix 3. I anticipated that organization leaders might have a difficult time talking about alliances within their movements, so I began by asking more general questions about alliance building. I then asked about alliances across and within movements more specifically, including questions about coalition work in statewide rights campaigns. At the end of each interview, interviewees completed a post interview demographic survey.

In conducting these interviews, I first identified potential interviewees through local newspaper articles and organization archives naming key advocates and leaders. After reaching out to all identified potential interviewees, I used a snowball sampling technique to identify additional potential interviewees who are active in intersectional advocacy in both states. Before each interview, participants were presented with an informed consent form. Each interview was recorded and lasted anywhere between about thirty minutes and two hours depending on the interviewee's availability. The interview analysis presented in this project is compiled from discourse patterns and common experiences recognized through the interview process and by using NVivo's qualitative research software to code patterns in transcribed interviews.[1]

In addition to the in-depth interviews, I also engaged in participant observations whenever possible in order to more fully flesh out my understanding of the coalition's legal rights advocacy, to connect with potential interviewees, and to give back to the organizations and individuals who agreed to participate in this study. As a researcher from a major university, I occupy a space of privilege that many of my interviewees do not. I am a white, cisgender woman; identify as queer; and come from a middle-class background. I had experience attending LGBTQ organization events and labor movement events through my graduate student union before beginning my fieldwork. I also interned for the civil rights law firm Columbia Legal Services while in law school in 2012, where I had the opportunity to meet local leaders involved in the immigrant rights movement in Washington State. During this internship, I assisted the law firm in litigating cases on behalf of organizations with large undocumented immigrant memberships and observed the multiracial task force on police accountability—a coalition of community of color organizations that formed to combat police violence in Seattle. The main immigrant rights case I worked on concerned the increased border patrol presence along the Washington State border, which local immigration advocacy organizations argued created a climate of fear in Washington's immigrant communities.[2]

Through these prior experiences, I developed contacts with local organizations in Washington State that I was able to go to when initially reaching out to interviewees. These experiences also taught me that many marginalized communities experience researcher intervention as exploitation and that white social justice advocates have a history of ignoring and marginalizing issues that matter to communities of color, undocumented people, and trans and queer people. In recognizing this, I developed a methodological model designed to prevent my researcher interventions from tending toward exploitation of minority communities. Specifically, I developed a volunteer-intensive participant observation component to my study that involved my volunteering at and participating in events designed to organize and provide services to the communities at the center of this study. In this way, I actively accounted for researcher positionality and subjectivity as a mechanism of transparency while conducting my research in line with contemporary critiques from qualitative and multimethod scholars in political science.[3]

Through the participant observation component, I was able to both connect with interviewees and give back through volunteer work with participant organizations. Because coalitions are the subject of the project, I was unable to volunteer with every organization. However, I did substantial volunteer work at coalition-based events. Most of the volunteer work I engaged in was through Trans Pride Seattle in 2015 and 2016, where I served as a volunteer lead and spent about two months each year working with the organizing committee to help plan the event, which draws between three thousand and five thousand participants and many local organizations each June. Event organizers were aware that I was both a researcher and a volunteer committed to trans, immigration, labor, and racial justice. In addition to volunteering, I identified potential moments for participant observation by following group announcements, press releases, and action alerts. Throughout the duration of my research, I also observed select public organization events such as protests, educational panels and forums, volunteer opportunities, and public membership meetings. Through these participant observations, I was able to identify the extent to which differing groups work together both during and after heated advocacy moments, and to identify new interviewees.

Unlike previous studies, which have focused on political movements by studying national groups, this study focuses on state-level, formal and informal organizations and, in doing so, explores the extent to which coalitions represent and serve intersectional and more marginalized communities. With this said, it is also important to recognize the limits of this research. This research does not provide a causal analysis or a comprehensive analysis of every legal and political campaign (or attempted campaign) that interviewees have been involved with in the past. Rather, it is designed to identify those moments that interviewees recollect as most important, with the understanding that memories of these moments and their believed importance may shift over time, but are crucial for learning about how communities form a collective subjectivity and about the limits of that subjectivity.

# Appendix 3

## INTERVIEW PROTOCOLS

### Interview Protocol I: Organization Leaders

Reference Number: _____ Date: _____ Time:_____ to _____
Interviewee: _____
Job Title: _____
Organization: _____
Contact Information: _____

Thank you for taking the time to meet with me. I know that you're very busy and I am grateful for your time. The purpose of this interview is to get some additional information about your work with cross-community rights advocacy. The interview will take about 45 minutes (or less upon request). I will start with a few general questions about your involvement with local organizations, followed by some questions about social and political activities you've participated in.

Before I begin, I want to make sure it's all right with you if I tape this interview. Anything you say will, of course, be kept completely anonymous if you would prefer. The information that I am collecting will be used for my own research and for educational purposes. Do you have any questions before I start?

GENERAL ORGANIZATION QUESTIONS
I'd like to begin with just a few background questions about your involvement with [organization].

(1) How did you first get involved and active with [organization]?

(2) How large is [organization]?

(3) What do you think are the goals and aims of [organization] in your own words?

(4) What is [organization's] general structure?

  (a) Is it a 501(c)(3) organization, a 501(c)(4), or another type of organization?

  (b) [If the organization uses an alternative model, ask:] What is the philosophy behind this alternative organizational model?

  (c) What are your organization's primary funding sources?

  (d) If possible, can you tell me what [organization's] annual budget is?

GENERAL SOCIAL AND POLITICAL ADVOCACY
Now I'd like to talk about your social and political advocacy.

(5) What are the biggest problems facing the _____ community in the state and nationwide? [When asking this question, fill in the blank with the community the interviewee has worked with and that is relevant to the state case. If the interviewee has worked with multiple communities, ask this question for each community the interviewee has worked with.]

  (a) What social and political advocacy has your organization done to address these problems?

(6) What are some of the biggest issues your organization has been involved with in the past?

  (a) What advocacy has your organization done on behalf of these issues?

COALITION WORK: CROSS-COMMUNITY ALLIANCES
Next, I would like to discuss how your organization has worked with other groups.

(7) What organizations do you see as allies?

(8) On what issues does [organization] work on with other local organizations?

(a) How much of [organization's] energy is devoted to these issues?

(b) How long has [organization] worked on these issues?

(c) Did you face any challenges, obstacles, or pushback from [organization] members and/or staff when you first began to work on these issues?

   (i) [If answer is yes] How did you overcome these challenges?

   (ii) [If answer is no] Why don't you think you faced any challenges with [organization] members when you first began to work on these issues?

   (iii) What did you do in order to convince others to work with your organization on these cross-community issues?

(9) After doing some background research on your organization, I've seen that you've worked with other groups on the following events: [list several concrete events]. Did any of your members react negatively when you announced that you were working on these events or did they have difficulty seeing how these events aligned with your group's mission?

(10) How has [major legislation, court case, or political campaign] like [example] impacted your activism? Did you work with any other organizations on actions surrounding this legislation?

(a) What about the [court case]? Did you work with any other organizations on actions surrounding this lawsuit?

(b) What about [state legislation]? Did you work with any other organizations on actions surrounding this legislation?

(c) What about [political campaign]? Did you work with any other organizations on actions surrounding this proposition?

(d) What about [other legislation, court case, political campaign, or political action]? Did you work with any other organizations on advocacy surrounding these legal actions?

(11) What do you think are the most effective tactics for accomplishing social change?

(12) What role do you think the law plays in movements for social change?

(13) Are there any [community or communities relevant to the state

case] issues your organization has decided not to work on or devotes less time and energy on due to resource constraints?

(14) What do you think are some of the benefits and constraints of coalition [or campaign] work you've been involved with in the past?

INTERVIEW WRAP-UP

(15) Do you have any organization archives (like emails, press releases, pamphlets, flyers, or organization publications) that I might look through for my research?

(16) Finally, can you suggest any other members of the community who might be interested in an interview? If so, can you provide me with their name and public contact information?

Thank you for taking the time to speak with me today. I really value having had the opportunity to hear your experiences and you have provided me with crucial information for my project.

## Interview Protocol II: Local Advocates

Reference Number: _____ Date: _____ Time:_____ to _____
Interviewee: _____
Job Title: _____
Organization: _____
Contact Information: _____

Thank you for taking the time to meet with me. I know that you're very busy and I am grateful for your time. The purpose of this interview is to get some additional information about your work with cross-community rights advocacy. The interview will take about 45 minutes (or less upon request). I will start with a few general questions about your involvement with local organizations, followed by some questions about social and political activities you've participated in.

Before I begin, I want to make sure it's all right with you if I tape this interview. Anything you say will, of course, be kept completely anonymous if you would prefer. The information that I am collecting will be used for my own research and for educational purposes. Do you have any questions before I start?

GENERAL ORGANIZATION QUESTIONS

I'd like to begin with just a few background questions about your involvement with any local organizations.

(1) Which local organizations have you worked with?

(2) How long have you been active with these organizations?

(3) How would you describe the goals and aims of these organizations in your own words? Which populations/communities do these organizations serve?

GENERAL SOCIAL AND POLITICAL ADVOCACY

Now I'd like to talk about your social and political advocacy.

(4) What are the biggest problems facing the _____ community in the state and nationwide? [When asking the question, fill in the blank with the community the interviewee has worked with and that is relevant to the state case. If the interviewee has worked with multiple communities, ask this question for each community the interviewee has worked with.]

(a) What social and political advocacy, if any, have you done on behalf of these problems?

(b) How do you think this advocacy has helped address these problems? Has any advocacy exacerbated these problems?

(5) What are some of the biggest issues (other than those already described) that you have been involved with in the past?

(a) What advocacy have you done on behalf of these issues if any?

(b) How do you think this advocacy contributed to social change?

COALITION WORK: CROSS-COMMUNITY ALLIANCES

Next, I would like to discuss how your organization has worked with other groups.

(6) Just a moment ago, I asked you about your advocacy on [community or communities relevant to the state case and interviewee] rights issues separately. Are there any issues you've worked on that you believe impact these communities collectively?

(a) How long have you worked on these issues?

(b) Did you face any challenges or obstacles when you first began to work on these issues?

    (i) [If the answer is yes] How did you overcome these challenges?

    (ii) [If the answer is no] Why don't you think you faced any challenges when you first began to work on these issues?

(7) Did any of the other organization members or people in your life react negatively when they found out that you were working on events that impact the [community or communities relevant to the state case and interviewee] communities? Why or why not?

(8) Did anyone have difficulty seeing how the issues you've described aligned with their other advocacy (including their prior cross-community rights activism)? Why or why not?

(9) How has [major legislation, court case, or political campaign] like [example] impacted your activism? Did you work with any other organizations on actions surrounding this legislation?

    (a) What about the [court case]? Did you work with any other organizations on actions surrounding this lawsuit?

    (b) What about [state legislation]? Did you work with any other organizations on actions surrounding this legislation?

    (c) What about [political campaign]? Did you work with any other organizations on actions surrounding this proposition?

    (d) What about [other legislation, court case, political campaign, or political action]? Did you work with any other organizations on advocacy surrounding these legal actions?

(10) What do you think are the most effective tactics for accomplishing social change?

(11) What role do you think the law plays in movements for social change?

(12) Are there any [community or communities relevant to the state case] issues you have decided not to work on or devote less time and energy on due to resource constraints?

(13) What do you think are some of the benefits and constraints of coalition [or campaign] work you've been involved with in the past?

Interview Wrap-Up

(14) Do you have any organization archives (like emails, press releases, pamphlets, flyers, or organization publications) that I might look through for my research?

(15) Finally, can you suggest any other members of the community who might be interested in an interview? If so, can you provide me with their name and public contact information?

Thank you for taking the time to speak with me today. I really value having had the opportunity to hear your experiences and you have provided me with crucial information for my project.

# NOTES

Introduction

1. Brewer 2010.

2. Pitzi 2016.

3. Interviewee names in this book are pseudonyms, except for politician interviewees who gave nonconfidential interviews. Interview excerpts are lightly edited to eliminate extraneous words (such as "um" and "you know").

4. See, e.g., McAdam 1999: 36.

5. See, e.g., Van Dyke and McCammon 2010.

6. Eskridge 2001.

7. See, e.g., Keck 2009, Andersen 2006, Epp 1998, Tushnet 2005.

8. Cathcart and Gabel-Brett 2016, Becker 2015, Kaplan and Dickey 2015, Solomon 2014.

9. See e.g., Murib 2017, Price 2017, Chávez 2013, Stone 2012, Ward 2008, Levitsky 2007.

10. Eng 2010: 12–16.

11. Cohen 1999, Piven and Cloward 1979.

12. Majic 2014.

13. See e.g., Chávez 2013.

14. Chua 2019, 2014; Gleeson 2012; Ernst 2010; Lovell 2012; Levitsky 2007; Strolovitch 2007; Merry 2000; McCann 1994; Engel 1984.

15. Simpson 1998:163.

16. Tarrow 2011: 32–33; Meyer and Minkoff 2004; McAdam 1999; McAdam, Tarrow, and Tilly 1996; Gamson and Meyer 1996.

17. McAdam, McCarthy, and Zald 1996: 2; see also Tilly 1978, Tarrow 1983.

18. Ward 2008: 2.

19. Strolovitch 2007.

20. See e.g., Cramer 2015, Chua 2014, Nielsen 2004, Merry 2003.

21. Beltrán 2010, Merry 2003, Butler 1990.

22. In her article on how domestic violence survivors in Hilo, Hawai'i, experience empowerment through the law, Merry (2003) argues that people can adopt an autonomous rights-bearing subjectivity or subject position when they have positive experiences with the law (e.g., when they go to court and a judge decides a case in their favor). According to Merry, domestic violence survivors have more difficulty adopting this subjectivity when they have negative experiences with the legal system—for instance, when a police officer responding to a domestic violence dispute refuses to treat the dispute as a serious criminal offense. A negative response like this de-emphasizes a survivor's autonomous rights-bearing subjectivity, thereby minimizing the survivor's ability to develop a rights consciousness through the law.

23. McCann 1994.

24. See e.g., Zemans 1983.

25. Legal mobilization researchers have studied how the right to same-sex marriage moved from the aspirations of activists to an institutionalized legal reality (NeJaime 2014), why civil rights movement activists chose to pursue school desegregation before economic justice (Goluboff 2005), and how women and minorities have mobilized the law in the movement against discrimination in the workplace (Burstein 1991).

26. Klarman 2014, 2014; Rosenberg 2008; Kluger 2004.

27. McCann 1994, Chua 2019, Lovell 2012, Bernstein et al. 2009, Andersen 2006, Goldberg-Hiller 2004, Marshall and Barclay 2003, Zemans 1983, Scheingold 1974.

28. McCann 1994: 307–308.

29. See, e.g., Duam 2009, Keck 2009, Andersen 2006, Goldberg-Hiller 2004; however, there are notable exceptions in legal mobilization scholarship that focus on local contexts, such as Mello 2016, Hull 2004, and Fisher 2009, which examine same-sex marriage at the state level, although these studies focus primarily on a small subset of organizations rather than cross-community coalitions.

30. See, e.g., Rosenberg 2008.

31. Adam 2017.

Chapter 1

1. Klarman 2014, 2004; Rosenberg 2008; Rimmerman 2002.

2. Cummings and NeJaime 2010; Keck 2009; Pinello 2006; Eskridge 2002.

3. Rosenberg 2008.

4. McCann 1994, Chua 2014.

5. See, e.g., Dorf and Tarrow 2014, Fetner 2008, Mansbridge 1986.

6. Webley 2013.

7. Gregory 2015.

8. Confessore 2016.

9. Ward 2008.

10. Gregory 2015.

11. Gregory 2009.

12. Bui 2015.

13. Johnson 2017.

14. Seattle Civil Rights and Labor History Project.

15. Silva 2017.

16. Davenport 2017.

17. Speidel 2017.

18. Balk 2014, Stuteville 2014, Hobbs and Stoops 2002.

19. McKenna 2017, Atkins 2003.

20. McKenna 2017.

21. McKenna 2017, Gregory 2015.

22. Sanders 2012, Sanders 2006.

23. Sanders 2012.

24. Boucai 2015.

25. *Singer v. Hara* 522 P.2d 1187, 1190 (Wash. 1974).

26. *Singer v. Hara* 522 P.2d 1187, 1195 (Wash. 1974).

27. Sanders 2012.

28. *We're Here to Stay* 1998.

29. *Baehr v. Lewin* 852 P.2d 44 (Hawaii 1993).

30. *We're Here to Stay* 1998.

31. *We're Here to Stay* 1998.

32. Atkins 2003.

33. *We're Here to Stay* 1998.

34. De Leon 1997, Murakami 1997.

35. Locke and Rigby 1997, Murakami 1997, "Washington Initiative Shot Down" 1997.

36. Dao 2004.

37. Washington Office of the Secretary of State 1997a, 1997b; "Rights Bill Would Protect Gays' Jobs" 1997.

38. See, e.g., HB 1130: Reaffirming and Protecting the Institution of Marriage, Floor debate remarks, Bill Thompson, February 4, 1998.

39. HB 1130: Reaffirming and Protecting the Institution of Marriage, floor debate remarks, Larry Sheahan, March 10, 2009.

40. SHB 1130: Reaffirming and Protecting the Institution of Marriage, floor debate remarks, Dow Constantine, February 4 1998. HB 1130: Reaffirming and Protecting the Institution of Marriage, floor debate remarks, Ed Murray, February 4, 1998.

41. Mapes 1998.

42. Melo 2014.

43. *Goodridge v. Department of Health* 798 N.E.2d 941 (Mass 2003).

44. Savage 2004, Young 2004.

45. Dorf and Tarrow 2014, NeJaime 2014.

46. O'Hagan 2013.

47. *Andersen v. King County* 138 P.3d 963, 973 (Wash. 2006); Melo 2014: 17.

48. Sanders 2006, citing State Representative Jamie Pedersen, who argued that, "looking back . . . we really lost this in the 2004 elections."

49. Melo 2014.

50. *Andersen v. King County* 138 P.3d. 963, 990 (Wash. 2006); Melo 2014.

51. *Andersen v. King County* 138 P.3d. 963, 963 (Wash. 2006).

52. Turnbull 2009a.

53. SB 5688: Expanding the Rights and Responsibilities of State Registered Domestic Partners, floor debate remarks, Val Stevens, March 10, 2009.

54. Melo 2014. SB 5688: Expanding the Rights and Responsibilities of State Registered Domestic Partners, floor debate remarks, Ed Murray, March 10, 2009.

55. Roesler 2009.

56. Wyman 2013.

57. La Corte 2009, Turnbull 2009b.

58. American Civil Liberties Union Washington 2009. Some of the thirty-one community of color organizations that supported the "everything but marriage" campaign in 2009 may have supported same-sex couples in the *Andersen* case as well if given the opportunity. For example, the Japanese American Citizens League (JACL) did not intervene in *Andersen* in 2004, but has supported same-sex marriage since 1994 (Japanese American Citizens League 2007). However, cross-community coalition building in Washington State, especially with LGBTQ rights organizations that have historically been dominated by white lesbian and gay leaders, was relatively fragile in the early 2000s. Hence, lesbian and gay leaders may not have reached out extensively to the array of organizations that endorsed Referendum 71, when *Andersen* was filed in 2004, nor had they yet engaged in deep, cross-community conversations.

59. Tu 2009.

60. Andrew 2009.

61. Brunner 2011.

62. Calmes and Baker 2012.

63. O'Donnell 2011, Pew Research Center 2016.

64. SB 6239: Concerning Civil Marriage and Domestic Partnerships, floor debate remarks, Dan Swecker, February 1, 2012; SB 6239: Concerning Civil

Marriage and Domestic Partnerships, floor debate remarks, Debbie Regala, February 1, 2012.

65. *Andersen v. King County* 138 P.3d 963 (Wash. 2006); *Hollingsworth v. Perry* 671 F.3d 1052 (9th Cir. 2012); SB 6239: Concerning Civil Marriage and Domestic Partnerships, floor debate remarks, Jamie Pedersen, February 8, 2012; SB 6239: Concerning Civil Marriage and Domestic Partnerships, floor debate remarks, Jay Rodne, February 8, 2012.

66. Turnbull 2012.

67. Associated Press 2012.

68. "Referendum 74 Ballot Question without the Spin" 2012; Baker 2012.

69. "Latinos for the Freedom for Marry" 2012, emphasis as it appears in the advertisement. The advertisement appears following the quotation here.

70. "Asian/Pacific Islanders for the Freedom to Marry" 2012, emphasis as it appears in the advertisement. The first page of the advertisement appears following the quotation here.

71. *Obergefell v. Hodges* 576 U.S. 1, 23 (2015).

72. Dorf and Tarrow 2014.

Chapter 2

1. *The State of Arizona* 2014.

2. SB 1070 (2010) The Support Our Law Enforcement and Safe Neighborhoods Act, Forty-Ninth Legislature, Second Regular Session.

3. Lynch 2010: 23.

4. González de Bustamante 2012: 26.

5. González de Bustamante 2012.

6. Lynch 2010: 23.

7. Lynch 2010.

8. González de Bustamante 2012.

9. Águila 2013: 134–135.

10. González de Bustamante 2012: 28.

11. González de Bustamante 2012.

12. Sinema 2012: 73.

13. Epps 2011, US Department of Justice 2015.

14. Lynch 2010; see also Gottschalk 2008, Pestritto 2000, Sarat 1999, Christianson 1998, and Dumm 1987 on the development of American law-and-order politics.

15. Lynch 2010.

16. Terry 1998; *Ruiz v. Hull* 957 P.2d 984; *Arizonans for Official English v. Arizona*, 520 US 43 (1997).

17. Amira 2013.

18. Cart 1990.

19. Ye Hee Lee 2012.

20. Engel 2016, Canaday 2011.

21. Beard Rau 2017b, Huerta 1996, Wasser 2016.

22. Harmon Cooley 2015: 1009, Eskridge 2000.

23. Harmon Cooley 2015, Chokshi 2014, Hendley 2014.

24. Kaur 2019.

25. FAIR was founded in 1979 by Jon Tanton and others whose activism originated in the reproductive rights movement and the environmentalist population control movement. Tanton's FAIR grew out of movements that were affiliated with left-wing politics in the US (HoSang 2010). The national organization seeks to end all undocumented immigration and eventually "permit no more than 300,000 immigrants and refugees" to gain entry into the US each year (Sinema 2012: 65). The 1988 effort to amend the state's constitution to make English the official language of Arizona was sponsored and funded by Tanton (Sinema 2012: 66). ALEC and FAIR worked with local politicians in Arizona to pass the mass of anti-immigration bills and ballot initiatives in the 2000s (discussed in the following section) and have diligently labored to thwart legal challenges to these efforts initiated by immigrant rights movement advocates.

26. Chin et al. 2012.

27. Kiefer 2015, Lacey and Seelye 2011.

28. Singer 2012, Passel and Suro 2005.

29. Sinema 2012: 73, Magaña 2013: 153.

30. Rex 2011.

31. Cárdenas et al. 2012.

32. Arizona Secretary of State 2000.

33. Johnson 2005.

34. *Sotomayor v. Burns* 13 P.3d 1198 (Ariz. 2000).

35. Sinema 2012.

36. Beard Rau 2017a.

37. Sinema 2012.

38. Villagra 2006.

39. McDonnell 1999.

40. Calavita 1996, Nesbet and Sellgren 1995.

41. Suro 1994.

42. *Plyer v. Doe* 457 U.S. 202 (1982); McDonnell 1997.

43. *League of United Latin American Citizens v. Wilson* 997 F.Supp. 1244 (C.D. California 1995); American Civil Liberties Union 1999; McDonnell 1999.

44. Arizona Secretary of State 2004a.

45. Arizona Secretary of State 2004b.

46. *Friendly House v. Napolitano* 419 F.3d 930 (9th Cir. 2005); *Gonzalez v. Arizona* (9th Cir. 2007); Campbell 2011.

47. Díaz and Sherwood 2005.

48. *Arizona v. Inter Tribal Council of Arizona* 133 S.Ct. 2447 (2013); Sanders 2013.

49. Sinema 2012.

50. Schmidt and Larimer 2017.

51. Arizona Secretary of State 2006a.

52. See, e.g., Committee on Appropriations, "Minutes of Meeting: SCR 1031," Arizona House of Representatives, March 29, 2006; Committee on K–12 Education, " Minutes of Meeting: SCR 1031," Arizona House of Representatives, March 29, 2006.

53. Arizona Secretary of State 2006b.

54. Arizona Secretary of State 2008a.

55. Arizona Together 2008, 2006; Arizona Secretary of State 2008b, 2006c.

56. Chávez 2013: 113.

57. Campbell 2011.

58. Beltrán 2010: chapter 5.

59. Archibold 2006.

60. Beltrán 2010: 132.

61. Chin et al. 2012.

62. SB 1070 created a variety of new crimes targeting undocumented immigrants in Arizona. For example, Section 3 makes "willful failure to complete or carry" documentation of one's immigration status, in violation of federal law, a state misdemeanor. Section 5 further makes it a state misdemeanor (1) for a driver to stop and "attempt to hire or hire and pick up passengers for work" if doing so blocks traffic; (2) for a person to enter a stopped vehicle "in order to be hired by an occupant of the motor vehicle" if the vehicle blocks traffic; (3) for an undocumented immigrant to "knowingly apply for work, solicit work in a public place, or perform work as an employee or independent contractor"; and (4) for a person who is "in violation of a criminal offense" to transport, conceal, harbor, or shield an undocumented immigrant or "encourage" an undocumented immigrant to come into the state. Section 10 of SB 1070 also allows police to impound a vehicle driven by someone who is "transporting, harboring, concealing, or shielding" an undocumented immigrant in the state.

In addition to the new crimes enacted by SB 1070, Section 2 of the bill includes a provision against sanctuary cities and requires local law enforcement officers to inquire about immigration status—the controversial "show me your papers" provision. Under the anti–sanctuary cities clause of Section 2, *any* legal resident of Arizona can sue *any* official, state agency, or state county, city, town, or political subdivision that implements "a policy or practice that restricts the enforcement of federal immigration laws." This section effectively makes it impossible for cities or localities to pass ordinances that prohibit local law enforcement officers from working with federal immigration officials—one of the key goals of immigrant rights advocates' sanctuary cities movement—without risking citizen lawsuits. The "show me your papers" segment of Section 2 requires local law enforcement officers to make a "reasonable attempt . . . to determine the immigration status" of someone they stop, detain, or arrest if officers have a "reasonable suspicion" that the person is undocumented. This was the most controversial section of the law and the section that most galvanized rights movement advocates after SB 1070 passed. Immigrant rights advocates argued that it would encourage law enforcement officers to racially profile all Latinx people in Arizona, regardless of immigration status, in the process of locating undocumented immigrants (Seldon et al. 2011; SB 1070 [2010] The Support Our Law Enforcement and Safe Neighborhoods Act, Forty-Ninth Legislature, Second Regular Session).

63. SB 1070 (2010) The Support Our Law Enforcement and Safe Neighborhoods Act, Forty-Ninth Legislature, Second Regular Session.

64. The quotes used in this paragraph all came from testimony on SB 1070 given at the Arizona legislature's Committee on Public Safety and Human Services. All direct quotations were transcribed by the author after reviewing video available on the state legislature's website. Committee on Public Safety and Human Services, "Video Testimony: SB 1070," Arizona Senate, January 20, 2020.

65. Pew 2010.

66. Riccardi 2010.

67. ¡Alto Arizona! 2010.

68. ¡Alto Arizona! 2010. Section 287(g) is a part of the federal Immigration and Nationality Act that provides for the creation of programs that foster partnerships between local and federal law enforcement, essentially allowing local departments to carry out federal immigration laws. Sheriff Joe Arpaio's Maricopa County Sheriff's Office (MCSO) operated a 287(g) program with the federal government between 2007 and 2011. In 2011, the US Department of Homeland Security, under the leadership of former Arizona governor Jan Brewer, revoked the MCSO's 287(g) authority (Stern 2011, Rivas 2011). This followed a US Department of Justice investigation, which determined that the MCSO was engaging in discriminatory practices in violation of the 1964 Civil Rights Act under Sheriff Arpaio's leadership, and the initiation of a civil rights lawsuit, *Melendres v. Arpaio*, which eventually found that the MCSO engaged in racial profiling and

unlawful traffic stops of Latinxs (*Melendres v. Arpaio* 989 F.Supp.2d 822 [D. Ariz. 2013]; US Department of Justice 2010).

69. Secure Communities was another federal program that linked local law enforcement with federal immigration authorities. It allowed local law enforcement to share digital fingerprints from everyone booked into local jails with federal immigration authorities. Federal immigration officials could then review the shared digital fingerprint data to identify and deport undocumented immigrants. Secure Communities was replaced by the Priority Enforcement Program (PEP) in 2015 (US Immigration and Customs Enforcement 2016; Associated Press 2014).

70. *Arizona v. United States* 567 US 387 (2012).

71. Scherer 2012, Weigel 2012.

72. Fitz and Kelley 2010.

73. State Senator Pearce  was involved in a scandal that involved the failure to report receiving $40,000 in gifts from Fiesta Bowl officials (Lacey and Seelye 2011, Roberts 2011).

74. Lacey and Seelye 2011, Thomason et al. 2011, Weiner 2011.

75. Beard Rau 2014.

Chapter 3

1. The paradoxical effects of political movement formation resonate with scholarship that focuses on shared ideology, political threats, and culturally resonant framing strategies (Dorf and Tarrow 2014; Cornfield and McCammon 2010; Benford and Snow 2000; Benford 1997; McAdam, McCarthy, and Zald 1996; Zald 1996). There are very few systematic, empirical studies that examine movement dynamics across cases, movements, and time (Benford 1997: 411–412). For this reason, scholarship that examines how political movements form often obscures how power relations shape movements (Feree 2003, Steinberg 1999, Ellingson 1995). As a result, the important roles that marginalized constituencies within political movements play in movement formation and expansion are frequently overlooked.

2. Interviewees' discussions of the importance of opponents in the formation of collective narratives are aligned with LGBTQ and political movement scholarship which argues that opponents play a prominent role in movement activism and that shared ideology and political threats are factors that contribute to coalition formation (Dorf and Tarrow 2014; Cornfield and McCammon 2010; Isaac 2010; McCammon and Van Dyke 2010; Fetner 2008).

3. As discussed earlier, Proposition 300 was a referendum that passed by popular vote in Arizona in 2006; it prohibited college students who are unable to prove that they are documented residents from receiving state financial aid for college (McKinley 2008).

4. One-to-one conversations are considered an essential element in union organizing. This is quickly apparent in the online organizing materials of three prominent unions: the Service Employees International Union (SEIU), the American Federation of Labor and Congress of Industrial Organizations (AFL-CIO), and the American Federation of Teachers (AFT) (SEIU, *The Complete Stewards Manual*; AFT, *Why One-to-One Communication Is Essential to Effective Organizing*; AFL-CIO, "FAQs about the AFL-CIO Organizing Institute").

5. The DREAM Act (the Development, Relief, and Education for Alien Minors Act) was a federal bill that would have created a pathway to citizenship for some undocumented people who arrived in the US as children. It failed to pass in 2010 largely due to opposition from Republicans in Congress and, most notably, Senator John McCain of Arizona, who had supported similar legislation in the 2000s (Ye Hee Lee 2016, Hing 2010). Undocumented people who would have qualified for this act adopted the name DREAMers during advocacy efforts in 2010.

6. Goth 2015; MovePHX, "List of Supporters."

7. Thornburgh 2010.

8. Alonzo 2014.

9. Because State Senator Quezada is a public official who gave a nonconfidential interview, his real name is used.

10. Sheriff Joe Arpaio was the sheriff of Maricopa County, Arizona, during this study. He is world renowned as America's "toughest sheriff" and instituted a wide range of anti-immigrant policies within the Maricopa County Sheriff's Department, including raids of local businesses in order to locate undocumented immigrants (Kiefer 2015). In one incident in 2008, a "swarm of 230 law officers" descended upon the streets of Mesa, Arizona, in order to round up undocumented people (Scarborough et al. 2008). *Melendres v. Arpaio*, a federal civil rights lawsuit filed by Latinx and immigrant community members in Arizona with the help of the ACLU, recently found that Sheriff Arpaio has engaged in racial profiling and unlawful traffic stops of Latinxs. Former state senator Russell Pearce orchestrated SB 1070 in 2010, which was signed by then governor Jan Brewer.

11. Mananzala and Spade 2008. The next section describes in more detail how the divide between mainstream and marginalized communities epitomized by the Nonprofit Industrial Complex impacts coalition building.

12. Puar 2014: 78; see also Hancock 2016, Strolovitch 2007.

13. Cházaro 2016, Parker 2014, Parker and Martin 2013, Johnson 2009.

14. National Day Laborer Organizing Network 2014.

15. Cházaro 2016; Bacon 2013, 2015; #Not1More 2014.

16. Both the expanded DACA and DAPA programs were never fully

implemented. Republican-led states challenged the programs' constitutionality in *Texas v. United States*, an appellate case that declared the immigration relief offered by the programs unconstitutional. Shortly before the 2016 election of Donald Trump, the US Supreme Court, left with an even number of justices after the death of Justice Antonin Scalia, deadlocked over the case, preventing the Obama administration from implementing these programs before the end of his term (*Texas v. United States* 787 F.3d 733 [5th Cir. 2015]; American Immigration Council 2016; Liptak and Shear 2016).

   17. Strolovitch 2007.

Chapter 4

   1. Merry 2006.
   2. Merry 2006: 192–194.
   3. Merry 2006: 194.
   4. Ayoub 2016; Tarrow 2005.
   5. Cho et al. 2013: 787.
   6. Hancock 2016; Cho et al. 2013; Crenshaw 1991, 1989; Collins 1989.
   7. Reddy 2011, Albiston 2009, Kandaswamy 2008, Bagenstos 2006, Brown 1995.
   8. Murib 2015; Chávez 2013; Stone 2012: chapter 6; Spade 2015; Puar 2011, 2007; Eng 2010; Duggan 2003; Yoshino 2000; Harris 1993.
   9. Luft and Ward 2009: 33.
   10. Tungohan 2016, Montoya 2013, Doetsch-Kidder 2012, Weldon 2011, Townsend-Bell 2011, Strolovitch 2007, Ernst 2010, Kurtz 2002, Cohen 1999.
   11. Strolovitch 2007.
   12. Strolovitch 2007: 192, Levi and Murphy 2006.
   13. See also Spade 2015, Arkles et al. 2010.
   14. Strolovitch 2007, Cohen 1999.
   15. See, e.g., Arkles et al. 2010, Gan 2007, Vaid 1995.
   16. Geidner 2015.
   17. Geidner 2015.
   18. Brydum 2013.
   19. The 2014 attempts to expand DACA and create a new DAPA program for the parents of those who qualified for DACA ultimately failed to get implemented before President Obama left office. These programs were attempts to expand the DACA program, created in 2012, which enabled certain people who arrived in the US as children without documentation to qualify for work authorization and deferred action from deportation proceedings for a period of two years (US Citizenship and Immigration Services 2017).
   20. Rupert 2014.

Conclusion

1. Hancock 2011; see also Sameh 2014, Yuval-Davis 2012, Collins 1999.

2. Hancock 2011: 65.

3. Collins 1999: 236–237, Yuval-Davis 2012.

4. Skocpol 2016.

5. Hermans 2014, Askini 2014, "Transgender Health Care Exclusions No Longer Permissible in Washington State" 2014.

6. *Legal Voice* 2015, Coalition for Inclusive Healthcare 2015.

7. O'Leary and Sprigg 2015.

8. Shapiro 2016, Yan 2016.

9. Holden 2016.

10. Brownstone and Garland 2016.

11. Herz 2016.

12. Senate floor debate (2016, February 10) "Senate Floor Debate: SB 6443." Video from TVW. Washington State Senate.

13. Ryan 2017.

14. McCoy 2006; Sailor 2015a, 2015b; Shapiro 2016.

15. American Civil Liberties Union Washington 2017.

16. See, e.g., Brownstone 2017, O'Sullivan 2017.

17. Spade 2015.

18. *One Arizona* 2017.

19. CityofPhoenixAZ 2015, Hogan 2015.

20. Gardiner 2016, City of Phoenix 2016.

21. Beard Rau 2016.

22. Gardiner 2017a.

23. Boehm 2018.

24. Gardiner 2017a, 2017b.

25. Puente Movement 2017.

26. Ollstein 2016.

27. Living La Vida Jota 2016.

28. Sweet 2018, Witt 2018.

29. "Florida Student Emma Gonzalez to Lawmakers and Gun Advocates: 'We Call BS'" 2018, Klas 2018, McLaughlin and Yan 2018, *"Parkland Students Meet with Florida's Legislative Leaders"* 2018.

30. Mayo-Adam 2018, Scherer 2018.

31. Witt 2018.

32. Blythe 2018, Ranii 2016. The sections of HB2 that prevented people from using restrooms that conform with their gender identity was repealed in 2017. However, the replacement bill still allowed for discrimination against trans people (Hannah and McLaughlin 2017). In 2019, a federal court approved a

settlement agreement between the Democratic governor of North Carolina and transgender plaintiffs who challenged the replacement bill that approved trans people's right to use the restrooms that conform with their gender identity (Associated Press 2019).

33. Aronoff 2018, Bidgood 2018, "A Year after the Teacher Walkout, a Timeline of Arizona's #RedForEd Movement" (2019), Russakoff 2018.

34. Jacobson 2018.

35. Thompson 2018, Tumulty 2018.

36. Goldstein 2019.

Appendix 1

1. Logue 2015

Appendix 2

1. Interviews are lightly edited to eliminate excessive words (i.e., "yeah," "like," "um," and "that") and to explain acronyms and references to legislation used by interviewees in order to facilitate reading. Interviewees and other private individuals they referred to have been given pseudonyms to preserve anonymity.

2. Jayapal and Godoy 2012.

3. Büthe and Jacobs 2015, Showden and Majic 2014.

# REFERENCES

Adam, Erin (2017) "Intersectional Coalitions: The Paradoxes of Rights-Based Movement Building in LGBTQ and Immigrant Communities," *Law & Society Review* 51 (1), 132–167.

Águila, Jaime R. (2013) "Immigration and Politics: Arizona Then and Now," *Aztlán: A Journal of Chicano Studies* 38, 131–149.

Albiston, Catherine (2009) "Institutional Inequality," *Wisconsin Law Review* 2009 (5), 1093–1167.

Alonzo, Monica (2014, March 19) "SB 1062 Was the Best Thing to Happen to Arizona's LGBT Community," *Phoenix New Times*. Available online at: http://www.phoenixnewtimes.com/news/sb-1062-was-the-best-thing-to-happen-for-arizonas-lgbt-community-6653581 (Accessed January 18, 2017).

¡Alto Arizona! (2010) "Arizona Boycott." Available online at: http://www.altoarizona.com/az-boycott.html (Accessed March 22, 2017).

American Civil Liberties Union (1999, July 29) "CA's Anti-Immigrant Proposition 187 Is Voided, Ending State's Five Year Battle with ACLU, Rights Groups." Press release. Available online at: https://www.aclu.org/press-releases/cas-anti-immigrant-proposition-187-voided-ending-states-five-year-battle-aclu-rights?redirect=immigrants-rights/cas-anti-immigrant-proposition-187-voided-ending-states-five-year-battle-aclu-righ (Accessed February 21, 2017).

American Civil Liberties Union Washington (2017) "Victory: Initiative Attempting to Roll Back Protections for Transgender Washingtonians Defeated Again." Press release. Available online at: https://www.aclu-wa.org/pages/victory-initiative-attempting-roll-back-protections-transgender-washingtonians-defeated-again (Accessed August 19, 2019)

American Civil Liberties Union Washington (2009, December 8) "Organizations for Communities of Color Endorse Referendum 71." Press release. Available online at: https://aclu-wa.org/news/organizations-communities-color-endorse-referendum-71 (Accessed February 21, 2017).

American Federation of Labor and Congress of Industrial Organizations (AFL-CIO), "FAQs about the AFL-CIO Organizing Institute." Available online at:

http://www.aflcio.org/Get-Involved/Become-a-Union-Organizer/Organizing-Institute/FAQs-about-the-AFL-CIO-Organizing-Institute (Accessed January 18, 2017).

American Federation of Teachers (AFT), *Why One-to-One Communication Is Essential to Effective Organizing*. Available online at: http://www.aft.org/sites/default/files/preparing_building_reps_for_the_organizing_conversation.pdf (Accessed January 18, 2017).

American Immigration Council (2016, April 11) *Special Report: Defending DAPA and Expanded DACA before the Supreme Court*. Available online at: https://www.americanimmigrationcouncil.org/research/defending-dapa-and-expanded-daca-supreme-court (Accessed January 25, 2017).

Amira, Dan (2013, January 21) "The Eight Current Members of Congress Who Voted against Martin Luther King Jr. Day," *New York Magazine*. Available online at: http://nymag.com/daily/intelligencer/2013/01/voted-against-mlk-day-mccain-hatch-grassley-shelby.html (Accessed March 13, 2017).

Andersen, Ellen Ann (2006) *Out of the Closets and into the Courts: Legal Opportunity Structure and Gay Rights Litigation*. Ann Arbor: University of Michigan Press.

Andrew, Mike (2009, October 2) "An Injury to One Is an Injury to All—Organized Labor Mobilizes for Referendum 71," *Seattle Gay News*. Available online at: http://sgn.org/sgnnews37_40/page3.cfm (Accessed February 22, 2017).

Archibold, Randal C. (2006, May 2) "Immigrants Take to Streets in Show of US Strength," *New York Times*. Available online at http://www.nytimes.com/2006/05/02/us/02immig.html (Accessed April 25, 2017).

Arizona Secretary of State (2008a) "2008 General Election Results: Proposition 102." Available online at: http://apps.azsos.gov/results/2008/general/BM102.htm (Accessed March 20, 2017).

Arizona Secretary of State (2008b) "Arizona 2008 Ballot Propositions: Proposition 102," *2008 General Election Pamphlet*. Available online at: http://apps.azsos.gov/election/2008/info/PubPamphlet/english/Prop102.htm (Accessed March 20, 2017).

Arizona Secretary of State (2006a) "2006 General Election Results: Proposition 300." Available online at: http://apps.azsos.gov/results/2006/general/BM300.htm (Accessed March 20, 2017).

Arizona Secretary of State (2006b) "2006 General Election Results: Proposition 107." Available online at: http://apps.azsos.gov/results/2006/general/BM107.htm (Accessed March 20, 2017).

Arizona Secretary of State (2006c) "Arizona 2006 Ballot Propositions: Proposition 107," *2006 General Election Pamphlet*. Available online at: http://apps.azsos.gov/election/2006/info/PubPamphlet/english/prop300.htm (Accessed March 20, 2017).

Arizona Secretary of State (2004a) "Arizona 2004 Ballot Propositions: Proposition 200," *2004 General Election Pamphlet.* Available online at: http://apps. azsos.gov/election/2004/Info/PubPamphlet/english/prop200.pdf (Accessed March 17, 2017).

Arizona Secretary of State (2004b) "2004 General Election Results: Proposition 200." Available online at: http://apps.azsos.gov/results/2004/general/BM200. htm (Accessed March 17, 2017).

Arizona Secretary of State (2000) "2000 General Election Results: Proposition 203." Available online at: http://apps.azsos.gov/results/2000/general/BM203. htm (Accessed March 16, 2017).

Arizona Together (2008) "Supporters: Vote No Again. Trust the People." Available online at: https://web.archive.org/web/20081015111149/http://www. aztogether.org/supporters/ (Accessed March 20, 2017).

Arizona Together (2006) "Our Team: Look Who Opposes Prop 107." Available online at: https://web.archive.org/web/20061114121836/http://www. noprop107.com/supporters/index.cfm (Accessed March 20, 2017).

Arkles, Gabriel, Pooja Gehi, and Elana Redfield (2010) "The Role of Lawyers in Trans Liberation: Building a Movement for Social Change," *Seattle Journal for Social Justice* 8, 579–641.

Aronoff, Kate (2018, March 2) "West Virginia Teachers Are Now Out on a Wildcat Strike. The Labor Movement Should Follow Their Lead," *In These Times.* Available online at: https://inthesetimes.com/working/entry/20955/ west_virginia_teachers_strike_wildcat (Accessed August 26, 2019).

Askini, Danni (2014, June 25) "Victory! Insurance Commissioner: Companies Can't Discriminate against Transgender Washingtonians." Press release. Available online at: http://www.genderjusticeleague.org/victory-insurance-commissioner-companies-cant-discriminate-against-transgender-washingtonians/ (Accessed May 16, 2017).

Associated Press (2019, July 23) "Agreement Affirms North Carolina Transgender Restroom Rights," *NBC News.* Available online at: https://www. nbcnews.com/feature/nbc-out/agreement-affirms-north-carolina-transgender-restroom-rights-n1033046 (Accessed August 19, 2019).

Associated Press (2014, November 21) "Obama Ends Secure Communities Program That Helped Hike Deportations," *NBC News.* Available online at: http://www.nbcnews.com/storyline/immigration-reform/obama-ends-secure-communities-program-helped-hike-deportations-n253541 (Accessed February 20, 2017).

Associated Press (2012, February 14). "Gay Marriage Referendum Renumbered," *Seattle Times.* Available online at: http://www.seattletimes.com/ seattle-news/gay-marriage-referendum-renumbered/ (Accessed February 21, 2017).

Atkins, Gary L. (2003) *Gay Seattle: Stories of Exile and Belonging.* Seattle: University of Washington Press.

Ayoub, Phillip M. (2016) *When States Come Out: Europe's Minorities and the Politics of Visibility*. New York: Cambridge University Press.

Bacon, David (2015, January 5) "Viewpoint: Concerns about Obama's Immigration Announcement. Available online at: http://labornotes.org/blogs/immigration?language=es (Accessed January 24, 2017).

Bacon, David (2013, February 6) "The Dignity Campaign's Alternative Vision for Immigration Reform," *The Nation*. Available online at: https://www.the-nation.com/article/dignity-campaigns-alternative-vision-immigration-reform/ (Accessed January 25, 2017).

Bagenstos, Samuel R. (2006) "The Structural Turn and the Limits of Antidiscrimination Law," *California Law Rev* 94, 1–47.

Baker, Mike (2012, June 6). "Opponents Place Washington Gay Marriage Law on Hold," *Seattle Times*. Available online at: http://www.seattletimes.com/seattle-news/opponents-place-wash-gay-marriage-law-on-hold/ (Accessed February 21, 2017).

Balk, Gene (2014, October 21) "Seattle Is Getting Whiter, Census Finds," *Seattle Times*. Available online at: http://blogs.seattletimes.com/fyi-guy/2014/10/27/seattle-is-getting-whiter-census-finds/ (Accessed May 23, 2017).

Beard Rau, Alia (2017a, February 27) "Anti-Immigrant Group Is behind What Could Be Arizona's Next SB 1070," *Arizona Republic*. Available online at: http://www.azcentral.com/story/news/politics/politicalinsider/2017/02/25/anti-immigration-group-behind-what-could-arizona-next-sb-1070/98376130/ (Accessed March 16, 2017).

Beard Rau, Alia (2017b, February 6) "Anti-LGBT Legislation Gets the Cold Shoulder with the Arizona Legislature. Here's Why," *Arizona Republic*. Available online at: http://www.azcentral.com/story/news/politics/arizona/2017/02/03/3-years-later-arizonas-religious-freedom-bill-sb-1062-still-affects-lgbt-legislation/97305546/ (Accessed March 13, 2017).

Bear Rau, Alia (2016, January 13) "Republican Bill Would Halt Phoenix Plan to Issue IDs to Undocumented Immigrants, Others," *Arizona Republic*. Available online at: http://www.azcentral.com/story/news/arizona/politics/2016/01/13/legislation-would-handcuff-phoenix-id-card-efforts/78748916/ (Accessed May 18, 2017).

Beard Rau, Alia (2014, March 1) "Activist Cathi Herrod a Political Force behind the Scenes," *Arizona Republic*. Available online at: http://archive.azcentral.com/news/politics/articles/20140225activist-cathi-herrod-political-force.html (Accessed March 29, 2017).

Becker, Jo (2015) *Forcing the Spring: Inside the Fight for Marriage Equality*. New York: Penguin Books.

Beltrán, Cristina (2010) *The Trouble with Unity: Latino Politics and the Creation of Identity*. New York: Oxford University Press.

Benford, Robert D. (1997) "An Insider's Critique of the Social Movement Framing Perspective," *Sociological Inquiry* 67, 409–430.

Benford, Robert D., and David A. Snow (2000) "Framing Processes and Social Movements: An Overview and Assessment," *Annual Review of Sociology* 26, 611–639.

Bernstein, Mary, Anna-Maria Marshall, and Scott Barclay (2009). "The Challenge of Law: Sexual Orientation, Gender Identity, and Social Movements," in S. Barclay, M. Bernstein, and A. Marshall, eds., *Queer Mobilizations: LGBT Activists Confront the Law*. New York: New York University Press 1–20.

Bidgood, John (2018, March 6) "West Virginia Teachers' Pay to End Statewide Strike," *New York Times*. Available online at: https://www.nytimes.com/2018/03/06/us/west-virginia-teachers-strike-deal.html (Accessed August 26, 2019).

Blythe, Anne (2018, April 30) "'We Will Continue to Resist.' 5 Years after First Moral Monday, Their Fight Continues," *News & Observer*. Available online at: https://www.newsobserver.com/latest-news/article210185774.html (Accessed January 23, 2019).

Boehm, Jessica (2018, February 12) "Controversial Phoenix ID Cards for Immigrants Dies before It Ever Began," Available online at: https://www.azcentral.com/story/news/local/phoenix/2018/02/12/controversial-phoenix-id-cards-immigrants-dies/308987002/ (Accessed January 22, 2019).

Boucai, Michael (2015) "Glorious Precedents: Why Gay Marriage Was Radical," *Yale Journal of Law and the Humanities* 27, 1–82.

Brewer, Jan (2010, April 23) "Arizona Governor Jan Brewer Explains Signing Nation's Toughest Illegal Immigration Law," *Los Angeles Times*. Available online at: http://latimesblogs.latimes.com/washington/2010/04/jan-brewer-arizona-illegal-immigration.html (Accessed April 25, 2017).

Brown, Wendy (1995) *States of Injury: Power and Freedom in Late Modernity*. Princeton: Princeton University Press.

Brownstone, Sydney (2017, February 14) "Anti-Trans Activists Will Soon Start Gathering Signatures for Their Ballot Initiative," *The Stranger*. Available online at: http://www.thestranger.com/slog/2017/02/14/24870725/anti-trans-activists-will-soon-start-gathering-signatures-for-their-new-ballot-initiative (Accessed February 23, 2017).

Brownstone, Sydney, and Alex Garland (2016, February 16) "Pro- and Anti-Trans Rights Protests Compete within 200 Feet at the State Capitol," *The Stranger*. Available online at: http://www.thestranger.com/blogs/slog/2016/02/15/23573427/pro-and-anti-trans-rights-protests-compete-within-200-feet-at-the-state-capitol (Accessed May 16, 2017).

Brunner, Jim (2011, November 12) "New Effort to Legalize Same-Sex Marriage Begins," *Seattle Times*. Available online at: http://www.seattletimes.com/seattle-news/new-effort-to-legalize-same-sex-marriage-begins/ (Accessed February 21, 2017).

Brydum, Sunnivie (2013, April 1) "HRC and Coalition Apologize for Silenc-

ing Undocumented, Trans Activists at Supreme Court Rally," *The Advocate.* Available online at: http://www.advocate.com/politics/marriage-equal-
ity/2013/04/01/hrc-and-coalition-apologize-silencing-undocumented-trans
(Accessed February 2, 2017).

Bui, Quoctrung (2015, February 23) "50 Years of Shrinking Union Membership, in One Map," *National Public Radio: Planet Money.* Available online
at: http://www.npr.org/sections/money/2015/02/23/385843576/50-years-of-
shrinking-union-membership-in-one-map (Accessed May 23, 2017).

Burstein, Paul (1991) "Legal Mobilization as a Social Movement Tactic: The
Struggle for Equal Employment Opportunity," *American Journal of Sociology* 96 (5), 1201–1225.

Büthe, Tim, and Alan M. Jacobs (2015) "Introduction to the Symposium" in
T. Büthe and A. Jacobs, eds., *Newsletter of the American Political Science
Association Section for Qualitative and Multi-Method Research* 13 (1), 2–8.

Butler, Judith (1990) *Gender Trouble: Feminism and the Subversion of Identity.*
New York: Routledge.

Calavita, Kitty (1996) "The New Politics of Immigration: "Balanced-Budget
Conservatism" and the Symbolism of Proposition 187," *Social Problems* 43,
287–305.

Calmes, Jackie, and Peter Baker (2012, May 9). "Obama Says Same-Sex Marriage Should be Legal," *New York Times.* Available online at: http://www.
nytimes.com/2012/05/10/us/politics/obama-says-same-sex-marriage-should-
be-legal.html (Accessed April 3, 2017).

Campbell, Kristina M. (2011) "The Road to SB 1070: How Arizona Became
Ground Zero for the Immigrants' Rights Movement and the Continuing
Struggle for Latino Civil Rights in America," *Harvard Latino Law Review*
14, 1–21.

Canaday, Margot (2011) *The Straight State: Sexuality and Citizenship in Twenti-
eth-Century America.* Princeton: Princeton University Press.

Cárdenas, Vanessa, Sophia Kerby, and Rachel Wilf (2012, February 28) "Arizona's Demographic Changes: A Look at the State's Emerging Communities
of Color," *Center for American Progress.* Available online at: https://www.
americanprogress.org/issues/poverty/news/2012/02/28/11060/arizonas-demo-
graphic-changes/ (Accessed March 14, 2017).

Cart, Julie (1990, November 8) "It's No Holiday for Arizona: Voters' Rejection
of King Day Causes More Than Just a Lot of Hot Air in the State," *Los
Angeles Times.* Available online at: http://articles.latimes.com/1990-11-18/
sports/sp-6921_1_king-holiday (Accessed March 13, 2017).

Cathcart, Kevin, and Leslie Gabel-Brett (2016) *Love Unites Us: Winning the
Freedom to Marry in America.* New York: New Press.

Chávez, Karma (2013) *Queer Migration Politics: Activist Rhetoric and Coalitional Possibilities.* Champaign: University of Illinois Press.

Cházaro, Angélica (2016) "Challenging the Criminal Alien Paradigm" *UCLA Law Review* 63, 594–664.

Chin, Gabriel J., Carissa Bryne Hessick, and Mark L. Miller (2012) "Arizona Senate Bill 1070: Politics through Immigration Law," in O. Santa Ana and C. González de Bustamante, eds., *Arizona Firestorm: Global Immigration Realities, National Media, and Provincial Politics*. New York and Plymouth: Rowman & Littlefield 73–96.

Cho, Sumi, Kimberlé Williams Crenshaw, and Leslie McCall (2013) "Toward a Field of Intersectionality Studies: Theory, Applications, and Praxis," *Signs: Journal of Women in Culture and Society* 38, 785–810.

Chokshi, Niraj (2014, February 3) "Eight U.S. States Have Policies Similar to Russia's Ban on Gay 'Propaganda,'" *Washington Post*. Available online at: https://www.washingtonpost.com/blogs/govbeat/wp/2014/02/03/eight-u-s-states-have-policies-similar-to-russias-ban-on-gay-propaganda/?utm_term=.f86892bcac41 (Accessed March 14, 2017).

Christianson, Scott (1998) *With Liberty for Some: 500 Years of Imprisonment in America*. Boston: Northeastern University Press.

Chua, Lynette J. (2019) *The Politics of Love in Myanmar: LGBT Mobilization and Human Rights as a Way of Life*. Palo Alto: Stanford University Press.

Chua, Lynette J. (2014) *Mobilizing Gay Singapore: Rights and Resistance in an Authoritarian State*. Singapore: National University of Singapore Press.

City of Phoenix (2016, August 31) "Phoenix City Council Approves Secondary Municipal ID and Unified City Services Card." Press release. Available online at: https://www.phoenix.gov/news/citymanager/1438 (Accessed May 17, 2017).

CityofPhoenixAZ (2015, November 18) "Phoenix City Council Formal Meeting - November 18, 2015," *YouTube*. Available online at: https://www.youtube.com/watch?v=6e_WKKNGfHw (Accessed May 18, 2017).

Coalition for Inclusive Healthcare (2014, July 31) "Public Employees Benefits Board Implements Transgender Inclusive Healthcare." Press release. Available online at: http://www.pridefoundation.org/wp-content/uploads/2014/07/7.31.14-Coalition-for-Inclusive-Healthcare-PEBB-statement-FINAL.pdf (Accessed May 16, 2017).

Cohen, Cathy J. (1999) *Boundaries of Blackness: AIDS and the Breakdown of Black Politics*. Chicago: University of Chicago Press.

Collins, Patricia Hill (1999) *Black Feminist Thought: Knowledge, Consciousness, and the Politics of Empowerment*. New York: Routledge.

Collins, Patricia Hill (1989) "The Social Construction of Black Feminist Thought," *Signs: A Journal of Women in Culture and Society* 14, 745–773.

Confessore, Nicolas (2016, April 29) "Microsoft Will Not Donate to Republicans' Convention," *New York Times*. Available online at: https://www.nytimes.com/politics/first-draft/2016/04/29/microsoft-will-not-donate-money-to-republicans-convention/?_r=0 (Accessed May 23, 2017).

Cornfield, Daniel B., and Holly J. McCammon (2010) "Approaching Merger: The Converging Public Policy Agendas of the AFL and CIO, 1938–1955," in N. Van Dyke and H. McCammon, eds., *Strategic Alliances: Coalition Building and Social Movements*. Minneapolis: University of Minnesota Press 79–98.

Cramer, Renée Ann (2015) *Pregnant with the Stars: Watching and Wanting the Celebrity Baby Bump*. Palo Alto: Stanford University Press.

Crenshaw, Kimberlé (1991) "Mapping the Margins: Intersectionality, Identity Politics, and Violence against Women of Color," *Stanford Law Review* 43, 1241–1299.

Crenshaw, Kimberlé (1989) "Demarginalizing the Intersection of Race and Sex: A Black Feminist Critique of Antidiscrimination Doctrine, Feminist Theory, and Antiracist Politics," *University of Chicago Legal Forum* 8, 139–167.

Cummings, Scott L., and Douglas NeJaime (2010) "Lawyering for Marriage Equality," *UCLA Law Review* 57, 1235–1331.

Dao, James (2004, November 4) "Same-Sex Marriage Issue Key to Some GOP Races," *New York Times*. Available online at: http://www.nytimes.com/2004/11/04/politics/campaign/samesex-marriage-issue-key-to-some-gop-races.html?_r=0 (Accessed April 20, 2017).

Davenport, Sarah (2006) "Battle at Boeing: African Americans and the Campaign for Jobs 1939–1943," Seattle Civil Rights and Labor History Project. Available online at: http://depts.washington.edu/civilr/boeing_battle.htm (Accessed May 23, 2017).

Doetsch-Kidder, Sharon (2012) *Social Change and Intersectional Activism: The Spirit of Social Movement*. London: Palgrave-Macmillan.

De Leon, Virginia (1997, October 22). "I-677 Focuses on Bias Law Would Ban Employment Discrimination Based on Sexual Orientation," *Spokesman Review*. Available online at: http://www.spokesman.com/stories/1997/oct/22/i-677-focuses-on-bias-law-would-ban-employment/ (Accessed February 23, 2017).

Díaz, Elvia, and Robbie Sherwood (2005, June 5) "Proposition 200's Effect Minimal," *Arizona Republic*. Available online at: http://archive.azcentral.com/12news/news/articles/0605Immigration-illegal05-CP.html (Accessed March 17, 2017).

Dorf, Michael, and Sidney Tarrow (2014) "Strange Bedfellows: How an Anticipatory Countermovement Brought Same-Sex Marriage into the Public Arena" *Law & Social Inquiry* 39, 449–473.

Duam, Courtenay W. (2009) "Deciding under the Influence? The "One Hit Wonders" and Organized-Interest Participation in U.S. Supreme Court Gay Rights Litigation," in S. Barclay, M. Bernstein, and A. Marshall, eds., *Queer Mobilizations: LGBT Activists Confront the Law*. New York: New York University Press 76–102.

Duggan, Lisa (2003) *The Twilight of Equality? Neoliberalism, Cultural Politics, and the Attack on Democracy.* Boston: Beacon Press.

Dumm, Thomas L. (1987) *Democracy and Punishment: Disciplinary Origins of the United States.* Madison: University of Wisconsin Press.

Ellingson, Stephen J. (1995) "Understanding the Dialectic Discourse and Collective Action: A Public Debate and Rioting in Antebellum Cincinnati," *American Journal of Sociology* 101, 100–144.

Eng, David L. (2010) *The Feeling of Kinship: Queer Liberalism and the Racialization of Intimacy.* Durham: Duke University Press.

Engel, David M. (1984) "The Oven Bird's Song: Insiders, Outsiders, and Personal Injuries in an American Community," *Law & Society Review* 18, 551–582.

Engel, Stephen M. (2016) *Fragmented Citizens: The Changing Landscape of Gay and Lesbian Lives.* New York: New York University Press.

Epp, Charles R. (1998) *Rights Revolution: Lawyers, Activists, and Supreme Courts in Comparative Perspective.* Chicago: University of Chicago Press.

Epps, Garrett (2011, September 12) "Arizona's Case against the Voting Rights Act," *Atlantic.* Available online at: https://www.theatlantic.com/national/archive/2011/09/arizonas-case-against-the-voting-rights-act/244548/ (Accessed March 13, 2017).

Ernst, Rose (2010) *The Price of Progressive Politics: The Welfare Rights Movement in an Era of Colorblind Racism.* New York: New York University Press.

Eskridge, William N. (2002) *Equality Practice: Civil Unions and the Future of Gay Rights.* New York: Routledge.

Eskridge, William N. (2001) "Identity-Based Social Movements and Public Law," *University of Pennsylvania Law Review* 150, 419–525.

Eskridge, William N. (2000) "No Promo Homo: The Sedimentation of Antigay Discourse and the Channeling Effect of Judicial Review," *New York University Law Review* 75, 1327–1411.

Feree, Myra Marx (2003) "Resonance and Radicalism: Feminist Framing in the Abortion Debates of the United States and Germany," *American Journal of Sociology* 109, 304–344.

Fetner, Tina (2008) *How the Religious Right Shaped Lesbian and Gay Activism.* Minneapolis: University of Minnesota Press.

Fisher, Shauna (2009) "It Takes (at Least) Two to Tango: Fighting with Words in the Conflict Over Same-Sex Marriage," in S. Barclay, M. Bernstein, and A. Marshall, eds., *Queer Mobilizations: LGBT Activists Confront the Law.* New York: New York University Press 231–256.

Fitz, Marshall, and Angela Marie Kelley (2010, November 18) "Stop the Conference: The Economic and Fiscal Consequences of Conference Cancellations Due to Arizona's SB 1070," Center for American Progress. Available online at: https://www.americanprogress.org/issues/immigration/reports/2010/11/18/8657/stop-the-conference/ (Accessed March 29, 2017).

"Florida Student Emma Gonzalez to Lawmakers and Gun Advocates: 'We

Call BS'" (2018, February 17) *CNN*. Available online at: https://www.cnn.com/2018/02/17/us/florida-student-emma-gonzalez-speech/index.html (Accessed August 22, 2019).

Gamson, William A., and David S. Meyer (1996) "Framing Political Opportunity," in D. McAdam, J. D. McCarthy, and M. N. Zald, eds., *Comparative Perspectives on Social Movements: Political Opportunities, Mobilizing Structures, and Cultural Framings*. New York: Cambridge University Press 275–290.

Gan, Jessi (2007) "Still at the Back of the Bus: Sylvia Rivera's Struggle," *Centro Journal* 19, 124–139.

Gardiner, Dustin (2017a, February 21) "Arizona Bill to Block Phoenix ID for Undocumented Immigrants Fails in the Senate," *Arizona Republic*. Available online at: http://www.azcentral.com/story/news/politics/legislature/2017/02/21/arizona-bills-block-phoenix-identification-cards-undocumented-immigrants/98162832/ (Accessed May 18, 2017).

Gardiner, Dustin (2017b, June 7) "Fearing President Donald Trump's Hardline Policies, Immigrant Activists Drop Support of Phoenix ID Card," *Arizona Republic*. Available online at: https://www.azcentral.com/story/news/local/phoenix/2017/06/07/fearing-president-donald-trumps-hard-line-policies-immigrant-activists-drop-support-phoenix-id-card/323201001/ (Accessed January 22, 2019).

Gardiner, Dustin (2016, August 31) "Phoenix Council OKs ID Cards for Undocumented Immigrants," *Arizona Republic*. Available online at: http://www.azcentral.com/story/news/local/phoenix/2016/08/31/phoenix-city-council-id-cards-undocumented/89613748/ (Accessed May 17, 2017).

Geidner, Chris (2015, June 3) "Internal Report: Major Diversity, Organizational Problems at Human Rights Campaign," *BuzzFeed News*. Available online at: https://www.buzzfeed.com/chrisgeidner/internal-report-major-diversity-organizational-problems-at-h?utm_term=.wuDGerBO6#.iaKzmly97 (Accessed February 2, 2017).

Gleeson, Shannon (2012) *Conflicting Commitments: The Politics of Enforcing Immigrant Worker Rights in San Jose and Houston*. Ithaca: Cornell University Press.

Goldberg-Hiller, Jonathan (2004) *The Limits to Union: Same-Sex Marriage and the Politics of Civil Rights*. Ann Arbor: University of Michigan Press.

Goldstein, Dana (2019, February 19) "West Virginia Teachers Walk Out (Again) and Score a Win in Hours," *New York Times*. Available online at: https://www.nytimes.com/2019/02/19/us/teachers-strikes.html (Accessed August 26, 2019).

Goluboff, Risa Lauren (2005) "'Let Economic Equality Take Care of Itself': The NAACP, Labor Litigation, and the Making of Civil Rights in the 1940s," *UCLA Law Review* 52, 1393–1486.

González de Bustamante, Celeste (2012) "Arizona and the Making of a State of

Exclusion, 1912–1912," in Otto Santa Ana and Celeste González de Bustamante, eds., *Arizona Firestorm: Global Immigration Realities, National
Media, and Provincial Politics.* New York and Plymouth: Rowman & Littlefield 19–42.

Goth, Brenna (2015, August 26) "Phoenix Voters Pass Prop. 104 Transit
Tax," *Arizona Republic.* Available online at: http://www.azcentral.com/
story/news/local/phoenix/2015/08/25/phoenix-elections-transit-results-
prop104/32283455/ (Accesses January 18, 2017).

Gottschalk, Marie (2008). "Hiding in Plain Sight: American Politics and the Carceral State," *Annual Review of Political Science* 11, 235–260.

Gregory, James N. (2015) "Seattle's Left Coast Formula," *Dissent.* Available
online at: https://www.dissentmagazine.org/article/seattles-left-coast-formula
(Accessed May 23, 2017).

Gregory, James N. (2009) "Introduction," *Communism in Washington State:
History and Memory.* Available online at: http://depts.washington.edu/lab-
hist/cpproject/ (Accessed May 23, 2017).

Hancock, Ange-Marie (2016) *Intersectionality: An Intellectual History.* New
York: Oxford University Press.

Hancock, Ange-Marie (2011) *Solidarity Politics for Millennials: A Guide to Ending the Oppression Olympics.* New York: Palgrave Macmillan.

Hannah, Jason, and Eliott McLaughlin (2017, March 30) "North Carolina Repeals 'Bathroom Bill," *CNN.* Available online at: https://www.cnn.
com/2017/03/30/politics/north-carolina-hb2-agreement/index.html (Accessed
August 19, 2019).

Harmon Cooley, Amanda (2015) "Constitutional Representations of the Family
in Public Schools: Ensuring Equal Protection Regardless of Parental Sexual
Orientation or Gender Identity," *Ohio State Law Journal* 76, 1007–1050.

Harris, Cheryl I. (1993) "Whiteness as Property," *Harvard Law Review* 106 (8)
1701–1791.

Hendley, Matthew (2014, February 4) "Arizona's Anti-Gay Law Similar to
Russian Law, Yale Professors Say," *Phoenix New Times.* Available online
at: http://www.phoenixnewtimes.com/news/arizonas-anti-gay-law-similar-to-
russian-law-yale-professors-say-6640154 (Accessed March 14, 2017).

Hermans, Kris (2014, June 26) "Breaking News: Victory for Transgender Health
Care Access." Available online at: https://www.pridefoundation.org/break-
ing-news-victory-transgender-healthcare-access/2014/06/ (Accessed May 16,
2017).

Herz, Ansel (2016, February 10) "This Anti-Transgender Bathroom Bill Couldn't
Get through the Republican Controlled State Senate," *The Stranger.* Available online at: http://www.thestranger.com/blogs/slog/2016/02/10/23554000/
this-anti-transgender-bathrom-bill-couldnt-get-through-the-republican-con-
trolled-state-senate (Accessed May 16, 2017).

Hing, Julianne (2010, December 18) "DREAM Act Fails in Senate, 55 to 41,"

*Colorlines.* Available online at: http://www.colorlines.com/articles/dream-act-fails-senate-55-41 (Accessed January 18, 2017).

Hobbs, Frank, and Nicole Stoops (2002) *Demographic Trends in the 20th Century: Census 2000 Special Reports,* US Census Bureau. Available online at: https://www.census.gov/prod/2002pubs/censr-4.pdf (Accessed May 23, 2017).

Holden, Dominic (2016, February 5). "Anti-Transgender Bills in Washington State Look Doomed—for Now," *BuzzFeed News.* Available online at: https://www.buzzfeed.com/dominicholden/anti-transgender-bills-in-washington-state-look-doomed-for-n?utm_term=.cbjdPP9Z#.wb6prrRX (Accessed February 23, 2017).

Hogan, Shana (2015, December 17) "Phoenix Joins Cities in Approving Municipal ID Card," *Phoenix New Times.* Available online at: http://www.phoenixnewtimes.com/news/phoenix-joins-progressive-cities-in-approving-municipal-id-card-7901639 (Accessed May 18, 2017).

HoSang, Daniel Martinez (2010) *Racial Propositions: Ballot Initiatives and the Making of Postwar California.* Oakland: University of California Press.

Huerta, Grace C. (1996) "Implementing AIDS Education: Policies and Practices," *Education Policy Analysis Archives* 4, 1–17.

Hull, Kathleen E. (2004) *Same-Sex Marriage: The Cultural Politics of Love and Law.* New York: Cambridge University Press.

Isaac, Larry (2010) "Policing Capital: Armed Countermovement Coalitions against Labor in Late Nineteenth-Century Industrial Cities," in N. Van Dyke and H. McCammon, eds., *Strategic Alliances: Coalition Building and Social Movements.* Minneapolis: University of Minnesota Press 22–49.

Jacobson, Louis (2018, February 26) "Precedent Says West Virginia Teacher's Strike Isn't Lawful," *In These Times.* Available online at: https://www.politifact.com/truth-o-meter/statements/2018/feb/26/patrick-morrisey/precedent-says-west-virginia-teachers-strike-isnt-/ (Accessed August 26, 2019).

Japanese American Citizens League (2007, September 26). "JACL Supports Marriage Equality." Press release. Available online at: https://jacl.org/jacl-supports-marriage-equality/ (Accessed February 21, 2017).

Jayapal, Pramila, and Angelina Snodgrass Godoy (2012) "The Growing Human Rights Crisis along Washington's Northern Border," OneAmerica and University of Washington Center for Human Rights. Available online at: https://jsis.washington.edu/humanrights/wp-content/uploads/sites/22/2017/02/EX-ECSUMM_northernborder-FINAL.pdf (Accessed January 23, 2020).

Johnson, Eric (2005) "Proposition 203: A Critical Metaphor Analysis," *Bilingual Research Journal* 29, 69–84.

Johnson, Jeff (2017, January 27) "Union Membership Is Up Again in Washington State," *The Stand.* Available online at: http://www.thestand.org/2017/01/union-membership-up-again-in-washington/ (Accessed May 23, 2017).

Johnson, Kevin R. (2009) "Comprehensive Immigration Reform Symposium:

Problems, Possibilities and Pragmatic Solutions: Ten Guiding Principles for Truly Comprehensive Immigration Reform: A Blueprint," *Wayne Law Review* 55, 1599–1639.

Kandaswamy, Priya (2008). "State Austerity and the Racial Politics of Same-Sex Marriage in the U.S.," *Sexualities* 11, 706–725.

Kaplan, Roberta, and Lisa Dickey (2015) *Then Comes Marriage: United States v. Windsor and the Defeat of DOMA.* New York: Norton.

Kaur, Harmeet (2019, April 11) "Arizona Just Repealed a Law That Banned Schools from Promoting a 'Homosexual Lifestyle,'" *CNN.* Available online at: https://www.cnn.com/2019/04/11/us/arizona-repeals-anti-lgbtq-law-trnd/index.html (Accessed September, 25 2019).

Keck, Thomas M. (2009) "Beyond Backlash: Assessing the Impact of Judicial Decisions on LGBT Rights," *Law & Society Review* 43, 151–186.

Kiefer, Michael (2015, November 9) "Sheriff Joe Arpaio Has Always Done It His Way," *Arizona Republic.* Available online At: http://www.azcentral.com/story/news/arizona/investigations/2015/09/11/sheriff-joe-arpaio-legacy/71888720/ (Accessed March 14, 2017).

Klarman, Michael J. (2014) *From the Closet to the Altar: Courts, Backlash, and the Struggle for Same-Sex Marriage.* New York: Oxford University Press.

Klarman, Michael J. (2004) *From Jim Crow to Civil Rights: The Supreme Court and the Struggle for Racial Equality.* New York: Oxford University Press.

Klas, Mary Ellen (2018, March 11) "Parkland Students and Parents Decide 'This Time Must Be Different.' And It Was," *Miami Herald.* Available online at: https://www.miamiherald.com/news/politics-government/state-politics/article204511654.html (Accessed August 22, 2019).

Kluger, Richard (2004) *Simple Justice: The History of Brown v. Board of Education and Black America's Struggle for Equality.* New York: Vintage Books.

Kurtz, Sharon (2002) *Workplace Justice: Organizing Multi-Identity Movements.* Minneapolis: University of Minnesota Press.

Lacey, Marc, and Katharine Q. Seelye (2011, November 10) "Recall Election Claims Arizona Anti-Immigrant Champion," *New York Times.* Available online at: http://www.nytimes.com/2011/11/10/us/politics/russell-pearce-arizonas-anti-immgration-champion-is-recalled.html (Accessed March 14, 2017).

La Corte, Rachel (2009, May 4). "Challenge to Domestic Partnership Expansion Filed," *Seattle Times.* Available online at: http://www.seattletimes.com/seattle-news/challenge-to-domestic-partnership-expansion-filed/ (Accessed February 21, 2017).

Legal Voice (2015, August 18) "Winning Inclusive Medicaid Coverage in Washington State." Available online at: http://www.legalvoice.org/single-post/2015/08/18/Winning-Inclusive-Medicaid-Coverage-in-Washington-State (Accessed May 16, 2017).

Levi, Margaret, and Gillian H. Murphy (2006) "Coalitions of Contention: The Case of the WTO Protests in Seattle," *Political Studies* 54, 651–670.

Levitsky, Sandra R. (2007) "Niche Activism: Constructing a Unified Movement Identity in a Heterogeneous Organizational Field," *Mobilization* 12, 271–286.

Liptak, Adam, and Michael Shear (2016, June 23) "Supreme Court Tie Blocks Obama Immigration Plan." Available online at: https://www.nytimes.com/2016/06/24/us/supreme-court-immigration-obama-dapa.html (Accessed January 25, 2017).

Living La Vida Jota (2016, November 4) "Selena Drag- Vota Con Esta Cumbia!" *YouTube*. Available online at: https://www.youtube.com/watch?v=RMaGSlDIIok (Accessed May 18, 2017).

Locke, Gary, and James Rigby (1997, October 30) "Pro/Con—Initiative 677: Gay Rights," *Seattle Times*. Available online at: http://community.seattletimes.nwsource.com/archive/?date=19971030&slug=2569266 (Accessed February 23, 2017).

Logue, Josh (2015, December 8) "Latina/o/x." *Inside Higher Ed.* Available online at: https://www.insidehighered.com/news/2015/12/08/students-adopt-gender-nonspecific-term-latinx-be-more-inclusive (Accessed December 2, 2019).

Lovell, George I. (2012). *This Is Not Civil Rights: Discovering Rights Talk in 1939 America.* Chicago: University of Chicago Press.

Luft, Rachel E., and Jane Ward (2009) "Toward an Intersectionality Just out of Reach: Confronting Challenges to Intersectionality as Practice," *Advances in Gender Research: Special Volume* 13, 9–37.

Lynch, Mona (2010) *Sunbelt Justice: Arizona and the Transformation of American Punishment.* Palo Alto: Stanford University Press.

Magaña, Lisa (2013) "SB 1070 and Negative Social Constructions of Latino Immigrants in Arizona," *Aztlán: A Journal of Chicano Studies* 38, 151–161.

Majic, Samantha (2014) *Sex Work Politics: From Protest to Service Provision.* Philadelphia: University of Pennsylvania Press.

Mananzala, Rickke, and Dean Spade (2008) "The Non-Profit Industrial Complex and Trans Resistance," *Sexuality Research and Social Policy* 5, 53–71.

Mansbridge, Jane R. (1986) *Why We Lost the ERA.* Chicago: University of Chicago Press.

Mapes, Lynda V. (1998, February 7). "Gay Marriage Ban Coasts into Law—Harried Democrats Help Override Veto," *Seattle Times*. Available online at: http://community.seattletimes.nwsource.com/archive/?date=19980207&slug=2733005 (Accessed February 20, 2017).

Marshall, Anna-Maria, and Scott Barclay (2003) "In Their Own Words: How Ordinary People Construct the Legal World," *Law & Social Inquiry* 28, 617–628.

Mayo-Adam, Erin (2018, March 15) "Yes, the Parkland Kids Could Change U.S. Gun Policy. Here's What It Would Take," *Washington Post*. Available online at: https://www.washingtonpost.com/news/monkey-cage/wp/2018/03/15/yes-the-parkland-kids-could-change-u-s-gun-policy-heres-what-it-would-take/ (Accessed August 22, 2019).

McAdam, Doug (1999). *Political Process and the Development of Black Insurgency, 1930–1970*, 2nd ed. Chicago: University of Chicago Press.

McAdam, Doug, John D. McCarthy, and Mayer N. Zald (1996) "Introduction: Opportunities, Mobilizing Structures, and Framing Processes—Toward a Synthetic, Comparative Perspective on Social Movements," in D. McAdam, J. D. McCarthy, and M. N. Zald, eds., *Comparative Perspectives on Social Movements: Political Opportunities, Mobilizing Structures, and Cultural Framings*. New York: Cambridge University Press 1–20.

McAdam, Doug, Sidney Tarrow, and Charles Tilly (1996) "To Map Contentious Politics," *Mobilization: An International Journal* 1, 17–34.

McCammon, Holly J., and Nella Van Dyke (2010) "Applying Qualitative Comparative Analysis to Empirical Studies of Social Movement Coalition Formation," in N. Van Dyke and H. J. McCammon, eds., *Strategic Alliances: Coalition Building and Social Movements*. Minneapolis: University of Minnesota Press 292–315.

McCann, Michael (1994) *Rights at Work: Pay Equity Reform and the Politics of Legal Mobilization*. Chicago: University of Chicago Press.

McCoy, Danny (2006, February 22). "Washington Campaign against Gay Discrimination," *Pink News*. Available online at: http://www.pinknews. co.uk/2006/02/22/washington-campaign-against-gay-discrimination/ (Accessed February 23, 2017).

McDonnell, Patrick (1999, July 29) "Davis Won't Appeal Proposition 187 Ruling, Ending Court Battles," *Los Angeles Times*. Available online at: http:// articles.latimes.com/1999/jul/29/news/mn-60700 (Accessed March 17, 2017).

McDonnell, Patrick (1997, November 15) "Proposition 187 Found Unconstitutional by Federal Judge," *Los Angeles Times*. Available online at: http://articles.latimes.com/1997/nov/15/news/mn-54053 (Accessed March 17, 2017).

McKenna, Kevin, "Special Section: LGBTQ Activism in Seattle History Project," Seattle Civil Rights and Labor History Project. Available online at: http:// depts.washington.edu/civilr/lgbtq_intro.htm (Accessed May 23, 2017).

McKinley, Jesse (2008, January 27) "Arizona Law Takes Toll on Nonresident Students," *New York Times*. Available online at: http://www.nytimes. com/2008/01/27/us/27tuition.html (Accessed January 20, 2017).

McLaughlin, Eliott, and Holly Yan (2018, February 22) "Florida Massacre Survivors Chant 'Vote Them Out' as Students Nationwide Walk Out in Solidarity," *CNN*. Available online at: https://www.cnn.com/2018/02/21/us/florida-school-shooting/index.html (August 22, 2019).

Mello, Joseph (2016). *The Courts, the Ballot Box, and Gay Rights: How Our Governing Institutions Shape the Same-Sex Marriage Debate*. Lawrence: University of Kansas Press.

Melo, Tania (2014). *An Institutionalist Love Story: Marriage Equality in Wash-*

*ington State*, conference paper presented at the annual meeting of the Western Political Science Association.

Merry, Sally Engel (2006) *Human Rights and Gender Violence: Translating International Law into Local Justice.* Chicago: University of Chicago Press.

Merry, Sally Engel (2003) "Rights Talk and the Experience of Law: Implementing Women's Human Rights to Protection from Violence," *Human Rights Quarterly* 25, 343–381.

Merry, Sally Engle (2000) *Colonizing Hawai'i: The Cultural Power of Law.* Princeton: Princeton University Press.

Meyer, David S., and Debra C. Minkoff (2004). "Conceptualizing Political Opportunity," *Social Forces* 82, 1457–1492.

Montoya, Celeste (2013) *From Global to Grassroots: The European Union, Transnational Advocacy, and Combating Violence against Women.* Oxford: Oxford University Press.

MovePHX, "List of Supporters." Available online at: https://web.archive.org/web/20150905124538/http://movephx.org/phoenician-support-movephx/supporters/ (Accessed January 18, 2017).

Murakami, Kery (1997, November 5) "Initiative 677—Gay-Rights Issue Loses; Foes See an Opening," *Seattle Times.* Available online at: http://community.seattletimes.nwsource.com/archive/?date=19971105&slug=2570520 (Accessed February 23, 2017).

Murib, Zein (2017) "Rethinking GLBT as a Political Category in U.S. Politics," in M. Brettschneider, S. Burgess, and C. Keating, eds., *LGBTQ Politics: A Critical Reader.* New York: New York University Press 14–33.

Murib, Zein (2015) "Transgender: Examining an Emerging Identity Using Three Political Processes," *Politics Groups and Identities* 2, 381–397.

National Day Laborer Organizing Network (2014 September 6) "Initial Reaction to Delay of Immigration Action." Press release. Available online at: http://www.ndlon.org/en/pressroom/press-releases/item/1087-reactions-delay-immigrant-rights-org (Accessed January 24, 2017).

NeJaime, Douglas (2014) "Before Marriage: The Unexplored History of Non-marital Recognition and Its Relationship to Marriage" *California Law Review* 102 (1), 87–172.

Nesbet, Barbara, and Sherilyn K. Sellgren (1995) "California's Proposition 187: A Painful History Repeats Itself," *Journal of International Law & Policy* 1, 153–175.

Nielsen, Beth (2004) *License to Harass: Law, Hierarchy, and Offensive Public Speech.* Princeton: Princeton University Press.

#Not1More (2014 April 10) "Blue Ribbon Commission Report on Deportation Review." Available online at: http://www.notonemoredeportation.com/2014/04/10/not1morebrc/ (Accessed January 24, 2017).

O'Donnell, Catherine (2011, October 31). "Washington Poll: Liquor Initiative Leads, Road Toll Measures Too Close to Call." Available online at: http://

www.washington.edu/news/2011/10/31/washington-poll-liquor-initiative-leads-road-tolls-measure-too-close-to-call/ (Accessed February 21, 2017).

O'Hagan, Maureen (2013, December 2) "Unlikely Allies: Immigration, LGBT Groups Seek Equality," *Truthout*. Available online at: http://www.truth-out.org/news/item/20366-unlikely-allies-immigration-lgbt-groups-seek-equality (Accessed February 21, 2017).

O'Leary, Dale, and Peter Sprigg (2015) *Understanding and Responding to the Transgender Movement*. Issue analysis, Family Research Council. Available online at: http://downloads.frc.org/EF/EF15F45.pdf (Accessed May 16, 2017).

Ollstein, Alice Miranda (2016, November 6) "The Downfall of Joe Arpaio," *Think Progress*. Available online at: https://thinkprogress.org/the-downfall-of-joe-arpaio-e3d63b1741e5 (Accessed May 18, 2017).

One Arizona, "Values." Available online at: http://www.onearizona.org/values (Accessed May 17, 2017)

O'Sullivan, Joseph (2017, January 9) "Groups Pushing Again to Repeal Washington State Transgender Bathrooms Rule," *Seattle Times*. Available online at: http://www.seattletimes.com/seattle-news/politics/group-pushing-again-to-repeal-state-transgender-bathrooms-rule/ (Accessed February 23, 2017).

Parker, Ashley, and Jonathan Martin (2013, June 27) "Senate, 68 to 32, Passes Overhaul for Immigration," *New York Times*. Available online at: http://www.nytimes.com/2013/06/28/us/politics/immigration-bill-clears-final-hurdle-to-senate-approval.html (Accessed January 25, 2017).

Parker, Christopher (2014, August 4) "The (Real) Reason Why the House Won't Pass Comprehensive Immigration Reform," Brookings Institute. Available online at: https://www.brookings.edu/blog/fixgov/2014/08/04/the-real-reason-why-the-house-wont-pass-comprehensive-immigration-reform/ (Accessed January 25, 2017).

"Parkland Students Meet with Florida's Legislative Leaders" (2018, February 21) *South Florida Sun Sentinel*. Available online at: https://www.sun-sentinel.com/local/broward/parkland/florida-school-shooting/95985061-132.html (Accessed August 22, 2019).

Passel, Jeffrey S., and Roberto Suro (2005, September 27) "Rise, Peak, and Decline: Trends in U.S. Immigration 1992–2004," Pew Research Center. Available online at: http://www.pewhispanic.org/2005/09/27/rise-peak-and-decline-trends-in-us-immigration-1992-2004/ (Accessed March 14, 2017).

Pestritto, Ronald J. (2000) *Founding the Criminal Law: Punishment and Political Thought in the Origins of America*. DeKalb: Northern Illinois University Press.

Pew Research Center (2016, May 12) "Changing Attitudes on Gay Marriage." Available online at: http://www.pewforum.org/2016/05/12/changing-attitudes-on-gay-marriage/ (Accessed February 21, 2017).

Pew Research Center (2010, May 12) "Broad Approval for New Arizona Immigration Law: Democrats Divided, but Support Key Provisions." Available online at: http://www.people-press.org/2010/05/12/broad-approval-for-new-arizona-immigration-law/ (Accessed March 22, 2017).

Pinello, Daniel (2006) *America's Struggle for Same-Sex Marriage*. New York: Cambridge University Press.

Pitzi, Mary Jo (2016, December 29) "Court: Arizona's New Minimum Wage Law Takes Effect Sunday," *Arizona Republic*. Available online at: http://www.az-central.com/story/news/politics/arizona/2016/12/29/arizona-supreme-court-refuses-to-block-minimum-wage-boost/95963314/ (Accessed April 25, 2017).

Piven, Frances Fox, and Cloward Richard A. (1979) *Poor People's Movements: Why They Succeed, How They Fail*. New York: Vintage Books.

Price, Kimala (2017) "Queering Reproductive Justice: Toward a Theory and Praxis for Building Intersectional Alliances," in M. Brettschneider, S. Burgess, and C. Keating, eds., *LGBTQ Politics: A Critical Reader*. New York: New York University Press 72–88.

Puar, Jasbir (2014) "Disability," *Transgender Studies Quarterly* 1, 77–81.

Puar, Jasbir (2011) "I Would Rather Be a Cyborg Than a Goddess': Intersectionality, Assemblage, and Affective Politics," *PhiloSOPHIA: A Journal of Feminist Philosophy* 2, 49–66.

Puar, Jasbir (2007) *Terrorist Assemblages: Homonationalism in Queer Times*. Durham: Duke University Press.

Puente Movement (2017, May 18) "The People vs. Arpaio: A Timeline." Available online at: https://puenteaz.org/blog/the-people-vs-arpaio-a-timeline/ (Accessed January 20, 2018).

Ranii, David (2016, April 9) "Organizers of 'Moral Monday' Protests Demand Repeal of HB2," *News & Observer*. Available online at: https://www.news-observer.com/news/local/article70925492.html (Accessed January 23, 2019).

Reddy, Chandan (2011) *Freedom from Violence: Race, Sexuality, and the US State*. Durham: Duke University Press.

"Referendum 74 Ballot Question without the Spin" (2012, March 20) *Seattle Times*. Available online at: http://www.seattletimes.com/opinion/referendum-74-ballot-question-without-the-spin/ (Accessed February 21, 2017).

Rex, Tom R. (2011) "The Latino Population in Arizona—Growth, Characteristics, and Outlook–with a Focus on Latino Education," W.P. Carey School of Business, Arizona State University.

Riccardi, Nicholas (2010, May 29) "Thousands in Phoenix Protest Arizona's Immigration Law," *Los Angeles Times*. Available online at: http://articles.latimes.com/2010/may/29/nation/la-na-arizona-protest-20100529-42 (Accessed March 22, 2017).

"Rights Bill Would Protect Gays' Jobs, Ban Preferences" (1997, October 15) *Washington Post*. Available online at: https://www.washingtonpost.com/archive/politics/1997/10/14/rights-bill-would-protect-gays-jobs-ban-preferences/198296ee-fa09-41ca-bc5c-7e8c92d8a819/ (Accessed February 23, 2017).

Rimmerman, Craig A. (2002) *From Identity to Politics: The Lesbian and Gay Movements in the United States.* Philadelphia: Temple University Press.

Rivas, Jorge (2011, December 15) "Department of Homeland Security and ICE End Sheriff Arpaio's 287(g) Contract," *Colorlines.* Available online at: http://www.colorlines.com/articles/department-homeland-security-and-ice-end-sheriff-arpaios-287g-contract (Accessed March 23, 2017).

Roberts, Laurie (2011, September 16) "Pearce: Fiesta Bowl Trips Good for Arizona," *Arizona Republic.* Available online at: http://archive.azcentral.com/members/Blog/LaurieRoberts/142042 (Accessed March 29, 2017).

Roesler, Richard (2009, May 18). "Gregoire Signs 'Everything but Marriage' Law," *Spokesman Review.* Available online at: http://www.spokesman.com/stories/2009/may/18/gregoire-signs-everything-marriage-law/ (Accessed February 21, 2017).

Rosenberg, Gerald N. (2008). *The Hollow Hope: Can Courts Bring About Social Change?* 2nd ed. Chicago: University of Chicago Press.

Rupert, Maya (2014, November 24) "Left out of Obama's Executive Action: Many LGBT Families," *New America Media.* URL no longer active.

Russakoff, Dale (2018, September 5) "The Teacher's Movement: Arizona Lawmakers Cut Education Budgets. Then Teachers Got Angry," *New York Times Magazine.* Available online at: https://www.nytimes.com/interactive/2018/09/05/magazine/arizona-teachers-facebook-group-doug-ducey.html (Accessed August 26, 2019).

Ryan, Lisa (2017, February 28) "An LGBTQ Suicide-Hotline Volunteer on Speaking with Trans Youth in Trump's America," *New York Magazine.* Available online at: http://nymag.com/thecut/2017/02/an-lgbtq-suicide-hotline-volunteer-on-talking-to-trans-youth.html (Accessed May 16, 2017).

Sailor, Craig (2015a, December 16) "Pierce, Kitsap YMCAs Release New Locker Room Policy," *Tacoma News Tribune.* Available online at: http://www.thenewstribune.com/news/local/article50174070.html (Accessed February 23, 2017).

Sailor, Craig (2015b, October 9) "Pierce, Kitsap YMCA Transgender Policy Sets Off a Storm," *Tacoma News Tribune.* Available online at: http://www.thenewstribune.com/news/local/article38264547.html (Accessed February 23, 2017).

Sameh, Catherine (2014) "From Tehran to Los Angeles to Tehran: Transnational Solidarity Politics in the One Million Signature Campaigns to End Discriminatory Law," *WSQ: Women's Studies Quarterly* 42 (3/4), 166–188.

Sanders, Eli (2012, June 6) "Gay Marriage's Jewish Pioneer: Faygele Ben Miriam," *Tablet.* Available online at: http://www.tabletmag.com/jewish-news-and-politics/101628/gay-marriages-jewish-pioneer (Accessed February 19, 2017).

Sanders, Eli (2006, August 3) "Marriage Denied: Reeling from the Recent Supreme Court Decision, the Gay Community Struggles to Answer the Question: What Next?" Available online at: http://www.thestranger.com/seattle/marriage-denied/Content?oid=45213 (Accessed February 19, 2017).

Sanders, Rebekah (2013) "The History of Proposition 200," *Arizona Republic*. Available online at: http://archive.azcentral.com/news/politics/articles/20130316proposition-200-history-timeline.html (Accessed March 17, 2017).

Sarat, Austin (1999) *The Killing State: Capital Punishment in Law, Politics, and Culture*. New York: New York University Press.

Savage, Dan (2004, March 11) "My Marriage License," *The Stranger*. Available online at: http://www.thestranger.com/seattle/my-marriage-license/Content?oid=17394 (Accessed May 23, 2017).

Scarborough, Senta, JJ Hensley, Dennis Wagner, and Ali Pfauser (2008, June 27) "28 Arrested in Mesa Sweep," *Arizona Republic*. Available online at: http://www.azcentral.com/news/articles/2008/06/27/20080627joe-arpaio-mesa-sweep.html (Accessed July 20, 2017).

Scheingold Stuart (1974) *The Politics of Rights*. Ann Arbor: University of Michigan Press.

Scherer, Michael (2018, March 9) "Florida Gov. Rick Scott Breaks with NRA to Sign New Gun Regulations," *Washington Post*. Available online at: https://www.washingtonpost.com/powerpost/florida-gov-rick-scott-breaks-with-nra-to-sign-new-gun-regulation/2018/03/09/e5d1f02e-23b2-11e8-86f6-54bfff693d2b_story.html (Accessed August 22, 2019).

Scherer, Michael (2012, February 22) "Why the Latino Vote in Arizona Could Be Decisive in 2012," *Time*. Available online at: http://swampland.time.com/2012/02/22/why-the-latino-vote-in-arizona-could-be-decisive-in-2012/ (Accessed March 29, 2017).

Schmidt, Samantha, and Sarah Larimer (2017, February 9) "For Years, Immigration Authorities Gave This Arizona Mother a Pass. Now She Has Been Deported," *Washington Post*. Available online at: https://www.washingtonpost.com/news/morning-mix/wp/2017/02/09/for-decades-immigration-authorities-gave-this-mother-a-pass-wednesday-when-she-checked-in-with-them-they-seized-her/?utm_term=.c1dce49df2d8 (Accessed March 17, 2017).

Seattle Civil Rights and Labor History Project, "Segregated Seattle." Available online at: http://depts.washington.edu/civilr/segregated.htm (Accessed May 23, 2017).

Seldon, David A., Julie A. Pace, and Heidi Nunn-Gilman (2011) "Placing SB 1070 and Racial Profiling into Context, and What SB 1070 Reveals about the Legislative Process in Arizona," *Arizona State Law Journal* 43, 523–561.

Service Employees International Union (SEIU), *The Complete Stewards Manual: Your Role, Part II*. Available online at: http://www.seiu.org/cards/the-complete-stewards-manual/your-role-part-ii/p16 (Accessed January 18, 2017).

Shapiro, Nina (2016, January 9) "State's Rule for Transgender Restroom Access Set Off Debate," *Seattle Times*. Available online at: http://www.seattletimes.com/seattle-news/politics/states-rules-for-transgender-restroom-access-set-off-debate/ (Accessed February 23, 2017).

"Sheriff Arpaio: An In-Depth Look at 'America's Toughest Sheriff'" (2015) *Arizona Republic*, Special issue. Available online at: http://www.azcentral.com/news/arpaio/arpaio-index.html (Accessed February 20, 2017)

Showden, Carisa R., and Samantha Majic (2014) "Introduction: The Politics of Sex Work," in C. Showden and S. Majic, eds., *Negotiating Sex Work: Unintended Consequences of Policy and Activism*. Minneapolis: University of Minnesota Press xiii–xl.

Silva, Catherine (2009) "Racial Restrictive Covenants: Enforcing Neighborhood Segregation in Seattle," Seattle Civil Rights and Labor History Project. Available online at: http://depts.washington.edu/civilr/covenants_report.htm (Accessed May 23, 2017).

Simpson, Andrea Y. (1998) *The Tie That Binds: Identity and Political Attitudes in the Post–Civil Rights Generation*. New York: New York University Press.

Sinema, Kyrsten (2012) "No Surprises: The Evolution of Anti-Immigrant Legislation in Arizona," in C. E. Kubrin, M. S. Zatz, and R. Martínez, eds., *Punishing Immigrants: Policy, Politics, and Injustice*. New York: New York University Press 62–90.

Singer, Audrey (2012, March 15) *Immigrant Workers in the U.S. Labor Force*, Brookings Institute. Available online at: https://www.brookings.edu/wp-content/uploads/2016/06/0315_immigrant_workers_singer.pdf (Accessed March 14, 2017).

Skocpol, Theda (2016, November 11) "Theda Skocpol Responds to Judis," *Talking Points Memo*. Available online at: http://talkingpointsmemo.com/edblog/theda-skocpol-responds-to-judis (Accessed May 15, 2017).

Solomon, Marc (2014) *Winning Marriage: The Inside Story of How Same-Sex Couples Took on the Politicians and Pundits—and Won*. Lebanon: University Press of New England.

Spade, Dean (2015) *Normal Life: Administrative Violence, Critical Trans Politics, and the Limits of Law*, 2nd ed. Durham: Duke University Press.

Speidel, Jennifer (2005) "After Internment: Seattle's Debate over Japanese Americans' Right to Return Home," Seattle Civil Rights and Labor History Project. Available online at: http://depts.washington.edu/civilr/after_internment.htm (Accessed May 23, 2017).

*The State of Arizona* (2014) A documentary by Carlos Sandoval, Independent Television Service. Available for purchase through PBS: Independent Lens: http://www.pbs.org/independentlens/films/state-of-arizona/.

Steinberg, Marc (1999) "The Talk and Back Talk of Collective Action: A Dialogic Analysis of Repertoires of Discourse among Nineteenth Century English Cotton Spinners" 105 *American Journal of Sociology* 736–780.

Stern, Ray (2011, December 15) "Feds Pull 287(g) from Maricopa County Jails Because of Civil Rights Violations," *Phoenix New Times*. Available online at: http://www.phoenixnewtimes.com/news/feds-pull-287-g-authority-from-maricopa-county-jails-because-of-civil-rights-violations-6631025 (Accessed March 23, 2017).

Stone, Amy L. (2012) *Gay Rights at the Ballot Box*. Minneapolis: University of Minnesota Press.

Strolovitch, Dara Z. (2007) *Affirmative Advocacy: Race, Class, and Gender in Interest Group Politics*. Chicago: University of Chicago Press.

Stuteville, Sarah (2014, November 4) "Confronting the Myth of Seattle as a 'White City,'" *Seattle Globalist*. Available online at: http://www.seattleglobalist.com/2014/11/14/seattle-white-city-myth-diversity-demographics/30637 (Accessed May 23, 2017).

Suro, Roberto (1994, November 11) "Proposition 187 Could Open Pandora's Box for GOP," *Washington Post*. Available online at: https://www.washingtonpost.com/archive/politics/1994/11/11/proposition-187-could-open-pandoras-box-for-gop/eb48e8bc-c27e-4a32-b432-bcfb5311d763/?utm_term=.5d4a06adb504 (Accessed March 17, 2017).

Sweet, Lynn (2018, June 16) "Parkland Students Arrive in Chicago, First Stop in U.S. Tour on Gun Violence," *Chicago Sun Times*. Available online at: https://chicago.suntimes.com/news/parkland-students-arrive-chicago-first-stop-national-tour-gun-violence/ (Accessed January 23, 2019).

Tarrow, Sidney (2011). *Power in Movement: Social Movements and Contentious Politics*, 3rd ed. New York: Cambridge University Press.

Tarrow, Sidney (2005) *The New Transnational Activism*. New York: Cambridge University Press.

Tarrow, Sidney (1983) "Struggling to Reform: Social Movements and Policy Change during Cycles of Protest," Western Societies Program Occasional Paper No. 15, New York Center for International Studies, Cornell University, Ithaca.

Terry, Don (1998, April 29) "Arizona Court Strikes Down Law Requiring English Use," *New York Times*. Available online at: http://www.nytimes.com/1998/04/29/us/arizona-court-strikes-down-law-requiring-english-use.html (Accessed March 13, 2017).

Thomason, Art, Jim Walsh, and John D'Anna (2011, November 8) "Russell Pearce on Verge of Historic Loss in Recall," *Arizona Republic*. Available online at: http://archive.azcentral.com/news/articles/2011/11/08/20111108russell-pearce-recall-trailing-jerry-lewis.html (Accessed March 29, 2017).

Thompson, Carolyn (2018, October 3) "After Arizona's #RedForEd Protests, Teachers in Drive to Win Offices across US," *Arizona Republic*. Available online at: https://www.azcentral.com/story/news/politics/elections/2018/10/03/arizona-redfored-education-protests-spurs-teachers-run-office-across-us/1515559002/ (Accessed August 26, 2019).

Thornburgh, Nathan (2010, April 26) "Arizona Gears Up for Protracted Immigration Fight," *Time*. Available online at: http://content.time.com/time/nation/article/0,8599,1984432,00.html (Accessed January 18, 2017).

Tilly, Charles (1978) *From Mobilization to Revolution*. Reading: Addison-Wesley.

Townsend-Bell, Erica (2011) "What Is Relevance? Defining Intersectional Praxis in Uruguay," *Political Research Quarterly* 64, 187–199.

"Transgender Health Care Exclusions No Longer Permissible in Washington State" (2014, June 25) *Seattle Lesbian*. Available online at: http://theseattlelesbian.com/transgender-health-care-exclusions-longer-permissible-washington-state/ (Accessed May 16, 2017).

Tu, Janet I. (2009, November 9) "Voters Approve Referendum 71," *Seattle Times*. Available online at: http://www.seattletimes.com/seattle-news/voters-approve-referendum-71/ (Accessed February 21, 2017).

Tumulty, Karen (2018, November 4) "This 31-Year-Old Woman Had Enough. So She Ran. And Won," *Washington Post*. Available online at: https://www.washingtonpost.com/opinions/this-31-year-old-had-had-enough-so-she-ran-and-won/2018/11/14/cd6a7046-e6c2-11e8-bbdb-72fdbf9d4fed_story.html (Accessed August 26, 2019).

Tungohan, Ethel (2016) "Intersectionality as Social Justice: Assessing Activists' Use of Intersectionality through Grassroots Migrant Organizations in Canada," *Politics, Groups, and Identities* 4, 347–362.

Turnbull, Lornet (2012, February 3) "Gregoire Signs Gay Marriage into Law," *Seattle Times*. Available online at: https://www.seattletimes.com/seattle-news/gregoire-signs-gay-marriage-into-law/ (Accessed January 15, 2020).

Turnbull, Lornet (2009a, May 18) "Gregoire Expands Same-Sex Partnerships," *Seattle Times*. Available online at: http://www.seattletimes.com/seattle-news/gregoire-expands-same-sex-partnerships/ (Accessed February 21, 2017).

Turnbull, Lornet (2009b, August 3) "Referendum 71 Backers Gather 138,000 Signatures," *Seattle Times*. Available online at: http://www.seattletimes.com/seattle-news/referendum-71-backers-gather-138000-signatures/ (Accessed February 21, 2017).

Tushnet, Mark V. (2005) *The NAACP's Legal Strategy against Segregated Education, 1925–1950*. Chapel Hill: University of North Carolina Press.

United States Citizenship and Immigration Services, "Consideration for Deferred Action for Childhood Arrivals (DACA)." Available online at: https://www.uscis.gov/humanitarian/consideration-deferred-action-childhood-arrivals-daca (Accessed February 6, 2017).

United States Department of Justice (2015, August 6) "Jurisdictions Previously Covered by Section 5." Available online at: https://www.justice.gov/crt/jurisdictions-previously-covered-section-5 (Accessed March 13, 2017).

United States Department of Justice (2010, September 2) "Justice Department Files Lawsuit against Maricopa County Sheriff's Office for Refusing Full Cooperation with Title VI Investigation." Press release. Available online at:

https://www.justice.gov/opa/pr/justice-department-files-lawsuit-against-mari-copa-county-sheriff-s-office-refusing-full (Accesses March 23, 2017).

United States Immigration and Customs Enforcement (2016, November 4) "Secure Communities." Available online at: https://www.ice.gov/secure-communities#tab1 (Accessed March 22, 2017).

Vaid, Urvashi (1995) *Virtual Equality: The Mainstreaming of Gay and Lesbian Liberation.* New York: Anchor Books.

Van Dyke, Nella, and McCammon, Holly J. (2010) "Introduction: Social Movement Coalition Formation," in N. Van Dyke and H. McCammon, eds., *Strategic Alliances: Coalition Building and Social Movements.* Minneapolis: University of Minnesota Press xi–xxviii.

Villagra, Hector O. (2006) "Arizona's Proposition 200 and the Supremacy of Federal Law: Elements of Law, Politics, and Faith," *Stanford Journal of Civil Rights & Civil Liberties* 2, 295–331.

Ward, Jane (2008) *Respectably Queer: Diversity Culture in LGBT Activist Organizations.* Nashville: Vanderbilt University Press.

"Washington Initiative Shot Down" (1997, December 9) *The Advocate* 16, 16.

Washington Office of the Secretary of State (1997a) *State of Washington Voter's Pamphlet: State General Election,* November 4, 1997. Available online at: https://wei.sos.wa.gov/agency/osos/en/press_and_research/PreviousElections/documents/voters%27pamphlets/1997_general_election_voters_pamphlet.pdf (Accessed February 23, 2017).

Washington Office of the Secretary of State (1997b) "November 1997 General Election Results." Available online at: https://www.sos.wa.gov/elections/results_report.aspx?e=6& (Accessed February 23, 2017).

Wasser, Miriam (2016, January 19) "Arizona's 'No Promo-Homo' Sex Education Law Targeted in Legislature," *Phoenix New Times.* Available online at: http://www.phoenixnewtimes.com/news/arizonas-no-promo-homo-sex-education-law-targeted-in-legislature-7982912 (Accessed March 14, 2017).

Webley, Kayla (2013, January 15) "A State Divided: As Washington Becomes More Liberal, Republicans Push Back," *Time.* Available online at: http://nation.time.com/2013/01/15/a-state-divided-as-washington-becomes-more-liberal-republicans-push-back/ (Accessed May 23, 2017).

Weigel, David (2012, February 24) "Arizona's House of Cards," *Slate.* Available online at: http://www.slate.com/articles/news_and_politics/politics/2012/02/the_arizona_gop_may_be_vulnerable_to_democrats_who_are_popular_with_the_growing_latino_community_.html (Accessed March 29, 2017).

Weiner, Rachel (2011, November 9) "Arizona Recall: Why Russell Pearce Lost," *Washington Post.* Available online at: https://www.washingtonpost.com/blogs/the-fix/post/arizona-recall-why-russell-pearce-lost/2011/11/09/gIQALj6a5M_blog.html?utm_term=.d6438cf9f31a (Accessed March 29, 2017).

Weldon, S. Laurel (2011) *When Protest Makes Policy: A Comparative Politics of Gender.* Ann Arbor: University of Michigan Press.

*We're Here to Stay* (1998) Documentary by Liz Latham, Lizard Productions. Available for purchase through Lizard Productions: http://www.lizardproductions.com/orderourvideos.html.

Witt, Emily (2018, June 26) "Launching a National Gun-Control Coalition, the Parkland Teens Meet Chicago's Young Activists," *New Yorker.* Available online at: https://www.newyorker.com/news/dispatch/launching-a-national-gun-control-coalition-the-parkland-teens-meet-chicagos-young-activists (Accessed January 23, 2019).

Wyman, Kim (2013) *Filing Initiatives and Referenda in Washington State,* Office of the Secretary of State. Available online at: https://www.sos.wa.gov/_assets/elections/Initiative%20and%20Referenda%20Manual.pdf (Accessed February 21, 2017).

Yan, Wudan (2016, February 5) "Seattle's Absurd, Discriminatory Trans Bathroom Panic," *Daily Beast.* Available online at: http://www.thedailybeast.com/articles/2016/02/05/seattle-s-absurd-discriminatory-trans-bathroom-panic (Accessed May 16, 2017).

"A Year after the Teacher Walkout, a Timeline of Arizona's #RedForEd Movement" (2019, April 11) *Arizona Republic.* Available online at: https://www.azcentral.com/story/news/local/arizona-education/2019/04/11/arizona-teacher-walkout-timeline-red-for-ed/3337757002/ (Accessed August 26, 2019).

Ye Hee Lee, Michelle (2016, May 4) "Rep. Ann Kirkpatrick Campaign's Misleading Attack on Senator John McCain's Support for the DREAM Act," *Washington Post.* Available online at: https://www.washingtonpost.com/news/fact-checker/wp/2016/05/04/rep-ann-kirkpatrick-campaigns-misleading-attack-on-sen-john-mccains-support-for-the-dream-act/?utm_term=.780e32fdbc68 (Accessed February 18, 2017).

Ye Hee Lee, Michelle (2012, January 15) "Recalling Arizona's Struggle for MLK Holiday," *Arizona Republic.* Available online at: http://archive.azcentral.com/arizonarepublic/news/articles/20120112martin-luther-king-holiday-dilemma.html (Accessed March 13, 2017).

Yoshino, Kenji (2000) "The Epistemic Contract of Bisexual Erasure," *Stanford Law Review* 52, 405–406.

Young, Bob (2004, March 9) "Officials Worried Gay Editor Would Beat Them to Court," *Seattle Times.* Available online at: http://old.seattletimes.com/html/stateofmarriage/2001874758_gaypolitics09m.html?mbaseid=2001874758 (Accessed May 23, 2017).

Yuval-Davis, Nira (2012) "Patricia Hill Collins Symposium: Dialogical Epistemology—An Intersectional Resistance to the 'Oppression Olympics'" *Gender & Society* 26 (1), 46–54.

Zald, Mayer N. (1996) "Culture, Ideology, and Strategic Framing," in D. McAdam, J. D. McCarthy, and M. N. Zald, eds., *Comparative Perspectives on Social Movements: Political Opportunities, Mobilizing Structures, and Cultural Framings.* New York: Cambridge University Press 261–274.

Zemans (1983) "Legal Mobilization: The Neglected Role of Law in the Public System," *American Political Science Review* 77 (3), 690–703.

# INDEX

The authorized representative in the EU for product safety and compliance is:
Mare Nostrum Group
B.V Doelen 72
4831 GR Breda
The Netherlands

www.ingramcontent.com/pod-product-compliance
Lightning Source LLC
Chambersburg PA
CBHW020858270326
41928CB00006B/756